Crisis in Korea

CRISIS IN KOREA

America, China and the Risk of War

Tim Beal

PlutoPress
www.plutobooks.com

First published 2011 by Pluto Press
345 Archway Road, London N6 5AA

www.plutobooks.com

Distributed in the United States of America exclusively by
Palgrave Macmillan, a division of St. Martin's Press LLC,
175 Fifth Avenue, New York, NY 10010

British Library Cataloguing in Publication Data
A catalogue record for this book is available from the British Library

ISBN   978 0 7453 3161 4   Hardback
ISBN   978 0 7453 3162 1   Paperback

Library of Congress Cataloging in Publication Data applied for

This book is printed on paper suitable for recycling and made from fully managed
and sustained forest sources. Logging, pulping and manufacturing processes are
expected to conform to the environmental standards of the country of origin.

10   9   8   7   6   5   4   3   2   1

Designed and produced for Pluto Press by Chase Publishing Services Ltd
Typeset from disk by Stanford DTP Services, Northampton, England
Simultaneously printed digitally by CPI Antony Rowe, Chippenham, UK and
Edwards Bros in the United States of America

Contents

APPENDICES
The following appendices do not appear in the printed book but are available on the web at <www.timbeal.net.nz/Crisis_in_Korea>.

1. Timeline
2. Statistical Appendix
3. Reports on the *Cheonan* Incident

List of Figures and Tables

Acknowledgements

No book gets written, and produced, without input from many people. This assistance comes in many forms; sometimes it is directly related to the book, in other cases it is rather a matter of long term support for the research and commitment that goes into writing. Debts, therefore, are boundless, and it is difficult just to identify a few individuals, leaving out the rest. Brevity however is necessary and I apologise to those I have not mentioned. Given the controversial nature of the book I should perhaps also apologise to those who are mentioned. Of course, any opinions expressed are mine and are not necessarily shared by others. Any mistakes are also mine alone.

I am grateful to Brent Efford for proofreading and to Tony Quinn for help with EndNote. Don Borrie, Peter Wilson, and Stuart Vogel, who share a commitment to peace and prosperity in Korea, have provided support over the years. I have a debt to many Koreans, North and South and in the diaspora but in particular to Chung Young Chul in Seoul who translated my first book on Korea, and might perhaps, be tempted to do the same with this one. My visits to North Korea have been facilitated by the Korea-New Zealand Friendship Society and I am very grateful for the insights, and friendships, these have provided. Most of what appears in a book comes from other books, and written matter in general, but actually walking the streets of Pyongyang and Seoul, travelling through both Koreas, gives an empathetic understanding that words alone cannot provide.

This book would not have been published without the support, encouragement and valuable criticism of Pluto publisher, Roger van Zwanenberg, and his team, specifically Alec Gregory, Tom Lynton, Jon Maunder, Charles Peyton, Robert Webb, and Jon Wheatley.

My greatest debt of all is to Ankie Hoogvelt. She criticised early drafts and laid the foundation for the index. She disagreed with much of what I originally wrote and this stimulated me, I hope, to do better. No doubt there are things in this final version with which she would take issue but that is in the nature of subjects which, by their nature, offer few certainties.

Preface

Korea is surprisingly important. It was Japan's takeover of Korea which led it to war with Russia, and provided the first victory over a European power by a non-European one for centuries. The colonisation of Korea then led Japan into war with China and ultimately with the United States; that brought us, among other things, Hiroshima and the atomic age. The Korean War, which broke out in 1950, ended America's post-Second World War demobilization and provided the impetus for the remilitarisation of its society and economy. This local 'forgotten war', as it has often been called, was the opening salvo of the Cold War, a war that, despite the collapse of the Soviet Union, continues today in a different form. The Soviet Union has been replaced as the main challenge to American hegemony by the hydra-headed Islamist 'global insurgency', and by China. And America's militarisation has proceeded apace, so that the US now accounts for half the world's military expenditure: it is the major international seller of arms, and weapons look set to become its major export. The business of America is no longer business, but war.

Things that happen in Korea have repercussions around the world, and this is due in no small measure to its strategic location. The Korean peninsula is where Russia, China, Japan and the United States collide and interact. Significantly, in 1950 Korea sparked the first Sino-American war; there are warning signs, that 60 years later, it may produce the second.

On 26 March 2010 the South Korean corvette, the *Cheonan*, sank in mysterious circumstances. The ship, named after the South Korean city of the same name – which ironically means 'heavenly peace' – took 46 men down with her. The sinking was not a major catastrophe as these things go; in 1999 a North Korean ship was sunk in the same waters with comparable casualties, and trains, planes, ships, let alone tsunamis and earthquakes, frequently inflict far more damage. What was important in this case was the response of the South Korean government. South Korean President Lee Myung-bak set up a military investigation which included the United States and some allies, and excluded neighbouring China and Russia, and pronounced North Korea guilty. North Korea demanded access to the evidence and was refused. There is widespread scepticism within South Korea, especially among younger and better-educated people, about the military's verdict, and both China and Russia have refused to accept it. Despite all this, Lee Myung-bak has used the incident to justify his hard-line stance towards the North and to increase tension on the peninsula. Indeed, there are strong indications, detailed in this book, that the South Korean government actually fabricated evidence in order to incriminate the North.

The *Cheonan* is not an isolated incident, but rather marks a further stage in the deterioration of relations between South and North since Lee came into power in 2008. Tension was further exacerbated by an artillery clash at Yeonpyeong Island in disputed waters off the west coast in November 2010. The relationship between the two Koreas had been improving over recent decades, and especially under the progressive administrations of Kim Dae-jung and Roh Moo-hyun, but under Lee Myung-bak it has plummeted.

Inter-Korean relations assume a particular importance because of the way they impact on global geopolitics. Foremost among these issues is the protracted dispute between North Korea and America. Since the 1960s, and with added urgency since the collapse of the Soviet Union, North Korea has been attempting to get the US to accept peaceful coexistence, to remove its military threat, and to lift wide-ranging sanctions that condemn the country to penury. The United States, for reasons of global strategy and the necessity to keep Japan and South Korea in an alliance against China, has baulked at this. Despite all the hyperbole, it apparently does not regard the North Korean nuclear weapons programme as sufficiently challenging to justify compromising more important objectives. The progressive administrations of Kim Dae-jung – famous for his 'sunshine policy' of engagement with the North – and Roh Moo-hyun tended to ameliorate the US position. Lee Myung-bak puts pressure in the other direction, and with the Obama administration floundering at home and abroad, with no clear idea how to reconcile policy and rhetoric, it seems that Lee has effectively captured Washington's North Korea policy.

All this comes at a time when there is a feeling in some quarters that sanctions have so destabilised North Korea that something like the death or incapacitation of leader Kim Jong Il will be sufficient to precipitate a crisis of some sort. This is what the military planners call 'contingencies'. This crisis, it is thought, would have two functions: it would justify, or be claimed to justify, an invasion; and it would make resistance short-lived and ineffective. A renewed war against North Korea has long been planned for, and every year there are a number of joint exercises between the US and South Korean military practising for such an event. Indeed, the *Cheonan* sunk while one of these exercises was being carried out. The difference now is the assumption that the North Korean state is on the verge of collapse.

But invasions, as we well know, often go awry. It might be that the Americans and South Koreans could launch an overwhelming attack that would swiftly take out the top leadership and military facilities and that resistance would crumble. More likely is that the North Koreans would counterattack, as they have threatened, with all means at their disposal. That includes attacking Seoul, which is within artillery range, and perhaps the use of nuclear weapons against US bases in South Korea and Japan. It is likely that there would also be fierce resistance to an invading force. Some American think tanks estimate that over 400,000 troops would be needed to pacify North Korea.

On top of this there is the question of the Chinese response. The centre-piece of China's foreign policy is not to offer the United States provocation, or a pretext, for war during its 'peaceful rise'. But it is likely that, as in 1950, an American army pushing up to the Yalu, the river dividing Korea from China, would be considered intolerable.

An invasion of North Korea would be catastrophic for the peninsula, and might well have a devastating impact on Japan. A second Sino-American war would have incalculable, but surely fearsome, consequences. Even if it were limited, as was the first one, the economic impact alone would be disastrous, the American and Chinese economies being now so inter-connected. China is much weaker than the United States militarily, but might prove more resilient. The British historian Niall Ferguson has called America the 'fragile empire', and for the United States this might be one war too many.

Possible consequences of such magnitude would seem to make war unlikely, but we should not discount the risk of accident or miscalculation sparking conflict in a tense and inflamed situation. We should also bear in mind the continued deterioration in Sino-American relations; the rivalry between the two nations, though it may take various forms, looks set to be the major issue of the coming decades.

Voices prophesying war have gained in number and strength over recent years, and especially since the sinking of the *Cheonan*. In both North and South Korea, and among foreign observers, there has been increasing discussion of the danger. However, even if there is no war, the anticipation of the collapse of North Korea has diminished the motive for negotiating peace. The Obama administration, which never had negotiations with North Korea high in its priorities, now seems to have turned its back on it, both bilaterally and in the Chinese-hosted Six-Party Talks. No doubt there will be protestations of a desire to reach a peaceful resolution – but examination of the small print, especially concerning preconditions, will mean this professed ambition will have no real substance. So there may not be war, but neither will there be peace; the crisis will rumble on.

This book attempts to set the *Cheonan* incident within its wider historical and geopolitical context. It is that context which makes the sinking of the *Cheonan* so ominous. A second Korean War is not pre-ordained, but the warning signs are there. Moreover, under prevailing policies, the absence of war does not mean movement towards peace. Sanctions will continue, as will the suffering of the North Korean people; estimates in South Korea based on the 2008 census gave a calculation of 340,000 'excess' deaths since 1993. If the North Korean economy is to recover – and up to the 1980s it was one the most successful developing economies, and for some decades ahead of South Korea – then peace is imperative. But not peace at any price. Tension on the Korean peninsula will continue to be an irritant in US–China relations, as well as providing an incentive and excuse for Japanese remilitarisation and the deepening militarisation of South Korea.

Whatever happens, unless there is peace, the prospects for peace and prosperity not only for the Korean peninsula but for the region and the wider world are much diminished. In these circumstances, an informed and critical analysis is vital. If a second war breaks out in Korea we need to understand why, and to be in a position to cut though the lies which will abound. If a second war is averted we need to know how close we were to it, and to understand and identify the drivers behind the situation. What happens in Korea has implications, and lessons, for all of us.

Part I

Korea and the Postwar Geopolitical Transformation

Context is vitally important if we are to situate events, their antecedents and their consequences into a pattern of causality. Without context, events can be stripped of meaning, or worse still, accorded a false meaning.

Chapter 1 focuses on Korea within the context of the struggle between imperialism and nationalism. Those who collaborate with American imperialism today, and seek to use it to their ends, are in a line of descent – political and often familial – with those who did the same in respect of Japan. Park Geun-hye, for instance, a leading member of the Grand National Party (GNP) who may well succeed Lee Myung-bak as the next president of the Republic of Korea, is the daughter of general/president Park Chung-hee, who first cut his teeth serving with the Japanese army in Manchuria in the 1930s. The familial connections on the other side are even more distinct. The current leader, Kim Jong Il, is the son of Kim Il Sung, who was a famous anti-Japanese guerrilla from the 1930s onwards. This chapter follows that historical thread up to the present.

Embedded within the struggle between imperialism and nationalism is the question of the reunification of Korea. Korea was divided into North and South in 1945 by the US, with Soviet acquiescence. In 1950 Kim Il Sung (and Syngman Rhee) attempted to unify the country by force. This failed, and Korea has remained divided. Despite claims that reunification remains a central objective, Kim Jong Il seems reconciled to the lesser aim of preserving the North Korean state. Lee Myung-bak, on the other hand, in the far richer and more powerful South, thinks that he can precipitate a collapse of the North and absorb it into a reunified Korea. To do that he needs American support and endorsement, and that raises the question of China's position. Lee must convince the Americans that there will be no substantial resistance in the North to a takeover, and that China will acquiesce. This is a complex game, with much subterfuge, deception and uncertainty. For example, one of the WikiLeaks cables, according to media reports, reported:

> China 'would be comfortable with a reunified Korea controlled by Seoul and anchored to the US in a 'benign alliance' as long as Korea was not hostile towards China,' then-South Korean vice foreign minister, Chun Yung-woo, is quoted as telling US ambassador to South Korea, Kathleen Stephens, in February.[1]

Much of the media took this as revealed truth, but in reality there are various possibilities:

1. Chun Yung-woo may have misinterpreted what the Chinese said;
2. Chun Yung-woo may have spoken to Chinese officials who were not in a position of sufficient authority to make such assurances;
3. the Chinese officials may have deliberately misled Chun Yung-woo for domestic political reasons;
4. Chun Yung-woo may have deliberately misled Ambassador Stephens to garner US support for a takeover of the North;
5. Ambassador Stephens may have misinterpreted what Minister Chun said.[2]

Chapter 1 introduces us to these fundamental issues, to which we return at the conclusion of the book.

The remaining chapters of Part I look at the postwar transformation of the geopolitical landscape. Korea is important because of its geographical location – it is where the United States, China, Japan and Russia (and the former Soviet Union) meet and interact. Were it placed in the South Pacific, it would still, because of its size, have some purchase on our attention, but far less than it has. Japan and Russia, America and China, have fought in and around Korea because of its location; they would not have travelled to the South Pacific to do that. Thus, we cannot begin to understand Korea without looking at the geopolitical environment in which it is located.

The geopolitical landscape of the postwar world has undergone immense changes, but four are particularly important in the context of this book:

1. decolonisation, the creation of new states, and the growing role of non-state actors;

2. the collapse of the Soviet Union and its impact on North Korea – the 'Arduous March';
3. the rise of China and the American dilemma;
4. the decline of the United States.

These are all complex and contested issues that have generated an extensive literature, and these chapters attempt to sketch out what seem to be their main aspects and the way in which they can throw light on the current situation. They are all interrelated, of course, though some more intimately than others. The rise of China, for instance, fits within the decolonisation process, and is its major success story – although purists may object that unlike, say, Korea, Vietnam or India, it was never a colony. That is formally correct, but misleading. China in the 1930s was a victim of imperialism, and of its own historical inadequacies. A substantial part of its territory, and a larger portion of its population, was under Japanese control. A small but highly significant portion was under the British (and a further, smaller part under the Portuguese). Large swathes of the former Qing territory enjoyed de facto independence (Tibet and Xinjiang in particular), and Outer Mongolia was in a half-way house between de jure and de facto independence. The Nationalist government was struggling, with incomplete success, to wrest control of the rest of the country from warlords, and from the Communists. In short, China was what in the modern cant term would be called a 'failed state'. Now things are remarkably different, and although Beijing has not (yet) achieved the re-absorption of all of the Qing territory – the status of Taiwan being still contested, and Outer Mongolia, it would seem, gone for good – China is now recognisably the same country that the Qianlong emperor ruled over in the eighteenth century, before the British started the dismemberment process. This reunified and reinvigorated China is commonly seen as one of the main reasons for American decline.

1
Imperialism, Nationalism, and the Division and Reunification of Korea

THE HISTORICAL AND GEOPOLITICAL CONTEXT

The *Cheonan* incident, and its possible consequences, can best be understood within the context of an overarching struggle between imperialism and nationalism. This is by no means a simple story, with good guys and bad guys, with forces of progress ranged against native backwardness, enunciating clearly delineated objectives and strategies. It is a complex, contradictory and confusing story, and no simple judgements, whether moral or factual, are possible. The next chapter looks at the broader picture: the changing geopolitical structure of the world since 1945. This chapter focuses on the Korean peninsula and perforce starts rather earlier, with the Japanese subjugation of Korea. Both aspects – the global and the Korean – fit together to form a historical context within which we can attempt to understand the *Cheonan* incident and the deepening crisis in Northeast Asia.

Japanese Imperialism and Its Defeat

Despite its complexity, the impact of imperialism on East Asia, and the reaction to it, has been the main historical driver of the last century and a half in the region. From the mid nineteenth century, in response to the unequal treaties imposed upon it by Western imperialism (in this instance led by the US), Japan attempted to carve out its own empire, creating something that towards the end went by the euphemism of the 'Greater East Asia Co-Prosperity Sphere'. Taiwan, seized from the flagging Qing dynasty, was the first conquest, although rather peripheral to imperial strategy. Not so Korea. The former Chosun was taken over in 1905, and formally became part of the empire in 1910. Korea was quite important in its own right: its land area is about 60 per cent of that of Japan, but it is its location that makes it so valuable. The Korean peninsula is a corridor between Japan and the Asian mainland. It has often been compared to a dagger, pointing either at China or Japan, depending on who is talking. It was no accident, therefore, that imperial Japan seized Korea.

Korea led Japan into Manchuria, now China's Dongbei, or Northeast, but then becoming the puppet state of Manchukuo. Next came unsuccessful forays into Mongolia and the Soviet Union, before the invasion of the rest of China in 1937. Japan's expansion inevitably brought it into conflict with Asian nationalism and other imperialisms. This created a complicated web of relationships, often shifting but always ambivalent and negotiated. Subhas Chandra Bose, for instance, saw the Japanese as allies in his fight for Indian independence from the British. Bose's stance was straightforward ('my enemy's enemy is my friend'), and his memory is respected, even revered, in India. Not so Wang Jingwei (Wang Ching-wei), who collaborated with the Japanese for reasons of personal ambition (he and Jiang Jieshi – Chiang Kai-shek – were bitter rivals), but also because, it has been argued, he saw the Japanese as protectors against Western imperialism. Wang has ended up being reviled as a traitor in both China and Taiwan, but had the Japanese prevailed, and had he survived into a postwar, Japanese-dominated China, he might have achieved the status that Park Chung-hee acquired in South Korea.

Japan's competition with other imperialisms, primarily the Americans but also the British, the French, the Dutch and the Soviet Union, led to its defeat and devastation. This defeat set the stage for postwar Asia. Of most relevance in this context was the liberation of Korea, and its division into two parts which after a few years solidified into the Republic of Korea (ROK) in the south, and the Democratic People's Republic of Korea (DPRK) in the north. This was an unnatural division: the Koreans are more homogenous than most peoples, and Korea had been in a unified state for centuries – much longer than, say, Germany. It is not surprising, therefore, that the economic, social, cultural and political imperatives for reunification remain strong. Reunification has had popular support since the division, though reports do suggest that young people in the South, at least, are less committed than their elders.

Elites in both Koreas have continuously advocated reunification, at least in public, but their attitudes in private are no doubt more nuanced. If one cannot have the whole cake, is it best to content oneself with half? Beyond that, given the blood-soaked history of the Korean peninsula since 1945, and especially during the Korean War 1950–53, defeated elites in a unified Korea might face imprisonment or death. At the very least, defeated elites tend to lose power, wealth and status. The number of East German diplomats, military officers and officials who enjoy uninterrupted careers in post-unification Germany is reportedly small – and that is without a civil war between the two Germanys. The reunification issue hangs over the Korean peninsula as both a promise and a threat. Ultimately it remains a necessity for sustainable economic growth and for political stability; the division is inherently unstable. However, if the reunification comes about through force – and that is a major concern of this book – the consequences will be catastrophic.

Reunification also has international ramifications. For countries at a distance it has little consequence, but for neighbouring countries there are enormous implications. Japan is averse, whatever the composition of the reunified state, because it would be a substantial economic, military and political competitor. This consideration does not weigh so heavily on the United States (which, despite the Pacific Ocean, must be considered a neighbour), China and Russia. None of these would be seriously challenged by an independent Korea, though none would want one that was dominated by one of the others. And that, in reality, means American domination. In fifty years' time it may well be different, and perhaps Korea will revert to a twenty-first-century version of its traditional tributary relationship with China; but for the immediate future, if it is a matter of forced reunification, only a US-dominated Korea seems possible.

Imperialism and Its Subjects: The Negotiated Relationship

Even the greatest of imperial powers are not all-powerful; crucially, they always have to work through local elites. The relationships involved vary greatly but there is always a degree of negotiation between superior and subordinate, between imperial proconsul and client politician or general. One of the lessons that the Americans brought away from their war in Vietnam is that dispensing with their local client, as they did with Ngo Dinh Diem and a few of his successors, can just make things worse. Incumbency can provide considerable leverage, even to the weakest of clients, if there are no obvious alternatives available; and even if there are, the 'transfer cost' of changing clients entails an admission of failure and poor judgement.

Hamid Karzai is an excellent case in point. His domestic support and power base are very weak, and even the American mainstream media acknowledge that he would not last long without US protection. And yet Karzai has considerable leverage, as was illustrated in a story in a *Rolling Stone* article on Stanley McChrystal that led to the general's downfall. In February 2010 he was preparing for the ill-fated Marja operation. This was meant to display and deploy American military superiority so that a 'government in a box' could be rolled out to administer the pacified Afghans. Before the operation went ahead, McChrystal needed the presidential signature, Afghanistan being in theory a sovereign country just getting a little help from its friends. The general went to the presidential palace, where he was kept waiting, according to the story, for some hours because Karzai was asleep recovering from a cold and could not be disturbed.[1] This anecdote might serve as a metaphor for the uneasy liaison between empire and local elites.

If imperial powers have difficult choices to make in the administration of their possessions, the decisions for the locals are of course usually much starker, and even existential. Within Korea there were a number of responses to the reality of Japanese, and subsequently American, imperialism, but they can be represented by three men: Yi Seungman (also Ri Seungman or Lee Seung-man) known by the anglicised form he preferred as Syngman Rhee; Park Chung-hee; and Kim Il Sung.

Syngman Rhee

Syngman Rhee was an aristocrat who became the first Korean to gain an American PhD. He had been active in opposing Japan, and lived for most of his life in Hawaii with his Austrian wife whom he married in 1933. He was for some years the president of the Korean provisional government in exile, based in Shanghai, though he spent little time there and was impeached in 1925. He returned to Korea from Hawaii in 1945 in General Douglas MacArthur's personal plane, and with American patronage became the first president of the Republic of Korea in 1947. Not having his own power base, and averse to disturbing the social hierarchy, he took advantage of American support in inheriting and utilising the Japanese colonial administration, and in particular the police and army. One reason his army was no match for that of the north was that it was geared for pacification rather than conventional war. After the outbreak of war, which took the North's Korean People's Army (KPA) down to the outskirts of the southern port of Pusan, he was saved by massive US intervention. He fled back to Hawaii in 1960 in a CIA plane, after being ousted in student-led riots.

Time magazine would say of him in 1953, with no hint of irony: 'The great strength of Syngman Rhee is his single-minded devotion to his country and its independence'.[2] The Americans, as we know, have curious ideas as to what constitutes another country's independence; having an American general in charge is no barrier to independent status. However, there was some truth to it. While he was clearly America's man, he was no poodle, and often relations with the United States were strained. He, no less than Kim Il Sung, wanted a unified Korea, and he had no qualms about war. In fact he refused to sign the armistice because he wanted to keep the Americans still fighting. This, incidentally, had a knock-on effect which has surfaced recently to complicate the post-*Cheonan* situation. China apparently suggested reconvening the Military Armistice Commission to investigate the sinking, and this would have brought together the four parties to that Commission – the US, China, North Korea and South Korea. North Korea objected, saying that the MAC had been in suspension since the US had unilaterally substituted a South Korean general for an American one in 1991.

Back in 1953 the Americans, constituted as the United Nations Command, went ahead and signed an armistice with China and North Korea. Rhee had no choice but to accept a fait accompli, the South Korean army not being in a position to continue the war on its own. Rhee lasted until the end of the decade, before being forced into exile. The man who took over, after a brief democratic hiatus, General Park Chung-hee, was yet another variation on the same dictatorial theme.

Park Chung-hee

Park was from a modest background, and he did what many ambitious men did: he trained as a primary school teacher to get an education, and then threw in his job and joined the army – the Japanese army, or more precisely the Manchukuo branch of it. So anxious was he to get in that he wrote a letter of loyalty to Japan in his own blood.[3] The Japanese went and the Americans came, and Park joined the new South Korean army. After a few adventures along the way, such as being accused of being a Communist, he came to power in a coup in 1961. Until his assassination by his spy chief in 1979, he led a South Korea firmly posted in the American camp. The country's major source of foreign exchange in the 1960s was the sending of soldiers to fight with the Americans in Vietnam.

So, in a sense, he was a servant of two masters. Yet again, Park was in many ways his own man as president of the Republic of Korea. One of the first things he did after coming to power was to set up an aggressive campaign to establish diplomatic relations with a wide range of countries. This was partly in competition with

North Korea, which was doing the same thing, but also to create an independent Korean international identity beyond Washington's direct control. The North Koreans were driven by much the same imperatives. His economic policies were very un-American, being firmly state-directed in the style of Meiji Japan or the Soviet Union. His pronouncements on the necessity of developing industry and on self-reliance mirrored what was being said in North Korea. Rapid economic growth gave him, and subsequent leaders, more leverage against American pressure.

His authoritarian, repressive style produced friction with Washington. The Americans, perhaps annoyed at his kidnapping of opposition leader Kim Dae-jung in Tokyo (the idea was to throw him from a helicopter into the sea, but this was foiled by American intervention) forced him to hold elections. The South Koreans were apparently not convinced by this display of democracy, and dutifully re-elected Park to the presidency a couple of times. In 2004 his killer was posthumously awarded a certificate for his contribution to the promotion of democracy. However, there was also a popular work of fiction in the 1990s which cast the Americans as being behind the assassination, suggesting that many thought his relationship with them was fractious. The US also clamped down on Park's attempt to develop nuclear weapons.

Kim Il Sung

The third person in this triumvirate, Kim Il Sung, faced many of the same choices as Syngman Rhee and Park Chung-hee. Like his son and successor, Kim Jong Il, he had to cope with the demands of patrons, in this case the Soviet Union/Russia and China, in somewhat the same way that Park had to deal with the Americans. But it was his first decision – how to address Japanese imperialism – that differentiates Kim Il Sung from Park Chung-hee, and to a lesser extent from Syngman Rhee. That decision, in turn, conditioned the way he was able to deal with his patrons.

Kim Il Sung chose the path of armed resistance to Japan, and while this liberation struggle did not have the success that, for instance, Albania or Yugoslavia had against the Germans it did establish Kim as the pre-eminent anti-Japanese nationalist.[4] Kim returned to Korea when Soviet forces entered northern Korea. While Syngman Rhee had campaigned against Japanese imperialism from Hawaii, and Park Chung-hee had collaborated, Kim built up a reputation as an independence fighter. He was not the only one, of course, but his ascendancy was not pre-ordained, or engineered from Moscow.

Reunifying the Peninsula

Kim Il Sung was adroit at playing off the Soviet Union against China, but was not so successful when it came to dealing with the Americans. Sixty years on, there are still debates and bitter recriminations about the Korean War. We know that both Kim Il Sung and Syngman Rhee were dedicated to a unified Korea (under their own control, of course) and that both regarded war as an acceptable instrument to obtain that. Nothing surprising, or especially morally reprehensible, in that. After all, the American Civil War was the bloodiest in US history, outranking both world wars in American casualties, and yet the moral opprobrium cast upon those who precipitated it is really quite muted; rightly or wrongly, we tend to judge civil wars differently from wars between nations.

In 1950 the greatest war in history was only five years in the past, and the Chinese Civil War was just coming to a close. War must have seemed a natural solution to achieving national reunification. Syngman Rhee's army was much weaker than Kim Il Sung's, although exactly how knowledgeable each was about the capacity of the other is another matter. There were many incursions from the south into the north prior to the outbreak of war in June 1950, but to what degree these were a deliberate attempt by Syngman Rhee to provoke a war that would bring in the Americans in sufficient force to reunify the country for him is unknown, and unknowable. This was the thesis advanced by the iconoclastic American investigative reporter I. F. Stone in his *The Secret History of the Korean War* (1952).[5]

Richard J. Bernstein and Richard Bernstein give the mainstream Western interpretation when they write of

> the generally accepted view that Kim Il Sung, with the somewhat nervous approval and military support of Joseph Stalin, began the conflict with a massive, premeditated attack across the 38th parallel on June 25, 1950, aimed at speedily defeating the ineffectual South Koreans and driving any American troops that came to their aid off the peninsula.[6]

They regret that the armistice of 1953 left 'the aggressor, North Korea's Kim Il Sung, in power unpunished and about to be celebrated as a living God in the half of the country he controlled'.[7] This is a simplistic and rather solipsistic assessment of historical complexity.

To blame Kim Il Sung for being foolhardy in instigating full-scale war in June 1950 is one thing, but judging that half the crime of 'North Korean aggression' was wanting to drive American troops off the peninsula rather gives the game away. If Kim Il Sung was at fault in wanting to drive American troops out of Korea, then what are we to make of George Washington and his desire to see the back of British troops? One suspects that if Syngman Rhee had had the military capability to invade and defeat North Korea in 1950, and had done so, the Bernsteins and their fellows would not have cried aggression. Or if a civil war had broken out in another country and the United States had had no strong interest in who won and who lost, then aggression would probably not have been discerned. And if the United States supported the victorious side in a civil war, as it did for instance in the Yemen in 1994, then the question of who started it would never be raised, and the war itself would remain scarcely noticed.

The historian Bruce Cumings has a much surer feel for the historical context when he points out that

> [t]he South Korean commander of the parallel in the summer of 1949 was Kim Sok-won, a quisling who had chased after Kim Il Sung and other guerrillas in Manchuria in the 1930s, on behalf of the Japanese Kwantung Army – an army well known for provoking incidents, such as the one resulting in Japan's invasion of Manchuria in 1931. My main point, though, was that the commanders of the respective Korean armies had chosen different sides in the long anticolonial struggle against Japan, and it should not have been surprising that once they had the means to do so, they would again clash with each other. What is more surprising is the direct American role, during the US occupation of Korea from 1945 to 1948, in putting in power an entire generation of Koreans in the military and the national police who had served Japanese imperialism.

This linking of the US decision to continue the Japanese imperial apparatus in South Korea to the outbreak of civil war is an important point. The Americans were caught in a dilemma, in Korea and elsewhere, most obviously Vietnam. They saw themselves taking over the defeated Japanese empire, and the collapsing European empires, in a new form of democratic imperialism in which local elites would willingly accept subordination to the United States for the privilege of belonging to the capitalist world system, in a more equal relationship than the old imperialist had allowed – and for protection, sometimes against foreign enemies, but also against their own people. This has in many ways been very successful – there are dozens of countries around the world that host US bases; that dutifully vote the correct way in the United Nations; that allow, at times reluctantly, US corporations into key positions in their markets; and that occasionally send troops to support American invasions or pacifications in the far reaches of the empire. This is a reasonable description of contemporary South Korea. But it was not possible in the 1940s, when a left-leaning popular government was the most likely outcome if the Japanese control apparatus was dismantled. So the Americans retained the police and military inherited from Japanese colonialism, and civil war became perhaps the inevitable outcome.

Cumings concludes that the various theses that have tried to explain the outbreak of war as a deliberate, calculated move by the Soviets or the Americans – something that could be understood outside of Korean history, and specifically the struggle against Japanese colonialism – as inadequate. The right saw the Korean War as Soviet expansion, and the left saw it in terms of American imperialism consolidating its place in the postwar world. The ROK paints the war as aggression from the north, and the DPRK sees it as provoked by the US imperialists and 'the south Korean puppet army'.[8] Cumings, perhaps with the American Civil War in mind, suggests that 'all the theses were wrong, because civil wars do not start, they come along after years or even decades of internecine conflict – as in Korea'.[9]

Finally, as Professor Jae-Jung Suh of Johns Hopkins University notes, the Korean War is still unresolved:

The war is not over. It is not simply that the armistice has yet to be replaced with a peace treaty or that the two Koreas remain at war, heavily armed across the wrongly named Demilitarized Zone. It is also because the Korean War is engaged in multiple conflicts and contradictions.[10]

Strange Symbiosis: South Korea and America

When South Korean soldiers stand at the border, at Panmunjom, and look across, all they will see, apart from Chinese tourists, are North Korean troops. No Russians, no Chinese – only Koreans. When North Korean soldiers look south they, too, see Korean faces, but also American ones. And they know that the general in charge is an American. The DPRK is authentically nationalist, and sovereign; but the ROK, more than 60 years after its creation, has still not achieved full sovereignty. Indeed, one of the main issues over the years, which became prominent during the administration of Roh Moo-hyun and which has resurfaced under Lee Myung-bak and been given extra impetus by the *Cheonan* incident, is what the Americans call OPCON – operational control of the ROK military.

Syngman Rhee ceded control to the US in 1950, as well he might. Presumably the KPA came under the command of the Chinese People's Volunteers sometime after the Chinese intervention. The Korean Civil War, in effect, turned into a Sino-American war, with the Koreans reduced to bit players. However, all the Chinese troops had been withdrawn by the late 1950s (and there had never been a substantial Soviet military presence), so by then we can assume that the DPRK had full operational control over its military. It might also be mentioned that, although North Korean pilots were seconded to the Vietnamese, there was no wholesale despatch of troops to that theatre, as there was from the south. ROK troops have been stationed in Afghanistan, and returned in 2010 after having been withdrawn by Roh Moo-hyun; but there were no DPRK troops there during the Soviet intervention. Nor, unlike the ROK, does the DPRK conduct military exercises with foreign countries.[11]

While the DPRK has been jealous of its military independence – neither sending forces abroad to fight for its patrons, the Soviet Union/Russia and China, nor allowing them command over its forces at home – the ROK has had perforce to follow a different line. Park Chung-hee did attempt to recover OPCON in the late 1960s, but was rebuffed. Back then, the US had complete command of the ROK military – not merely in the case of war ('wartime control') but also on a day-to-day basis in peacetime. When general Chun Doo-hwan mounted his coup in 1979, it is said that he needed American permission to move troops from the border to Seoul. In 1994, during the Kim Young-sam administration, the South Koreans regained peacetime control of their military, and in 2007, under Roh Moo-hyun, it was agreed that wartime control would revert to Seoul on 17 April 2012. But there has been vociferous opposition from the right to this move, and in the aftermath of the *Cheonan* incident it was agreed to delay OPCON until 1 December 2015.[12]

To an outsider, this all seems very strange. In no other substantial independent country at peace is the military under foreign control. And South Korea is a formidable military power, with the tenth-largest military expenditure and the world's sixth-largest military; even standing alone, which it does not, it is much more powerful than North Korea.[13] Even in terms of numbers of soldiers, it is on a par with or effectively superior to North Korea. The press regularly tells us that North Korea has a regular army of 1.2 million, but a recent analysis suggests its size is 700,000 – slightly more than in the south. Apart from the huge disparity in military equipment and materiel, including fuel, the North Korean army spends much of its time growing food and carrying out other economic activities, with correspondingly less time available for military training.

The reason for the foreign control of the military would seem to be that the South Korean right, including President Lee Myung-bak, thinks it important to lock the US military into any war on the Korean peninsula, partly because of the difficulties of overcoming the north, but also because of the Chinese.

Since the end of the Japanese empire, the relationship with the United States, for both Koreas, has been paramount – although it is now being challenged by the rise of China. China has always been important, of course, particularly during the Korean War; but the importance of history and proximity is now being hugely augmented by that of economics. Nevertheless, despite its decline, the United States is still hegemon, and occupies centre-stage. Most, probably all, South Korean leaders have had a complex, negotiated relationship with the United States. Lee Myung-bak seems, at least so far, to have had a relatively frictionless association that has transcended administrations. He transferred his allegiance from Bush to Obama as easily as Blair did his from Clinton to Bush. He has preserved good relations with Washington despite two US-related issues that are potentially very damaging – the importation of US beef in 2008 (in the 'mad cow disease' scare) and the ongoing refusal of the US Congress to ratify the South Korea–United States Free Trade Agreement (KORUS FTA).

Lee's rapport with Washington stands in some contrast to the demeanour of his progressive predecessors, Kim Dae-jung and, especially, Roh Moo-hyun. Roh, as we have seen, wanted to regain full operational control of the ROK military, and he wanted to position South Korea as a political balancing force in Northeast Asia – and as an economic and logistic hub. In other words, he was striving for greater independence of the ROK from the United States. Lee Myung-bak has a different approach. He sees the ROK taking a stronger role within the American imperium, in some ways echoing John Howard's desire to become America's sheriff. Lee, it would seem, seeks to serve Washington in order to manipulate Washington.

He has suffered a number of setbacks over his handling of the *Cheonan* incident – widespread scepticism within South Korea, and the refusal of Russia and China, in their different ways, blindly to accept his investigation of the sinking. This in turn has led to their refusal to condemn North Korea, and their sceptical stance in the United Nations Security Council and elsewhere. However, he has had no such problems with the Americans – and once you have the endorsement of Washington, others follow, including the EU parliament and at least 80 countries around the world.[14] If the New Zealand government is anything to go by, those countries do not even bother to examine the evidence, or notice the opposition to the government verdict in South Korea.

This seemingly unreflective and unnuanced support is rather astounding given its possible consequences. Whereas China and Russia have trod cautiously, the United States has rushed ahead. Among other things, this has cut off negotiations, limited though they were, with the DPRK, sunk the Six-Party Talks, and adversely affected relations with China. These consequences might conceivably be sensible if they were the result of considered policy choices; but they seem to have come about in a policy vacuum, with the Obama administration floundering in strategic incoherence. This is happening at home of course – in the Mexican Gulf, most obviously – and globally, as exemplified by the paralysis in the Middle East. But nowhere, it seems – except perhaps in Israel – has the United States so relinquished strategic planning as in Korea. The distinguished Russian Korea expert Georgy Toloraya draws these threads together:

The *Cheonan* tragedy is being seen by some as an opportunity to get Kim Jong Il, especially in a difficult time of economic and succession problems. So after two months of thorough preparations the tactical response seems to be aimed at accomplishing the following goals:

- to isolate [the] North Korean regime internationally;
- to deprive North Korea of Chinese support (this seems to be the main cause, as China has been threatened that unless it acts the way the West wants it to, the response, including increased military build-up in the area, will hurt its own interests); and
- to weaken the regime by imposing new sanctions, breaking financial and trade life-lines [and] pushing the impoverished country to implosion.

Interestingly, in a manner of 'tail wagging the dog,' the US has been reluctantly pulled into this plot by South Korea. One anonymous expert commented in the widely-circulated Nelson Report that the US is now wedded to Lee Myung-bak's policy of 'regime change' and this has broad policy implications not just for the peninsula, but across the board [in] US-China issues.[15]

It would seem that Lee Myung-bak has been astonishingly successful in manipulating the Obama administration into accepting his agenda, and that agenda is fraught with dangers.

Others see the United States as much more in control of the post-*Cheonan* game-plan than this. The North Koreans, publicly at least, put the US in the driving seat:

Recently the US secretary of State [*sic*] let loose a spate of sheer lies to brand the DPRK as the chief culprit of the warship sinking during her junkets to Japan, China and south Korea.

But a scrutiny into who is to benefit from the 'story about a torpedo attack by north Korea' and what will be gained from it makes it clear that the case was orchestrated by the US and the south Korean authorities. Firstly, the Obama administration is using the recent case for orchestrating with utmost efforts a farce to make it appear 'strong' with the Congress mid-term election slated for coming November at hand as it was known to be weak externally in the first year of its administration. Secondly, the US hyped the 'threat from north Korea' to sound real, finally making the ruling Democratic Party of Japan, which had been keen to drive the US forces out of Okinawa, yield to it. This is the reason why the 'results of investigation' were announced within May. Thirdly, the US has come to justify its policy of 'strategic patience' designed to degrade the environment for international investment in the DPRK and steadily suffocate its economy. Fourthly, it became possible for the US to put China into an awkward position and keep hold on Japan and south Korea as its servants.[16]

It is common for North Korea to castigate the 'south Korean authorities' (note the capitalisation) as American puppets, but where the analysis ends and the rhetoric, and negotiating ploys, begin is difficult to discern.

Somewhat between these positions (Lee Myung-bak as driver of the crisis versus Lee as American puppet serving US strategy) is the argument of Alexander Vorontsov and Oleg Revenko:

> At this point the question arises naturally what force could have been behind the *Cheonan* incident and in whose interests it was inflated to become a global problem. One must be naive to believe that S. Korea could independently – without its patron's blessing and support – make such far-reaching decisions and, in a matter of days, float the broad international campaign. Whoever is actually responsible for the *Cheonan* tragedy, the very developments warrant the hypothesis that they are a result of careful a priori planning ...
>
> Preoccupied with Iran and Afghanistan, the US can't at the same time focus on the six-party talks. The present US negotiating team headed by Stephen Bosworth is clearly weak and even has no specific plan for breaking the stalemate should N. Korea revert to the negotiations. Accordingly, there could be an intention to freeze the negotiating situation under some pretext, for example blaming a provocation on Pyongyang, and, for the time being, rely on sanctions against N. Korea. Perhaps, the freeze of the six-party talks became the option of choice for Washington not only because the US cannot afford to stretch its resources thin, but also because – contrary to official claims – the White House and the Pentagon do not regard the threat posed by N. Korea's nuclear program as truly serious due to the more than modest proportions of the country's nuclear arsenal and missile capability.[17]

This book attempts to tease out the complex relationship between Seoul and Washington. South Korea is clearly more than a pawn in US grand strategy, but can we go so far as to say that the Korean tail is wagging the American dog? Lee Myung-bak would not have been able to implement his hardline exploitation of the *Cheonan* incident without American approval, and that approval was forthcoming because it was consistent with American strategies – in particular the containment of China. Moreover, the United States has made moves to curtail Lee's autonomy: it has reclaimed control of the joint exercises, and it has backed down on anti-submarine games in the face of Chinese protests.[18] Nevertheless, on balance it does seem that Lee Myung-bak has the initiative, and at the moment has effectively captured US North Korea policy.

NORTH KOREA: THE EXISTENTIAL CHALLENGE OF AMERICAN HOSTILITY

The United States is no less important to Pyongyang than to Seoul, although that importance takes a very different form. The relationship is one of hostility, but not quite the mutual hostility that is usually portrayed. No doubt there is a huge amount of resentment on the part of North Korea because of the division of Korea, and because of the war and the decades of military threat and economic and political sanctions since then.[19] But this is tempered by an awareness that the DPRK needs to have a 'normal', even friendly relationship with the United States – normal enough to remove the threat and the sanctions, and friendly enough to offer some counterbalance to Chinese influence.[20]

For some decades after the Korean War the North outperformed the South, even despite American hostility, but with the collapse of the Soviet Union the economy went into crisis. According to the South Korean government the disparity between the two economies is now huge:

> South Korea's gross national income (GNI) for 2009 was 1,680 trillion won – 37.3 times more than the North's 28 trillion won. (GNI is the total value produced within a country, its gross domestic product, together with income received from other countries.[21])
>
> South Korea's per-capita GNI was 21.92 million won last year, 17.9 times more than the North's 1.22 million won.
>
> Total trade volume for the South reached $686.6 billion last year. North Korea's total trade was $3.41 billion.[22]

The DPRK, for its part, has calculated that sanctions have cost it $13.8 trillion in the six decades from 1945 to 2005.[23]

Whatever the accuracy of those estimates, it is clear that the DPRK economy cannot be rehabilitated and produce the 'great prosperous and powerful nation', as the current slogan has it, by 2012, the 100th anniversary of Kim Il Sung's birth, unless there is a peaceful relationship with the United States.[24] It is imperative for Pyongyang somehow to get Washington to drop its policy of hostility, without surrendering its independence. This has been the main thrust of its foreign policy, especially since the demise of the Soviet Union. The nuclear weapons programme clearly has a deterrent component, but nuclear weapons are essentially a bargaining device. Many dispute this, and argue that Pyongyang will never relinquish nuclear weapons; but former President Jimmy Carter got it right when he remarked: 'It could be worked out, in my opinion, in half a day."[25]

Not merely is a deal with the United States essential for North Korea's economic recovery, but the rapid decline in relations with the South since Lee Myung-bak came to power, now much exacerbated by the *Cheonan* incident, has caused a return to economic decline. Trade and tourism between the two Koreas had grown considerably, especially under Kim Dae-jung and Roh Moo-hyun. Lee Myung-bak has brought tourism to a halt and, putatively in response to the *Cheonan* sinking, has cut off trade as well.

These economic problems, combined with reports of Kim Jong Il's ill health and presumed problems around his succession (see Chapter 8), have greatly excited the right in the South who now, it would seem, anticipate that the North might now be ripe for the picking. The contingency plans for invading the North, which had been put aside under Kim and Roh, have been taken out again and dusted down.

2
Korea and the Postcolonial World

DECOLONISATION, THE CREATION OF NEW STATES, AND THE GROWING ROLE OF NON-STATE ACTORS

There is a difficulty in discussing decolonisation, because the concept and practice of colonisation, and hence of decolonisation, is very slippery. Manchukuo, described by its opponents as a 'puppet state' of Japan, was never formally a colony; and today, as we look around the world, we can see many nominally independent states that are not really so. The United States arguably has the largest empire in the history of the world, with perhaps a thousand military bases around the globe.[1] The Republic of Korea, in particular, is a state of constrained sovereignty, as we saw in Chapter 1, with its military under the 'wartime command' of the United States. Bases are not the only instrument of 'neocolonial' control, but its most visible symbol. But control beyond recognised boundaries is only part of the definitional problem, because there are few parts of the old world without contested areas: the Basques, the Scots, the Tibetans, the Kashmiris, and the Tamils in Sri Lanka, among many others, all have advocates for independence. The New World of European settlement largely escaped these problems of historical legacy – the result of waves of migration – largely because its original inhabitants were decimated or exterminated – or occasionally, as in the case of the Maori people, dispersed and assimilated in such a way that separatism is not viable.

Nevertheless, it is meaningful to consider decolonisation as a seminal characteristic of the postwar world. In the words of the United Nations: 'When the United Nations was established in 1945, 750 million people – almost a third of the world's population – lived in Territories that were non-self-governing, dependent on colonial Powers. Today, fewer than 2 million people live in such Territories.'[2]

In pre-war Korea, as in many other parts of the world, many considered it natural that they should be ruled by foreigners. Some, no doubt, welcomed it – colonisation does bring benefits, at least to segments of the population. Many, in their various ways, resisted it. Today, while we can discern, if we chose to look, continuity in patterns of control, hegemony and influence, it is clear that the modes in which these are exercised are greatly changed. Today, whatever the realities of submerged power, it is the norm for countries to have their own national government, flag, armed forces and football team. Aspiration does, to quite some extent, determine or at least influence reality. Slaves are slaves partly because they accept slavery. Mental emancipation is an essential component of liberation. Similarly, the belief in superiority – of race, religion, technology – is crucial to the ability to rule an empire, and if that belief falters, then things tend to fall apart. There are signs of such anxiety in contemporary American discussions of the decline of the US.

The decolonisation process, and the concomitant creation, or re-creation, of nation-states, has been inexorable – though often long drawn-out (30 years of struggle passed between the declaration of Vietnamese independence in 1945 and the departure of American troops in 1975) and frequently unsuccessful. Lack of success in nation-building is a variable construct, and it may result in states such as Egypt that appear to be functioning but are in fact teetering on the brink, and others, such as Somalia, that are dismissed as 'failed states'. This term is cant, in that it obscures the role of foreign forces in stifling the nascent state. However, one characteristic that these unconsummated states have is that the role of defending and administering the country has passed to non-state actors. We return to that issue below, because it has important implications for US policy towards North Korea.

KOREA'S UNCONSUMMATED NATIONAL REVIVAL

The boundaries of states are seldom fixed for a long time. They ebb and flow with changes in power. States may be created from pre-existing entities, and sometimes, as in the case of many of the European-created states of Africa, in disregard of the tribal structures that preceded them. In many cases tribal or ethnic groups straddle one or more modern states, often leading to great instability – the Kurds (Iraq, Turkey, Iran), the Pashtuns (Afghanistan, Pakistan), and the Baluchis (Pakistan, Iran) are particularly important contemporary examples. Germany is a particularly important case, and one which, because of its 1945 division and subsequent unification, resonates in Korea. Korea was divided, by American initiation and Soviet acquiescence, into two parts, north and south, which became formally established as states – the Democratic People's Republic of Korea (DPRK) and the Republic of Korea (ROK). Both were admitted as United Nations members on the same day – 17 September 1991 – and both are viable, functioning states. Coming from a homogenous ethnic group, they have many things in common but have, of course, moved apart in many ways over the last six decades.[3] One way this has happened is in the use of languages, and linguistic differences indeed became an issue during the *Cheonan* investigation (see Chapter 7). In the context of this book, it is worth noting that the ROK is a rich state with constrained sovereignty, while the DPRK is a poor state with full sovereignty.

The Republic of Korea

The ROK military is under the 'wartime control' of the United States (see Chapter 1), and there is a wide range of areas in which the latter has effective, if not formal, control. These include missiles, the purchase of weapons systems, and despatch of troops for America's foreign wars. The ROK is allowed ballistic missiles with a range of up 300 kilometres, with warheads of 500 kilograms of explosives or less (these constraints apparently do not extend to cruise missiles).[4] The purchase of weapons systems can not only be very expensive, but often carries far-reaching political implications. The United States restricts the sale of advanced systems, such as the F-22 Raptor, and there was visible disquiet in South Korea in 2007 when it was said that the US was contemplating selling these stealth fighters to Japan and not South Korea. The *Chosun Ilbo* agonised:

> In mock battles with F-15, F-16 and F-18 fighter jets, the F-22 won 144 dogfights and lost none. The South Korean Air Force, composed mainly of F-15 and F-16 fighters, would be powerless in front of the Japanese Air Self Defense Force equipped with F-22s.[5]

The sale of F-22s to Japan did not materialize, but the issue may well resurface. The United States is reportedly losing its edge in stealth technology, and Russia, China and Japan are catching up.[6] Arms sales are a very important part of the US economy, and it is common for it, like other weapon-producing countries, to produce for export as a way of keeping down the unit cost of the weapons systems used by its own military. There is always a need to balance the economic advantage of export with the desire to retain the technological lead (even over 'allies'), and the changing landscape of stealth technology might bring the export of F-22s back onto the agenda.

The F-22 is at the leading edge of the US arsenal, and so there are strategic constraints; but in general America is a very assiduous exporter of arms: only to selected clients, of course, but there are enough of them to make the US by far the world's leading seller of arms, hugely dwarfing the much-maligned DPRK's military exports, which are so small they scarcely register; the latest report from the Congressional Research Service does not mention them at all.[7] Indeed, so assiduous is the United States in its exporting endeavours that it sells weapons to rival states such as India and Pakistan 'to maintain neutrality', as well as 'creating new opportunities for American defense firms'.[8] One great advantage of selling arms to friendly states in rivalry with each other is that sales to one spur purchases from the others. The anticipated sale of an arms package worth $64 billion to Saudi Arabia, reported in September 2010, was expected to 'trigger additional purchases by nervous neighbors in the Middle East, and ensure continued US arms sales to Israel'.[9] There is an added twist to this story: Israel will get more advanced weapons than Saudi Arabia 'to maintain Israel's QME – qualitative military edge', and much of it will be paid for by the American taxpayer.[10] George Bernard Shaw's Andrew Undershaft, the arms manufacturer in Major Barbara who had no compunction about selling weapons to both sides, would feel quite at home.[11]

The global arms market is far from a level playing field. Straightforward pecuniary corruption plays a part, and the British seem to be the leaders in that field.[12] Where the Americans do excel is in applying political pressure to sell their weapons, and it may be that if you have the political leverage, as the US has, then resorting to bribes is not necessary. In addition, the Americans have a long tradition of frowning on foreign corruption, and on those nations, such as the French, that are perceived to tolerate it; US commentators frequently refer to the Foreign Corrupt Practices Act of 1977 as evidence of their probity in international business.[13] However, as Mark Thompson wrote in *Time* magazine, 'There's no business like the arms business', because virtually by definition most of the weapons bought are a waste of money from a military point of view.[14] The Saudis must have spent hundreds of billions of dollars since 1973 on arms purchases from the US, Britain and other countries anxious to recoup their expenditure on oil-price rises.

'Interoperability' is the mantra of both the US military and the arms industry: in other words, having weapons systems that allow selected 'allied' militaries to operate in coordination with (and under the control of) the United States. John Feffer outlines some of the implications of this for South Korea:

> Then there is the cost of maintaining the interoperability of allied forces through the import of US military goods. In 2007, South Korea bought about $900 million worth of arms, 95 percent of which came from the United States. This figure will likely grow as the US Congress recently upgraded South Korea's military procurement status to the level of Australia, New Zealand, Japan, and NATO members. The United States has used interoperability as a way to influence South Korea's purchasing decisions, for example, twisting arms to persuade South Korea to purchase Boeing F-15Ks rather than French Rafales or Russian Sukhoi Su-35s. Also, as the United States upgrades its forces in line with RMA [the Revolution in Military Affairs], South Korea has no choice but to do the same, for the dance partner who fails to follow the lead will eventually be exchanged for another.[15]

Feffer is not quite right about the danger to South Korea of being replaced as a dancing partner – nobody else on the dance floor is positioned between Japan, China, Russia and North Korea, and among US allies in the region, only Japan has a larger military budget. But the pressure is there, and the fact that the US took 95 per cent of the market in 2007 attests to its effectiveness.

The case of the Rafales was particularly illustrative, because the South Korean military reportedly preferred them, but the government (then under Kim Dae-jung) apparently succumbed to US pressure: 'European industry officials believe the Rafale built by French aircraft firm Dassault initially received more favorable reviews from the Korean military than Boeing's F-15K, but the Korean government selected the US fighter jet allegedly due to a political consideration.'[16] Dassault tried to fight the decision in the South Korea courts, but gave up and withdrew in 2002:

> 'We have every reason to believe that the Korean defense market is the private hunting ground of the US defense industry,' Yves Robins, vice-president of international relations at Dassault, said at a press briefing. Mr Robins said his firm would not bid for any defense contracts offered by South Korean government as long as the US firms dominate the Korean market.[17]

The issue subsequently resurfaced with the crash of an F-15K in 2006:

> Critics said the need to maintain Korea–US military cooperation held precedence over function and price at the time. But Air Force officials countered that the technology transfer and the large number of Korean components in the plane as well as technical localisation were major factors in the decision. The latest crash, however, is forcing them to reconsider the plane's continuous purchase.[18]

Pressure on the South Korean government to increase military expenditure – from the US and from its own military establishment, which of course has a vested interest – has proved irresistible, irrespective of the political complexion of the administration in power. As Jae-Jung Suh pointed out in 2009:

> The Republic of Korea has rapidly increased its defense budget in recent years. Last year's spending of 26.6 trillion won represents a twofold increase from ten years ago. Now the Ministry of National Defense projects an annual average increase of 7.6 percent to 53.3 trillion won by 2020, another doubling over the next decade. South Korea, notably, raised its defense spending at a higher rate than North Korea at a time when Seoul was taking a more conciliatory policy of engagement. While the Roh Moo-hyun administration increased defense spending ostensibly in response to its policy goal to build a more autonomous military, *the US–Korea alliance motivated and shaped South Korea's military transformation.*[19]

The purported 'threat from North Korea' is frequently brought forward as the reason for a number of things – South Korea's burgeoning military expenditure, US missile defence and Prompt Global Strike (PGS), the US military presence in East Asia and the West Pacific, and Japanese remilitarisation.[20] North Korea can inflict considerable local damage on its adversaries if attacked, but the idea that it poses a threat because it might *initiate* hostilities is preposterous given the huge disparity between North Korea's military and that of the United States, South Korea, or Japan – let alone all three of them. But fear is fed by relentless propaganda, not by facts. A US poll in 2009 indicated that

[f]ifty-two percent say that North Korea is a very serious threat, higher than the 43 percent who feel that way about Iran and much higher than the 20 percent who feel that way about China or the 11 percent who think Russia threatens the US.[21]

'Interoperability' has another function beyond driving the demand for high-tech, expensive American hardware. It enables subaltern militaries, such as that of South Korea, not merely to fight alongside the US at home, but also to help out in wars elsewhere in the empire. Again, this pressure is no respecter of the political leanings of the South Korean government, and indeed progressive administrations might be more susceptible than right-wing ones.

President Roh Moo-hyun sent troops to Iraq, against his ideological preference and better judgement, as part of a deal with George W. Bush. He was lucky in that there was only one military casualty, but it did erode his political support at home:

'I thought [then] and even now that sending troops to Iraq would go down in history as a mistake. As a president, however, it was an unavoidable, inevitable choice.' These were the thoughts of late President Roh Moo-hyun on the Iraq deployment, as revealed in his memoir, 'Success and Setbacks.'

The Roh administration tried to use the Iraq deployment as a lever to get the George W. Bush administration to ease its hardline policy on North Korea and resolve the nuclear issue. This was because in spring 2003, immediately after the launch of the Roh administration, hardline rhetoric coming from the United States was rife, including calls to bomb North Korea to eliminate its nuclear program.

At the end of April 2003, one month after the US invasion of Iraq, South Korea sent about 300 non-combat troops, including engineers and medics, to Iraq to help the United States. The controversy continued throughout 2003. Ultimately, after controversy, the National Assembly passed a resolution to send troops to Iraq in February 2004.

Roh, who pledged before his inauguration to say what he had to say to the United States, and get red in the face when it was time to get red in the face, explained that the Iraq deployment was an inevitable choice to stop the possibility of war on the Korean Peninsula resulting from the North Korean nuclear crisis.

Roh's base, which conducted a movement against the deployment, began turning its back on the Roh administration, saying it had participated in America's immoral war of aggression. Due to the Iraq deployment, a crack developed in the faith between the Roh administration and its base.[22]

There are parallels here in the way that the administration of Japanese Prime Minister Hatoyama Yukio collapsed after he reneged, under American pressure, on his promise to close the Marine Air Station Futenma base in the wake of the *Cheonan* incident.[23]

The current theatre of operations in which the United States is anxious to have 'allies' is, of course, Afghanistan. Roh pulled South Korean troops out of Afghanistan in 2007 as part of a deal with the Taliban, who had captured a group of South Korean missionaries and executed two of them.[24] Lee Myung-bak, ignoring Roh's presumed promise to the Taliban, recommitted South Korea troops towards the end of 2009, and they were deployed mid 2010. There are two components, a Provincial Reconstruction Team (PRT) and, to protect them, a combat unit, the Ashena Unit. The liberal press opposed the sending of troops and the right-wing press applauded it.[25] An American scholar maintained that 'Korea's troop deployment in Afghanistan serves Korea's national interest', and Secretary Clinton, realising that President Lee faced domestic opposition, 'welcomed the deployment', implying that she thought that not all Koreans would consider that to be the case, and that President Lee was due some thanks.[26] The right-wing *Chosun Ilbo*, a firm supporter of the deployment, rather plaintively demanded, 'Gov't Must Tell Muslim World of Ashena Unit's Mission of Peace', adding that 'the name Ashena means 'friend' or 'companion' in the local dialect'.[27] Whether the locals will be convinced is another matter, and attacks on Korean companies in Afghanistan have increased since the decision to redeploy troops.[28]

What all these reports had in common, despite their differences, was that the despatch of troops was not really about Afghanistan, but about South Korea's relationship with the United States.[29] The same underlying factor governed a subsequent commitment to the United States, but here the South Korean reaction was rather different. There seems little doubt that the ROK military welcomed the opportunity to return to Afghanistan: the risks are relatively slight; ROK participation, like that of most of the other Coalition partners, is primarily symbolic rather than military, and it seems that the US command does its best not to expose them to undue danger. Ironically, it makes sense for General Petraeus to shed American lives rather than those from countries where there is significant opposition to the war. On the positive side, the ROK troops get combat experience and the opportunity to work with the world's best-equipped, and currently most experienced, military. The Koreans are not alone in thinking this. Rick Rozoff points out that

> [t]here are 150,000 foreign troops in Afghanistan, 120,000 of them under the command of NATO's International Security Assistance Force (ISAF). Military personnel from over a quarter of the 192 members of the United Nations.
>
> They include soldiers from almost every European country, several Asia-Pacific states, and nations in the Americas and the Middle East ...
>
> The war in Afghanistan provides long-range integrated combat training for global NATO and a foundation for the US to build a far-reaching military network unprecedented in scope.[30]

The subsequent issue was the imposition of sanctions on Iran. This was another matter that transcended the left/right, civil/military schisms over Afghanistan. Iran is an important economic partner for South Korea:

> the United States is believed to have pressured Korea to freeze the assets of Bank Mellat, the second largest bank in Iran, which is believed to have funneled money to Iran's nuclear program. The bank's Seoul branch serves as its Asian hub and is one of only three branches outside Iran. According to Korean news reports, 70 percent of export transactions between Korea and Iran, involving some 2,000 Korean businesses, are handled by Bank Mellat. Most of these businesses are small and medium-sized enterprises that have already been affected by the new US sanctions, as Korean banks have stopped conducting transactions with Bank Mellat to maintain their access to the US banking system.
>
> This effort creates obvious problems for South Korea, which has recently enjoyed robust trade relations with Iran [, growing] to nearly $10 billion a year. Iran is Korea's second largest export market in the Middle East and is its fourth largest supplier of oil, providing about 10 percent of Korea's petroleum imports. Implementing sanctions against Iran and freezing the assets of Bank Mellat could lead to retaliatory measures by Iran, which could hurt many key Korean industries in the Middle East, including the construction industry.[31]

Symbolic of the economic relationship between Iran and South Korea, and the dilemma faced by South Korean industry, was the Kia Pride: 'Kia is a household name in the Islamic republic and its affordable, boxy Pride represents between 30 and 40 per cent of vehicles on the road.'[32] According to this *Financial Times* article, Kia will try to retain some foothold in the Iran market. But if, or when, the Americans do allow Kia, and other South Korean companies, back into Iran, they may well find that the Chinese have supplanted them.

The Democratic People's Republic of Korea

The DPRK is a poor state, especially in comparison with the South. Even allowing for exaggeration, uncertainty arising from lack of reliable data and assumptions over exchange rates, the gap between North and South is immense, with one South Korean scholar estimating that the North's GNI is only one percent of that of the South.[33] This poverty is primarily the result of US sanctions (see Chapter 11), broadly defined and including the continuing military threat that imposes such a heavy defence burden. There is no doubt that North Korea's economic performance was for some decades better than that of South Korea – although there is some dispute about how long that superiority lasted. There is also uncertainty about the degree to which high growth was reflected in better living standards. The Korean American economist, Joseph Sang-Hoon Chung, writing in the early 1970s, noted that both the priority given to industrial development and the defence burden limited growth of personal consumption, although with different consequences:

> Not atypically for a communist country, an average North Korean, though his lot has improved substantially, has not benefited fully from economic development. Priority development in heavy industry at the expense of the consumer and agricultural sector is one explanation. A high rate of defense spending is another. While sacrificing today's consumption for greater consumption tomorrow (North Korea's strategy of high-level capital formation) does make long-run economic sense, resources allocated to national defense bring no such beneficial effects.[34]

Whether defence spending yields beneficial effects really depends on whether it is necessary or not. Current US defence spending clearly goes well beyond any definition of necessity – it accounts for some 42 per cent of world military expenditure, and is as much as that of the next 15 countries put together – and many of those are 'allies'.[35] North Korea obviously has much more cause for heavy spending on defence, and providing that cause – through constant military threat – is part of US strategy, as it was against Soviet Union. Ronald Reagan is widely thought to have brought about the Soviet collapse by an escalation of military spending.

Professor Chung provides an interesting and not unrepresentative example, from an unlikely source, of the acknowledgement of the success of North Korean development:

> All in all the study shows that North Korea has made a giant stride since 1945 in her drive toward industrialisation and economic viability. Although recently her pace of growth has slowed, resulting in a readjustment of her economic plans, from all indications the dislocations of the early 1960s have long been contained and her progress continues …
>
> Calling the North Korean feat a miracle perhaps overstates the case but nevertheless dramatizes her achievements as evidenced by various indicators …[36]

North Korea not merely outperformed the South, but also did much better than China. Robert Ash, reviewing Chung's book for the *China Quarterly*, noted that although North Korea had not achieved self-sufficiency in food, the growth rate was very high:

> Perhaps predictably, agriculture has proved to be the weak link, although 'weak' here needs to be qualified, for the 6 per cent per annum growth of agricultural GVO (Gross Value of Output) between 1947 and 1963 (an annual 4–6 per cent per capita) is a figure which in, say, the Chinese context would be interpreted with some optimism. Nevertheless, it seems that North Korea has not yet attained self-sufficiency in food supplies.[37]

Agriculture was predictably the weak link, because it was constrained by geographical factors – shortage of arable land and a short growing season – and it was in industry that the North's economy really shone:

> By contrast, industrial development has been an outstanding success. Emphasis has been on the creation of a heavy-industry base and so rapidly has this been achieved that in recent years North Korea has been an exporter of industrial goods. Between

1949 and 1970 gross industrial output rose 69 times, a particularly important role having been played by the machine-building industry which in 1954–60 grew by 47 per cent per annum![38]

North Korea's drive for economic development and industrialisation was mirrored in the South, especially under Park Chung-hee, and in many ways the similarities between the two Koreas are stronger than their differences.[39] In this they are both 'developmental states', albeit of different complexions, and – crucially in this context – with differing international linkages.[40] Both Korean states are part of the decolonisation process and emerged from the same colonial experience, and they share the usual aspirations to be economically prosperous and economically and politically secure. There are huge differences between them, to be sure, but these are ultimately more the result of the international linkages than anything else.

In respect of the international environment, South Korea has had most of the advantages. One advantage the North had was that it had two patrons – the Soviet Union and China – and could play one off against the other. But that advantage disappeared with the collapse of the Soviet Union, which meant not only that Soviet (and East European) support was lost, but that its relationship with China, already moving towards some sort of capitalism, was also transformed, becoming much more commercial and calculating.

Even before the collapse of the Soviet Union, North Korea was in a disadvantageous international position. The Soviet Union was not a good economy to be partnered with; it was much poorer than the United States and the developed capitalist countries, and was geographically distant for practical purposes. Although North Korea and the Soviet Union shared a land boundary, the cost of transporting products between their heartlands must have been considerably greater than that of trans-Pacific trade. The construction of improved rail links across Eurasia – what Kim Dae-jung dubbed the 'Iron Silk Road' – may well transform these cost differentials in the future, but they have been a great burden in the past.[41]

South Korea, on the other hand, had untrammelled access to the richest markets, both developed and developing (construction projects in the Middle East, for example), relatively good access to advanced technology and to higher education overseas – especially in the US. Moreover, it received a huge amount of US aid, both civilian and military. The 'economic dimension' of military aid is, naturally, difficult to pin down. To the extent that it takes the form of direct payments to the recipient country, it has an economic impact – but data on the breakdown are not available. It should also be added, as a counterbalance to the costs mentioned above, that the stationing of US troops in South Korea, though not classified as military aid, does provide economic benefit in the form of purchases of local goods and services. Economic benefit also flowed to South Korea through its provision of troops to serve in Vietnam in the 1960s.

US aid has had an existential impact on South Korea. David Steinberg, who has produced the most authoritative work on the subject, claims that 'without United States military and economic support of almost $13 billion the Republic of Korea (ROK) would not exist'.[42] This figure, it should be noted, is given in current dollars, and so represents a far greater sum, if corrected for inflation, than it might appear. For instance, the Library of Congress country study on South Korea states: 'About US$3 billion was received before 1968, forming an average of *60 percent of all investment* in South Korea.'[43]

The United States was not the only donor to South Korea, although it was by far the largest: 'United States assistance to Korea totalled about $12.6 billion from 1946 to 1975. Over half of this was military aid. In addition, the Japanese provided about $1.0 billion and other foreign donors, $1.8 billion.'[44] The Japanese contribution is particularly significant, because it was in fact disguised reparations for the colonial period that were given after the establishment of diplomatic relations between Japan and the Republic of Korea in 1965. North Korea has naturally been hankering after similar reparations, and that has been one of the drivers behind its desire to normalise relations with Japan.[45]

North Korea also benefited from aid from the Soviet Union, Eastern Europe and China, although the amount it received was almost certainly much smaller. Uncertainties arise because of the lack of data, difficulties of classification (What is aid and what is a commercial transaction? How should we compare a grant with a loan?) and the problems of price and currency conversions. Soviet prices, for instance, were often very different from 'world prices'. It was reported that 'the North Koreans claim that the Russians sold them exports at prices that were higher than those of the world market while it imported goods from Korea at prices that were lower.'[46] How frequent – and how justified – such complaints were is unknown. After all, if the prices of some Soviet imports were higher than world averages, others were lower – oil being the most significant of the latter. When Russia raised the price of its oil exports to world prices after the collapse of the Soviet Union, North

Korea could not afford to keep up imports, which precipitated the economic crisis.

Despite methodological difficulties, we can be confident that North Korea received far less aid than the South – not surprising, of course, given the greater wealth of the United States and its allies. In the period up to 1962 it is reported that:

> North Korea had received an estimated $1.4 billion in economic assistance (of which $719 million was in the form of loans). Of this, 48.8 percent had come from the Soviet Union, 30.9 percent from China, and the remainder from Eastern Europe.[47]

However, what is more important, and more relevant in this context, than the amount of aid was the way in which it – and the economic relationship underlying it – fitted with the strategy for nation-building and development.[48] Kim Il Sung was wedded to the idea of *Juche*, usually translated as 'self-reliance', and the building of a nation that was independent economically as well as politically. According to Joungwon Alexander Kim, it was commitment to independence that brought about a rupture with the Soviet Union in 1962:

> And once again the regime introduced an economic plan aimed at 'independence'. The Seven Year Plan, introduced to the congress in 1961, once more defied Soviet efforts to induce 'cooperative planning' among the nations of the Communist bloc. In outlining the plan, Kim Il-song [Kim Il Sung] pointed out that as the previous Five Year Plan had laid the basis for an industrial economy, the Seven Year Plan would consolidate the basis of an 'independent national economy.' Insistence on this independent economy soon brought retaliation from the Soviet Union, which after 1962 cut off economic aid.[49]

The use of quotation marks around the word independence is telling, because in South Korea, which was nominally independent, the drive for autonomous nation-building, though not absent, was by comparison quite muted. Or, to put it another way, perhaps one could say that Park Chung-hee (who had taken South Korea by then) saw the way forward as being *through* America rather than in opposition to it. This, as already noted, reflects back on attitudes to Japanese colonialism. Park Chung-hee worked with it, perhaps to further Korean national aims as well as his own personal ones, while Kim Il Sung fought it as a guerrilla.

North Korea has suffered from its quest for 'real independence'. The Soviets disapproved of it, the Chinese were less than happy, and the Americans have been consistently hostile. The DPRK has received less in aid than the ROK; and while Russia, and particularly China, are now important economic partners of South Korea, the North faces embargo and sanctions. Terrible though the consequences of independence may be, this Korean nationalism is in many ways the defining characteristic of the DPRK: it is what differentiates it from the ROK. The South Korean military is under the wartime command of the Americans, American troops are still in the country 65 years after they arrived, and Korean troops go abroad to fight in American wars. The contrast with the North is stark. No foreigners control the North Korean military, or even have any substantial role within it. Soviet troops, who like their American counterparts took over from the defeated Japan in 1945, left in 1948; and the Chinese, who came during the Korean war in 1950, left in 1958.[50] There have been no reports of any joint military exercises between the Korean People's Army (KPA) and foreign armies, certainly in recent decades; and no North Korean troops are engaged abroad.

If nationalism is a defining characteristic of the DPRK, and a cause of many of its problems, it is also a source of great strength. It is nationalism that gave it the resilience to survive both the collapse of the Soviet Union and the rise of China, as discussed below. It is this nationalism which is likely to thwart the attempts of a takeover that are discussed in Part III of this book.

Despite all of its problems, and the frequent allegations to that effect, the DPRK is no 'failed state'. The state is less intrusive than it was, and less able to provide for its citizens through the Public Distribution System (PDS) and health services.[51] Nevertheless it functions as a state in that it has effective control over its territory, and if attacked or invaded it will fight back as a state. However, the possibility of an invasion of North Korea does intersect with the subject of non-state actors and terrorism, albeit as pretext rather than reality, so it is an issue which should be addressed.

Would the DPRK, as is frequently alleged, transfer nuclear assets to terrorists?[52] The growing role of non-state actors in defending states which have ceased to function effectively – the so-called 'failed states' – has been mentioned above. However, non-state actors are even more important in respect of states which are not deemed to have failed but have, in effect, lost sovereignty, usually through invasion. Iraq and Afghanistan are obvious examples. The loss of sovereignty may not be through physical invasion, and it may not be complete – here Pakistan comes to mind. However, in all these cases the state ceases to perform its basic traditional function of defending the nation, but rather becomes an instrument of its subjugation. As a result, what resistance there is to foreign domination comes from non-state actors, variously called insurgents, freedom-fighters, or terrorists. The corollary of this is that non-state actors are becoming increasingly a concern, perhaps the major concern, to imperialist powers, notably the United States. Most American casualties in its wars since the Korean War have been caused by non-state actors, although Vietnam might be considered a transition between the two. Defeating the armed forces of the Republic of Iraq was an easy matter; subjugating the resistance was not.

Conflict between states is basically symmetrical, even when the disparity between the two sides is immense, as was the case with Iraq and the US. However, as the conflict moves from the defeated state to non-state actors its nature changes, and it becomes asymmetrical. Soldiers take off their uniforms and become guerrillas, and in doing so their style of fighting changes. In so far as they blend in with the general population they become invisible to the occupying enemy, and hence invulnerable to the traditional weapons that overwhelmed them as an army. They attempt to redress the imbalance in military power by developing new weapons such as improvised explosive devices (IEDs), and new techniques, such as suicide bombers. The big guns have been the preserve of states, and the bigger the state, the bigger the gun. Nuclear weapons have been the symbol of this unequal access to violence. So far, only states have developed nuclear weapons, and they are constrained from using them against other nuclear-weapon states through fear of retaliation. Non-state actors do not face the constraint of nuclear retaliation, but they do not have the resources, up to now at least, to develop them. If, however, non-state actors can obtain nuclear weapons, probably from state arsenals, then the global balance of power and violence changes dramatically. That has become a spectre haunting military strategists in capitals around the world, but especially Washington, which has more enemies than most.

It is against this background that we must ask, would the DPRK, as is frequently alleged, transfer nuclear assets to terrorists?

Pyongyang has publically and privately condemned terrorism, especially in the immediate aftermath of 9/11.[53] That proves nothing, of course; governments routinely condemn things, such as violence and war, which they practise with gusto. However, the DPRK has always stressed that it sells arms only to governments, not to other entities. The nearest thing we have to evidence that this may not be so is an 'uncorroborated US intelligence report released by Wikileaks' in July 2010, and reported by the *Washington Post*.[54] This report claimed that two emissaries, one from the Taliban and one from al-Qaeda, went to North Korea in 2005 and signed a contract for the supply of anti-aircraft missiles which were to be delivered at the beginning of 2006. The *Washington Post* stated: 'If true, the report unearthed by Wikileaks illustrates the length to which North Korea will go to kick the United States – and generate cash for its sanctions-strapped economy, experts said.' However, the articles also admitted that '[n]o previous reports linking North Korea to the Afghan insurgency could be immediately located'. The article could only give one instance of the use of an anti-aircraft missile against the US in Afghanistan, and there was no mention of any evidence of its provenance. If the emissaries paid good money for missiles that were scheduled to be delivered in early 2006 but have yet to appear, they should return to Pyongyang and ask for their money back.

The United States originally put the DPRK on its 'Terrorism List' – the list of countries it classifies as a 'State Sponsor of Terrorism' – because of its alleged involvement in the bombing of KAL flight 858 in 1987, which killed all 115 people on board. There have always been suspicions about the bombing, because it happened shortly before the presidential election and was instrumental in General Roh Tae-woo's gaining of the presidency – what is called the 'North Wind' effect. The *Korea Times* in 2004 reported:

> There has been a suspicion that some spy agents loyal to Roh and his predecessor Chun Doo-hwan had plotted the bombing to bounce back the popularity of the then ruling camp in the lead up to the 1987 presidential election.
>
> It was common for the past regimes in the South to use the North's potential military threat as a bait for the public to vote for the ruling party candidates, who argued [that with their military background] they had strong and stable power to protect the country.
>
> The Supreme Court sentenced Kim Hyon-hee to death in March 1990. But Roh, the then head of state, gave her a special pardon the next month. In December 1997 she married a secret agent who had guarded her.[55]

There are interesting parallels – mainly revolving around the issue of motive – between the KAL 858 bombing, with the initial government investigation laying blame on North Korea, and the *Cheonan* incident. Just as with the *Cheonan*, the KAL bombing benefited the South, or more precisely the Chun Doo-hwan/Roh Tae-woo group, and damaged the North. This was not surprising – and claims that Kim Jong Il ordered the bombing in order to disrupt the Seoul Olympics and influence the elections against Roh do not bear serious examination, any more than does the suggestion that he sank the *Cheonan* in order to secure the succession of his second son, Kim Jong-Un. There was a rather inconclusive reinvestigation of the KAL 858 bombing during the Kim Dae-jung administration, in 2004. It is possible that, if a progressive administration succeeds that of Lee Myung-bak, the case might be reopened again – and, in the aftermath of the loss of credibility of government investigations over *Cheonan*, the conclusions about culpability might be different.

The issue of 'nuclear terrorism' is important, not because it is a realistic or plausible eventuality, but because if there is an invasion of the North, US participation will be sold to the public, and the world, as a necessary step to prevent nuclear technology and materials, and other WMD assets, 'falling into the wrong hands'. The 31st MEU (Marine Expeditionary Unit) of the US Marine Corps, based in Okinawa, is poised to strike: 'As a collapse of North Korea – rather than a North Korean invasion of South Korea – has become a more likely scenario, the 31st MEU can search and seize the North Korean nuclear arsenal, and prevent proliferation of those weapons.'[56] The problem with that scenario, as discussed in Chapter 12, is that it is a 'Rubicon event' that would precipitate full-scale war.

3
The Collapse of the Soviet Union and North Korea's 'Arduous March'

COLLAPSE OF THE SOVIET UNION

The collapse of the Soviet Union was a momentous and multifaceted affair, a seminal event of the twentieth century with many consequences, some of which are still unravelling. Here we will focus on its relevance to the Korean peninsula, particularly the DPRK.

Journalists are fond of describing North Korea as 'Stalinist', and many on the right have seen the DPRK as Stalin's creation. An article in the Sydney Morning Herald titled 'North Korea: A Living, Breathing Stalinist State' takes the origins of the DPRK out of the complexities of history and implies that it was a product of Stalin's 'iron-fisted rule':

> Half a century after the death of Joseph Stalin, the former Soviet dictator, North Korea remains the world's only country routinely referred to as Stalinist.
>
> The isolated, impoverished regime came into being after Soviet troops occupied the northern half of the Korean peninsula at the end of World War II and the southern half came under US control.
>
> North Korea's founding father Kim Il-Sung established power in Pyongyang during the Soviet occupation, and in 1948, while Stalin exerted his iron-fisted rule in the Kremlin, the Democratic People's Republic of Korea was born.[1]

The function of the labelling is not difficult to discern. 'Stalinism' has had negative connotations across much of the political spectrum since the 1930s, so attaching it to North Korea links the country into a deep, long-existing hostility. Actually, as Korean scholar Bruce Cumings (among others) has pointed out, the label does not really fit:

> Stalin is long dead, but Stalinism is apparently not, and it's still okay to say almost anything about Stalinism. Furthermore, lo and

behold, one set of Orientals has kept it alive: journalists use the term time and again to describe North Korea, without any hint of qualifying or questioning their position ... In the 1960s Kim Il Sung instituted sharp changes, recasting the state ideology in the direction of nationalism and self-reliance and causing sharp clashes with Moscow – enough to make Premier Alexei Kosygin and KGB head Yuri Andropov come running to Pyongyang, where Kim essentially told them to go to hell. Whatever North Korea has been since then, it hasn't been Stalinist. Stalin's speeches cranked with the newest gains in pig iron and machine tools; in their focus on ideas determining everything, the two Kims' ideology is closer to their Neo-Confucian forebears.[2]

Negative labelling aside, that Stalinist tag often surfaces in a question that perplexes many. If the North Korean state was created by Stalin's Soviet Union, how has it managed to survive both de-Stalinization in 1956 and then, decades later, the collapse of the Soviet Union itself? The answer goes beyond the clichés of Stalinism and the mechanics of authoritarian political rule, although the latter are clearly important. The DPRK survives because it is an expression of Korean nationalism. It was born out of the anti-Japanese struggle, and its nationalist credentials were strengthened, at least in the North, in the Korean War, where the enemy forces, which included Korean soldiers, were under the command of the United States. Indeed, the US still has ultimate control over the South Korean military, and if conflict breaks out again it will have direct military command over ROK forces.

The DPRK survives, but the collapse of the Soviet Union inflicted dreadful damage on its economy, both directly and indirectly. Despite the myth-making about *Juche*, both inside and outside the DPRK, the North Korean economy was very dependent on the pre-1990 economic relationship with the Soviet Union and the socialist bloc in eastern Europe. The DPRK never joined COMECON – again, a reflection of its nationalism – but trade with, and assistance from, the COMECON countries was vitally important. In particular it provided oil, in various forms, and fertiliser. The impact of the collapse of the Soviet system was felt across the economy, and the damage was all the greater because North Korea was a surprisingly industrialised country. By 1960 industry's share of gross national production had already reached 71 per cent, and by 1980 it was described by one scholar as a 'semi-advanced industrial society'.[3]

Belief in the importance of industrialisation was of course not confined to North Korea. It was, rather, the norm, and extended well beyond the socialist countries:

> Among developmentalist economists in the 1950s and 1960s, there was a broad consensus that development was a relatively easy task. They believed that industrialization would automatically lead to prosperity. This industrialization could be brought about by massive, although not lasting, state intervention. Markets were perceived as means to realizing the end of economic development; they were not ends in themselves.[4]

Industrialisation was the route to economic success for Japan, South Korea and China, to name just a few obvious examples. Other than in tax havens and small economies based on financial services, logistics, or tourism, industrialisation generally lies at the core of economic growth, and while the service sector has grown greatly in importance in developed societies in recent decades, that growth has really been built on a foundation of industrialisation. However, for relatively small countries with limited natural endowments – and crucially, in the modern world, with no indigenous oil – industrialisation inevitably deepens dependence on foreign trade. The DPRK might, like other countries, have sought self-reliance under the slogan of *Juche*, but this happened within the context of de facto economic interdependence:

> In the 1970s, the pattern of industrialization was outward. [The DPRK] introduced a great deal of foreign technology, especially from Western countries, and additional emphasis was placed on the development of export goods industries, such as ferrous and non-ferrous mining, building materials, light industry, and agricultural production in order to earn foreign currency. During the 1970s, their investment priority to heavy industry continued and allocated an annual average of 40–50 percent of state capital investment in this sector. During this period, the annual average growth rate of industry recorded 16–17 percent. As an index of industrial power it was claimed as of 1997 that the nation was 98 percent self-sufficient in machinery. The trend of recent [pre-1982] industrialization [suggests] that they rely more and more on foreign technology while they put more [investment into] producing exportable goods such as minerals and grains.[5]

Industrialisation extended to agriculture, with heavy investment in four main areas:

> To attain food self-sufficiency, agricultural modernisation was pursued, emphasising four major growth augmenting factors – irrigation, electrification, chemicalization (fertiliser, pesticide, herbicide, etc.) and mechanisation. A high level of success was achieved in the seventies and early eighties. Irrigation was extended (reaching 70 percent or more of the cultivated land by 1970); sufficient numbers of tractors (a total of 75,000 or more), transplanters, threshers, trucks and other farm machinery were provided; rural electrification was expanded rapidly (covering all rural areas by 1970 or so); and fertilisers and other chemicals were made available in large quantities.[6]

The sudden termination of the trading arrangement with the Soviet Union and eastern Europe meant a calamitous cut-off of the inputs necessary to sustain this industrial structure. This had repercussions across the economy – not merely on industry but also, because its output was based on industrial inputs, on agriculture. The latest FAO/WFP assessment of the food situation notes that grain production has plateaued at about 4.5 million tonnes, far below the '6 million tonnes experienced in the 1980s'.[7] I was told in Pyongyang in November 2010 that the aim of creating a 'great and prosperous' nation by 2012 – the 100th anniversary of Kim Il Sung's birth – meant getting the economy back to the peak production levels of the 1980s. Such a modest target is an indicator of just how serious, and long-lasting, the crisis was. When one thinks of the huge growth in the Chinese and South Korean economies over that quarter-century – a growth denied to the DPRK by its external environment – one is doubly struck by the economic catastrophe.

While the Soviet collapse had a direct impact on the North Korean economy and security, it also had a number of indirect ones. Firstly, North Korea could no longer play off China against the Soviet Union. China was, in any case, well on the capitalist road, and was increasingly managing its trade on a commercial basis rather than an ideological one. This also coincided with China's move from being an oil exporter to an importer, so 'friendship prices' for oil, as for other commodities, came off the agenda. Indeed, one recent study claims that, '[w]hereas North Korean coal and electricity exports are sold at sub-market "friendship prices," Chinese coal and oil products have been sold to North Korea at premium prices.[8]

Whether the Korean prices are really concessional 'friendship prices', or merely a reflection of quality differences or the lack of alternative export markets, is unclear. However, it does appear that China sells at world market prices, and has done so for a long time.

Secondly, the demise of the Soviet Union was followed by both the Russian Federation – its successor state – and China establishing diplomatic relations with the Republic of Korea. This in turn led to strong economic links – China has been South Korea's main trading partner for some time. Although Russia and China had put Cold War enmities behind them, this was not reciprocated by the United States (or by Japan). Indeed, far from peace and reconciliation being sought, the hostility of the United States, and subsequently of Japan, towards the DPRK actually increased. While the development of the Russian and Chinese relationships with South Korea did not have a direct bearing on the North, it clearly diminished its relative importance.

Thirdly, the collapse of the Soviet Union, and the relative cooling of the relationship with China, meant that the DPRK was exposed to the full force of American power in ways that had not been relevant before. Although US hostility had long been a burden to North Korea, both directly and through its hegemony over the capitalist world, the damage it could do was relatively limited. The DPRK had turned to the non-American West for trade and technology since the 1970s. The US continued to refuse to have any economic dealings with the DPRK, under its Trading with the Enemy Act and other constraints. Although these were partially lifted in 2008, the American embargo against the DPRK has essentially continued since 1950, and is the longest-standing one in US history – or that of any other country. However, while the United States refused to let its companies trade with North Korea, other capitalist countries were less restrictive. Japan and West Germany, in particular, became significant trading partners for the DPRK (see Table 3.1). In 1988 North Korea's exports to Japan surpassed her exports to China, and exports to West Germany were greater than those to any country in eastern Europe apart from the Soviet Union itself. It is worth noting that North Korea's foreign trade grew considerably over the period 1955–90, from $104 million to $4.8 billion. It is clear that the DPRK leadership recognised the need both to grow foreign trade and diversify the direction of exports and imports despite the constraints it faced.

These constraints became greater after the collapse of the Soviet Union, though not immediately. It is true that trade with Russia fell precipitously, although by 2001 there was some recovery. Although the Russian gap was filled to quite a large extent by a number of other countries, the pattern, duration and political context of trade with those countries had their own characteristics.

Table 3.1   Direction of DPRK Foreign Trade, Selected Years, Major Partners

Share of total trade (%)

	1955	1965	1975	1985	1988	1990
Total	100.0	100.0	100.0	100.0	100.0	100.0
Soviet Union	80.6	40.4	23.9	40.7	58.1	56.8
China	0.0	40.9	23.7	14.7	12.8	11.4
Japan	0.0	7.1	11.8	13.1	12.0	9.7
West Germany	0.0	0.0	6.1	2.5	1.8	2.5
Hong Kong	0.0	0.0	0.4	2.2	3.5	3.0
Thailand	0.0	0.0	0.0	0.6	0.8	0.8
Singapore	0.0	0.0	1.0	0.9	2.9	n/a
Indonesia	0.0	0.0	0.0	0.5	0.5	1.8
India	0.0	0.0	0.5	0.9	1.6	1.8

Source: Derived from Eui-Gak Hwang, *The Korean Economies: A Comparison of North and South* (Oxford and New York: Clarendon, 1993), Table 5.3.

The economy of the DPRK was devastated by the dissolution of the Soviet Union and the trade/aid relationship it embodied. The 1990s became known as the years of the 'Arduous March'. The number of its casualties is unknown, and is the subject of much – sometimes rather hysterical – debate. The latest estimates from South Korea range from 340,000 to 600,000.[9] Faced with an international environment dominated by countries whose attitude towards the DPRK ranged from hostility (the United States and its allies) to uncertain friendship (China), it is not surprising that North Korea does not release much in the way of statistics. Everything can be considered to have military significance when the world's military superpower is constantly threatening. However, at the same time the DPRK came increasingly to cooperate with international organisations such as UNICEF and the FAO, and this led to a substantial amount of data being collected and disseminated.[10] In particular, towards the end of 2008 a national census was conducted, and the final report was released in 2009, with an online version made available through the United Nations the following year.[11] The report is 278 pages long, and gives considerable demographic detail, which has led to the publication of a number of articles, especially in the South Korean press. Most of these concerned the effects of food shortages during the Arduous March.[12] One, however, used the census data to calculate the size of the North Korean army, and came up with a figure of 700,000 – far lower than the prevailing estimates of over a million.[13]

One area for which we do have a fair amount of data is that of foreign trade. Traditionally such data have been arrived at using partner data.[14] This is presumably what the International Monetary Fund (IMF) does when compiling data for North Korea for its Direction of Trade Statistics (DOTS), which is the main source for global trade data. DOTS only gives aggregate data (exports and imports) by country and group, so there are lots of unanswered questions. However, a glance at DOTS does reveal some interesting information about the DPRK, much of it contrary to conventional perception.

Firstly, as shown in Fig. 3.1, North Korea's 'foreign' trade has grown considerably since the collapse of the Soviet Union. 'Foreign' needs some explanation. Neither Korea regards the other as foreign, so inter-Korean trade is often left out, and this frequently leads to confusion. Here we will include trade between the two Koreas in foreign trade. Trade also includes aid in the form of trade goods. This appears to be particularly important in respect of South Korea, although the statistics are incomplete. Aid was a small part of the South's exports to the North until the mid 1990s, when it started growing in importance. During the first half of the next decade, aid comprised about three-quarters of the South's exports (i.e. the North's imports from the South). No data have been traced for the period after 2004.[15]

Since it was legitimised by Seoul in 1989, trade with the South has been a major growth area for North Korea – in 2009 it accounted for 34 per cent of exports and 13 per cent of imports.[16] Another important trading partner, not surprisingly, has been China. The third area of growth is, as we shall see, rather more surprising.

Fig 3.2 shows the main sources of North Korea's imports from 1993 to 2009. Aid, as we have noted, is an important part of imports from the South, and the spike in imports from Japan in 2001 is also aid. Aid is likely to have played a large role in imports from China, but probably not from the other countries shown – Algeria, India and Russia. Oil presumably accounts for the bulk of imports from Algeria. The decline in imports from Japan after 2001 and from South Korea after 2007 are readily explicable by political factors, to which we will return below. The reason for the decline in imports from China and Algeria during 2008/09 is not clear.

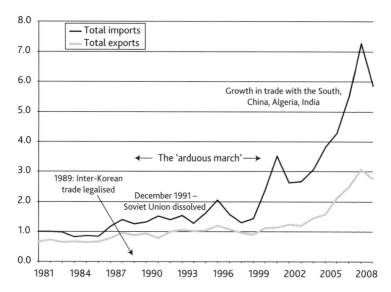

Figure 3.1   North Korea's 'Foreign' Trade, 1981–2009 (Source: 'Direction of Trade Statistics', *International Monetary Fund*, September 2010)

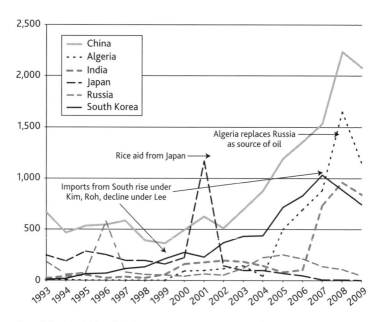

Figure 3.2   North Korea's Major Import Sources, 1993–2009 (Source: Statistical Appendix, Table A2)

South Korea and China also figure strongly in North Korea's exports (see Fig 3.3). However, what is most interesting here is the attempted diversification into other markets, principally Brazil, India and Venezuela. No information is available on the composition of the exports to these markets, but the fluctuation is noticeable. To what degree this is due to political pressure from the United States is unknown, but we can make some informed guesses. India's relations with the United States improved with the nuclear deal in 2005, by which the United States initiated nuclear cooperation with India in violation of the Nuclear Non-Proliferation Treaty (NPT) and its own laws (which had to be amended, taking some years).[17] India became a 'respectable' nuclear power, and the United States gained a new ally against China. Whether North Korea's exports to India were a casualty of the India–US rapprochement is unknown, but the timing is suggestive. They peaked at $348 million in 2006, representing 22 per cent of North Korea's total exports, but dropped to $222 million in 2007 and $72 million in 2008.[18]

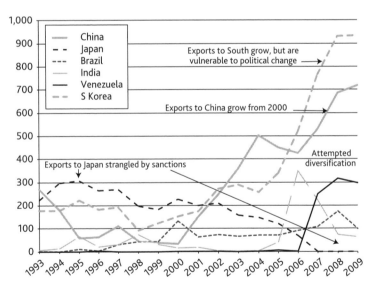

Figure 3.3 North Korea's Major Export Markets, 1993–2009 (Source: Statistical Appendix, Table A3)

In general, the disappearance of the Soviet Union meant that trade was much more likely to be interrupted for political reasons – the obvious case being Japan. In 1993 Japan had rapidly overtaken

Russia to become North Korea's second-largest source of imports, and in 2001, because of a shipment of rice aid presumably connected to the Kim–Koizumi summit of the following year, it became the largest. However, as relations soured after the summit and the Japanese government restricted trade, imports from Japan fell away rapidly, as did exports (see Fig 3.4). The question of why relations soured leads to an interesting story, the details of which are unclear. The deterioration was apparently driven from the Japanese side, on the pretext that North Korea had not fully accounted for the handful of Japanese abducted, for mysterious reasons, from the late 1970s until the early 1980s. The DPRK had no good reason to hide any abductees, and – as Fig. 3.4 shows – a lot to lose. Japanese politicians, on the other hand, were able to ride a rising tide of anti–North Korean (or perhaps just anti-Korean) feeling. Exploitation of the 'threat from North Korea' has been an important mechanism to propel Japanese remilitarisation and its drive to rehabilitation as a 'normal country' – that is, one with the legal right to belligerency which had been foresworn in the postwar Constitution.[19] Another twist to the story is the role of the United States, which had been horrified by the Kim–Koizumi summit of 2002, which it saw as outflanking its North Korea policy, and threatening the prospect of peace. It is likely, as Jonathan D. Pollack argues, that this was

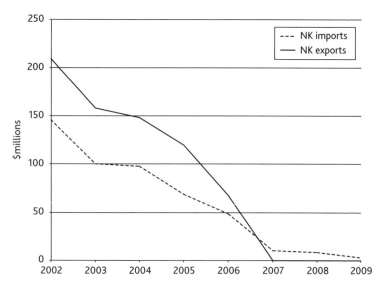

Figure 3.4 North Korea's Trade with Japan 2002–2009: Strangulation by Sanctions (Source: Statistical Appendix, Table A2 and A3)

the trigger that led the Bush administration to abrogate the Agreed Framework that the Clinton administration had signed with the DPRK in 1994.[20]

Whatever the roles of the DPRK and the United States, and of domestic considerations, in bringing about the hard-line anti-North Korea policy, one of the economic results can be seen in the dramatic decline of trade between the two neighbours after 2002. Exports to Japan were completely extinguished by 2007, and imports virtually so. The Japanese government did not stop there, making moves to stop the flow of remittances from Japanese-Koreans back to their relatives in North Korea. However, trade statistics can be misleading, and there are ways around sanctions. For North Korea, that means trading through China: 'For instance, Tokyo discovered that the DPRK was exporting sanctioned food items such as mushrooms to China and they were then sold to Japan at higher prices. The only losers may have been Japanese consumers.'[21] To which we might add Korean farmers. For all their awful consequences – the deaths, malnutrition and impoverishment that sanctions produce – they concern themselves with petty matters such as mushrooms. One is reminded of Hannah Arendt's phrase about the banality of evil.

During this period, trade between the Koreas became very important for the North – though not nearly so important for the South, of course, because of the difference in size between their economies, and the amount of foreign trade they conducted. In 2009, according to the South's Bank of Korea, South Korea's foreign trade was $686.6 billion and North Korea's $3.41 billion. Inter-Korean trade, which is not considered 'foreign' by the Bank of Korea, came to a further $1.7 billion.[22] Small though $1.7 billion is in comparison with $686.6 billion, it is still a substantial amount of money, and the constituency of South Korean businesses involved with North Korea cannot be just pushed aside. Moreover, there was a consciousness that, as South Korea withdrew from the North Korean economy, China would inevitably replace it. In particular, the small South Korean companies operating in the Kaesong Industrial Park – a South Korean economic enclave within North Korea – proved resilient, and trade through Kaesong actually increased in 2010.[23] As a result, Lee Myung-bak's squeeze on inter-Korean trade, which was formally prohibited on 24 May 2010, will take some time to have effect, but effect there will be.[24] No doubt some trade will survive, probably classified as trade with China – there have been reports of North Korean companies contacting South Korean firms in China; but for the moment inter-Korean trade looks as if it will suffer the same fate as trade between Japan and North Korea.

The collapse of the Soviet Union removed a formidable bulwark against the ongoing hostility of the United States and the fluctuating attitude of South Korea and Japan. It also enabled the United States to extend its sanctions mechanisms beyond the traditional Cold War device of the Coordinating Committee for Export Control (COCOM) and its post-Cold War successor, the Wassenaar Arrangement.[25] In particular, the United States was able to pressure the United Nations Security Council, by means of Japan acting on its behalf, to impose mandatory sanctions.[26] These were powerful weapons, and their effect on North Korea has been severe – but has also been mitigated by the third of our themes: the rise of China.

4
The Rise of China and the Decline of America

THE RISE OF CHINA

The rapid growth of China's powers across the spectrum – from economic to intellectual – is clearly one of the major transformative events of our time. The rise of China is important as reality and as symbol. It carries additional significance in the context of this book because of its crucial geographical location. Just as an American war with North Korea has involved China in the past and will surely do so in the future, so too does economic warfare. North Korea's main border with the outside world is that with China. If North Korea has been able to withstand the economic warfare that the United States has waged against it, it is to a large degree because of China.

China's rise is important not only in itself but as a symbol of a wider resurgence that complements and builds on the decolonisation process discussed earlier. As discussed in Chapter 2, China has a special significance because it is the only country never colonised or conquered by the Europeans or Americans.[1] There is a marked difference between European and American attitudes towards, say, India or Japan, and those towards China. India and Japan were both conquered, and tamed, while China – though enfeebled during the decline of the Qing and the first half or so of the twentieth century – was not. China remains the archetypal Other. Fear and distrust of China are never far from the surface, even when the words are effusive. The parallels with North Korea are obivous.

North Korea and China: Parallels and Differences

North Korea is the unconquered, untamed, alien part of Korea, in contradistinction to 'our' South Korea, a stalwart member of the 'international community'. In reality, South Korea has never been as subservient as the United States would like. The Northern Limit Line, for instance, which features so strongly in the contemporary narrative, was drawn by the American generals in order to stop Syngman Rhee from violating the Korean War Armistice Agreement, which he had refused to sign, and thereby reigniting fighting.[2] Indeed, one can readily discern in the blogosphere a fear among Americans in Korea that if you scratch a South Korean you will find a North Korean.

Similarly, in much American media coverage of East Asia the terms 'North Korea' and 'China' could be mutually substituted. However, there is clearly a huge difference in the way the contemporary US government (if not those of the 1950s and 1960s) approaches the two countries. Part of this is due to size and power; China is now so powerful that it cannot be treated in the same way it was in the 1950s, or North Korea is today.

Size is not the only difference, though it has formed the basis of others. The United States, not willing to recognise Asian nationalism for what it was, saw the decolonisation process as an expression of 'Chinese Communist expansion'.[3] North Korea, on the other hand, while frequently portrayed as a threat, is not seen as having territorial designs beyond the peninsula.

Crucially, China was seen to have something to offer. The United States needed to extricate itself from its failing war in Southeast Asia, and Chinese 'understanding' was seen as helpful for that.[4] More important in relation to global strategy was that China could be used as a counterbalance to the Soviet Union. Hence Henry Kissinger played the 'China card' by taking President Nixon to Beijing in 1972. The move took most by surprise, even allies; the Japanese, who felt much betrayed, called it the 'Nixon Shock', and have lived ever since with the fear that the Americans might do something similar again.[5] The South Koreans have had similar fears that the United States might cut a deal with the North, with China or with Japan, leaving them on the sidelines.[6]

The China Card and Unintended Consequences

The card was played, in a sense, in two games, but with the common aim of providing a counterbalance against the Soviet Union.[7] The first time was by Nixon and Kissinger in 1972, and the second by Carter and Brzezinski in 1978. The first game established de facto relations and the second de jure ones. As a piece of balance-of-power geopolitics it made good sense, the only question being why the Americans did not get round to it a decade earlier. However, it did have quite unintended, and unforeseen, consequences. By reducing the military threat and lowering the economic embargo, it created the economic opportunity and the political space for Deng Xiaoping's 'Opening'. As a result, investment from Hong

Kong and Taiwan began to flood in, and exports to surge out. Hong Kong and Taiwanese capitalists transferred production to China's south-eastern coastal provinces, which came to experience an export-led boom. Chinese productive capacities, even in the immediate postwar, post-liberation period of the 1950s, were potentially huge (as manifested in the steep growth of trade in that period); so when it was supplied with capital, voracious export markets and international marketing networks, the results were explosive, and China relatively soon became a major player in global trade (see Fig 4.1). It is today the world's leading exporter and, by some calculations, already the largest economy.[8]

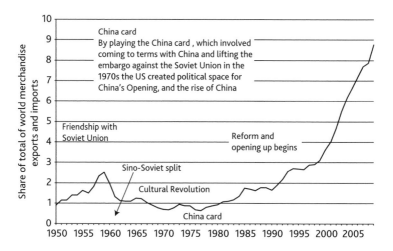

Figure 4.1   China's Share of World Trade, 1950–2009 (Source: Derived from WTO Trade Statistics Database, downloaded 24 December 2010)

But in fact the Americans had unleashed a tiger – one that in a couple of decades would come to challenge, and haunt them. One indicator of this is the balance of trade between the two countries. Fig 4.2 shows the export ratio in US trade with China from 1980 to 2009. In fact, 1980 was the last year in which the US achieved a surplus in recorded merchandise trade with China. The data have to be treated with some caution: they show only merchandise trade, and not services, in which – though much smaller – the United States has an advantage, and will retain a surplus for some time.[9] Moreover, as production has moved to China, trade statistics give a misleading impression of the flow of benefits. The US trade deficit with Japan, very much the topic of concern in the 1980s, now appears as part of the deficit with China, as Japanese companies produce in China for export to the American market. Some of America's imports from China are purchases from American companies manufacturing there – so, although their workers in America, or elsewhere, have lost their jobs, the owners and executives of the company still benefit. The off-shoring of jobs to China has become a matter of heated debate in America.[10] Nevertheless, the burgeoning deficit in merchandise trade is an indication of what is happening across the board: the loss of American competitiveness with China.

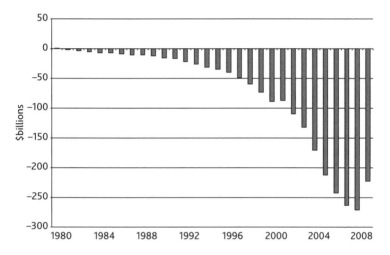

Figure 4.2   The American Trade Deficit with China, 1989–2009 (Source: 'Direction of Trade Statistics', International Monetary Fund, September 2010)

The rise of China is so obvious, and frequently reported, that it would be superfluous to document it. However, it is important to sketch its strengths, as well as its actual and potential weaknesses. China is taking a leading place in one area after another, including, for example: aerospace,[11] automobiles,[12] clean energy (solar, wind, etc.),[13] electric cars,[14] energy (fossil),[15] finance,[16] railways,[17] research and development,[18] science,[19] and telecommunications.[20]

Perhaps the most telling development of all is the surge in Chinese patents. China is the fastest-growing foreign register of patents in the United States (see Fig. 4.3). China, as the *Chosun Ilbo* put it, is transforming itself 'from Copycat to Patent Powerhouse':

China is emerging as a global patent powerhouse, cleaning up its image as 'the world's factory' relying on a huge pool of cheap labor or a hub for fake goods without original expertise. China's patent filings have risen dramatically on the back of innovative research and development efforts, putting the country on track to overtake the US and Japan in the worldwide patent race.[21]

If we look at the economy as a whole, the question is not whether China will overtake the United States, but when – if it has not done so already.[22]

China is also challenging the United States in unexpected fields. It has overtaken the US to become the favourite destination for South Koreans studying abroad.[23] And, to twist the knife, China is moving ahead in what many thought was America's prerogative: soft power.[24]

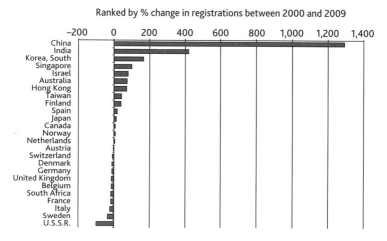

Figure 4.3 Rising and Falling Stars: Foreign Registrations of US Patents, 2000–09 (Source: Statistical Appendix, Table A6)

US Military Supremacy, Chinese Vulnerability: The American Dilemma

So the United States, which not so long ago was boasting of full-spectrum dominance, is facing challenges across the board.[25] In specific industries, in the economy as a whole, in R&D, in soft power – wherever we look, China is approaching or overtaking the United States. The challenge varies in intensity and urgency, but the one area in which the United States is currently far ahead is military power.

This might seem surprising given the frequent warnings by the US government, duly repeated in the media, about the increase in Chinese military power. Official pronouncements tend to be diplomatic:

> The pace and scope of China's military modernization have increased over the past decade, enabling China's armed forces to develop capabilities to contribute to the delivery of international public goods, as well as increase China's options for using military force to gain diplomatic advantage or resolve disputes in its favor.[26]

But the media are unhindered by the necessities of diplomacy, and get across the Pentagon's message with more vigour: 'China Military Build-Up Seems US-focused: Mullen',[27] 'China's "Aggressive" Buildup Called Worry',[28] 'Pentagon Sounds Alarm at China's Military Buildup',[29] 'Chinese Military Buildup Far Exceeds its Defensive Needs: US',[30] 'China Has More Warships than US',[31] 'China's Anti-Aircraft Carrier Missile "Closer to Completion"'.[32]

Despite the hype, China is still a military minnow compared with the American whale. Just looking at the navy, and leaving out of account all the other aspects of US military power, Secretary of Defense Robert Gates recently pointed out:

- The US operates 11 large carriers, all nuclear-powered. In terms of size and striking power, no other country has even one comparable ship.
- The US navy has 10 large-deck amphibious ships that can operate as sea bases for helicopters and vertical-takeoff jets. No other navy has more than three, and all of those navies belong to our allies or friends. Our navy can carry twice as many aircraft at sea as all the rest of the world combined.
- The US has 57 nuclear-powered attack and cruise missile submarines – again, more than the rest of the world combined.
- Seventy-nine Aegis-equipped combatants carry roughly 8,000 vertical-launch missile cells. In terms of total missile firepower, the US arguably outmatches the next 20 largest navies.
- All told, the displacement of the US battle fleet – a proxy for overall fleet capabilities – exceeds, by one recent estimate, at least the next 13 navies combined, of which 11 are our allies or partners.
- And, at 202,000 strong, the Marine Corps is the largest military force of its kind in the world and exceeds the size of most world armies.[33]

Another way to assess the balance of military power is to consider military expenditure. In 2009, according to the Stockholm International Peace Research Institute (SIPRI), US military expenditure stood at $661 billion, and that of China at $100.4 billion. If we look at the top 21 countries in terms of military expenditure, we find that the US and its allies account for some 75 per cent of world military expenditure.[34]

China has entered a very vulnerable period. Its overall challenge to the United States, and its global hegemony, are unmistakable. American power may be eroding, but its military strength will remain devastating for some time yet. Leaving aside the question of whether China will turn into another imperialist power like the United States and others before it, it will have the potential to do so. Before that point is reached, it will come to a point where the United States can no longer attack it with impunity. Until that day there will be the temptation to attack China 'before it is too late'. We must hope that will never happen, but the possibility does inform the context in which the current crisis around the Korean peninsula must be analysed. We return to this question at the end of the book.

AMERICAN DECLINE

A survey of the relevant elite media in the United States, ranging from *New York Times* to *Foreign Affairs*, would probably find that 'American decline' is an increasingly frequently canvassed issue. The elite debate is presumably repeated in the popular media, talk-back shows, and so on, but usually in a more upbeat, optimistic fashion. At times, no doubt, the popular version is more pessimistic, even apocalyptic, than the more measured worries of the elite. Clearly, popular concerns have an impact on elite decision-making, especially in a modern democracy; but it is necessary here, for reasons of space, to focus on the elite. In addition, public opinion is, after all, largely the creation of the elite, though it does take on an amplified voice of its own through the mechanisms of the media. It is not for nothing that radio broadcasters are commonly called 'shock jocks'.

Decline is also a perennial favourite. Back in 1985 Bruce Russett could write in *International Organization*: 'Mark Twain did die eventually, and so will American hegemony. But in both cases early reports of their demise have been greatly exaggerated.'[35] Russett was probably not the first to haul Mark Twain out of his grave to give this particular bit of comfort. Russett was right in that, despite all the Cassandras – in 1985, on the eve of one of its greatest triumphs, the collapse of the Soviet Union – the United States was still there, and still powerful. The French writer, Serge Halimi has traced talk of decline back to 1952:

> In 1952, when the US was at the very height of its power, General Douglas MacArthur – hero of the Republican right since President Harry Truman relieved him of his command in Korea – warned fellow Americans of 'our own relative decline, our inability to conserve resources, the rising burden of our fiscal commitments, an astronomically rising public debt mortgaging the future of our children.'[36]

However, talk of decline, and evidence of it, has gathered pace in recent years. For instance, Gideon Rachman, chief foreign-affairs commentator for the *Financial Times*, writing in the Washington-based magazine *Foreign Policy* in January 2011 – under the heading 'We've Heard All This About American Decline Before' – argues that 'this time it's for real':

> This time it's different. It's certainly true that America has been through cycles of declinism in the past. Campaigning for the presidency in 1960, John F. Kennedy complained, 'American strength relative to that of the Soviet Union has been slipping, and communism has been advancing steadily in every area of the world.' Ezra Vogel's *Japan as Number One* was published in 1979, heralding a decade of steadily rising paranoia about Japanese manufacturing techniques and trade policies.
>
> In the end, of course, the Soviet and Japanese threats to American supremacy proved chimerical. So Americans can be forgiven if they greet talk of a new challenge from China as just another case of the boy who cried wolf. But a frequently overlooked fact about that fable is that the boy was eventually proved right. The wolf did arrive – and China is the wolf.[37]

Rachman very much represents the mid-Atlantic media elite, and his words carry weight. Nevertheless, American decline is a much-contested area, though several strands can be teased out. First of all, how do we define America? What is it that is, or is not, declining?

Categorisations of American Power

- *Imperialism*
  Only the left uses the term 'imperialism', and since the left does not remotely influence US foreign policy there is little point spending much time on it here. Nevertheless, imperialism is ultimately the most important construct for analysing America's interaction with the world.[38]

- *Empire*
  The negative connotations of 'imperialism' are more or less universal; empire is different. Many regard it in a positive light, partly because they can add ameliorative epithets in front – liberal empire, benign empire, civilising empire. Not quite the sort of thing you can do with imperialism, hence its popularity with those who cannot deny the fact (1000 military bases around the world) but are happier not to consider its implications.[39]

- *Superpower/Hyperpower/Power*
  This is sometimes conflated within other descriptions, such as 'empire'. 'Power', along with its variants, is considered to be a neutral term having no particular connotations of approval or opprobrium, and is therefore very popular. It seems to be merely a statement of fact to which one could only object on grounds of fact – is it true or not? – rather than for political or ethical reasons.[40]

- *Hegemony*
  'Hegemony' is a very popular term, coming as it does between 'empire', which sits dangerously close to imperialism, and the bland 'superpower'.[41] 'Superpower' is essentially a description of size, albeit in relation to other countries whereas 'hegemon' has connotations about the relationships between countries. A hegemon is basically a dominating power, a master among servants.

- *Primacy*
  This is a term used by Peter Liberman in a very useful collection of essays in *Foreign Affairs*, entitled 'What to Read on American Primacy'.[42] It might be considered hegemony-lite, with a bit more bite to it than superpower but not straying into concepts of

dominance and subordination. It is associated with the concept *primus inter pares* – first among equals.

- *Indispensable/default power*
  Secretary of State Madeleine Albright described the US as the 'indispensable power'.[43] Hillary Clinton has come up with a variant – 'new American moment' – described by Mark Lander in the *New York Times* as 'not quite as lofty'.[44] Lofty or not, it carries with it connotations of benignity.

- *Leadership*
  Leadership is also a firm favourite, being a very positive term.[45] It is also used in conjunction with others, as exemplified by Hillary Clinton in her 'new American moment' speech:

  > In a speech meant to showcase the successes of the Obama administration's foreign policy, Mrs Clinton emphatically reasserted the primacy of American power in a dangerous world. Whether it is American aid after the floods in Pakistan or American brokering of the recently revived Middle East peace negotiations, she said, 'The world is counting on us.'
  > 'After years of war and uncertainty,' she said, 'people are wondering what the future holds, at home and abroad. So let me say it clearly: the United States can, must, and will lead in this new century.'

  The following week Secretary Clinton travelled to Israel and Egypt in another display of 'leadership'. A few months later, events in Egypt would demonstrate a certain hollowness to US pretensions of leadership.[46]

The Timing and Course of Decline

- *Collapse*
  The idea that decline might be not slow but apocalyptic owes something to chaos and complexity theory, and is illustrated here by an unlikely pair: an Anglo-American, Niall Ferguson, and a Russian, Igor Panarin. It is particularly relevant for this book because a war on the Korean peninsula, in which the United States is drawn into conflict with China, might precipitate such a crisis.[47]

- *Imminent*
  Some see American decline as imminent, if supremacy has not already been lost.[48]

- *Long way off/slow decline*
  Others accept the concept of decline but see it as being slow, and the tipping point as being a long way off.[49]

- *Never!*
  Others again see that tipping point as never being reached. There may be relative decline, but the United States will remain pre-eminent. This is usually the reserve of the gung-ho Right, but left/liberals such as Bruce Cumings also express reservations about the inevitability of decline.[50]

  Others see the United States staying ahead through 'reinvention', and see the possible alternatives to its hegemony as being less popular.[51]

- *Mission accomplished*
  This sees US hegemony as having established an international system that works to the benefit of most, if not all, countries.[52] The task then is to ensure that newcomers, such as China, behave as 'responsible members' of that system. If that happens, then the disappearance of US hegemony itself is of little consequence, because America will continue to reap the benefits of this stable, benign system.[53]

Manifestations of Decline

- *Internal*
  There is a widespread and growing feeling among many Americans that the country can no longer cope with its challenges in the way it could in the past. The bungled response to Hurricane Katrina and the financial meltdown of 2008 were perhaps prime examples, but they came on top of rising unemployment and stagnant or falling real wages for many ordinary people. A poll in a Kansas paper in 2010 found that 71 per cent of respondents answered 'yes' to the question, 'Do you think America's "can-do" spirit is faltering?' To what extent are the town of Lawrence (population about 92,000), and the 1,340 respondents to the poll, representative of Middle America? They seem to be articulating a widespread feeling.[54]

- *External: rising China, global Islamist insurgency*
  Sometimes the two come together. The US invasion of Iraq led
  to a great increase in Iranian presence and influence, as well
  as that of China, and the invasion of Afghanistan opened the
  way for Chinese companies.[55] Most forecasts focus on China's
  economic challenge.[56] However, as might be anticipated, the
  military-industrial-security complex highlights China's rising
  military expenditure, though that remains a very long way
  behind America's.[57]

The previous section gave a number of statistics measuring the
United States against China's rise, but China is just the leading
element of a global challenge to America. One key indicator of
America's faltering standing in the world is share of GDP. Fig 4.4
shows the declining share of the United States since its heyday
in the immediate postwar period. Much of that declining share
was inevitable as competitor economies recovered from the war.
However, much of the erosion of American economic supremacy,
and an increasing share of it, comes from 'emerging' economies – in
particular, China

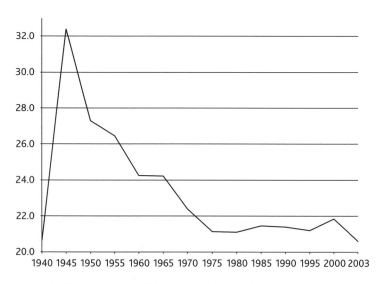

Figure 4.4 US Share of World GDP, 1940–2003 (Source: Derived from Angus Maddison,
The World Economy: Historical Statistics, [Development Centre Studies], Paris: OECD,
2004. Maddison does not give an estimate for world GDP in 1945, and I have extrapolated
from his estimates for 1940 and 1950)

Anxiety and the Search for Comfort

China's challenge is primarily civilian, and that is where the United States has depleted and squandered its advantages. Significantly, Barack Obama used an analogy with Sputnik in his second State of the Union address, in January 2011. This time, he said, the response would not be in space research but in 'biomedical research, information technology, and especially clean energy technology'. He also noted the focus of China, India and South Korea on education, but offered the usual reassurances without any plan of action:

> We're the home to the world's best colleges and universities, where more students come to study than any place on Earth.
>
> What's more, we are the first nation to be founded for the sake of an idea – the idea that each of us deserves the chance to shape our own destiny. That's why centuries of pioneers and immigrants have risked everything to come here. It's why our students don't just memorize equations, but answer questions like 'What do you think of that idea? What would you change about the world? What do you want to be when you grow up?'[58]

At least he eschewed the 'axis of evil' nonsense that marked Bush's State of the Union address in 2002. Despite some fine words, however, there was little indication that the United States would really address the new Sputnik challenge.

The indications are that the Obama administration will respond to the challenge of China, and the decline of America's place in the world, not by seriously addressing the problems of social and physical infrastructure, but by relying increasingly, like the British before them, on the siren comforts and consolations of militarisation.[59]

5
Obama's Strategic Paralysis

The first chapters in this section positioned the Korean experience within the context of the struggle between imperialism and nationalism, and the changed configuration of the postcolonial world – especially the increasing importance of non-state actors. We then looked at the collapse of the Soviet Union and the effect this had on Korea. Chapter 4 looked at the rise of China and the decline of the United States. That decline is inevitably and increasingly calibrated in terms of the rise of China. However, the waning of the United States preceded the emergence of the Chinese economic challenge and had its roots in the continued militarisation of the United States. That was a consequence of the permanent war economy and its political manifestation, known for convenience as the 'military-industrial complex', but in fact a triangular relationship between the political, military and economic power elites, informed and guided by the security industry.[1] Military spending, though a smaller part of the economy than it was in the early days of the Cold War and during the Second World War itself, has been sufficiently large to distort America's economy and society: over 50 per cent of the US discretionary budget goes to the military, and the next-largest power in terms of military expenditure only spends one-tenth of the American amount.[2] It is a canker which replenishes itself through the damage it does to its host. The military canker also deforms American foreign policy: the theme of this chapter.

THE US–DPRK RELATIONSHIP

The relationship between the United States and North Korea has been fraught for all of its 60 or so years. This really requires some explanation: it is uncommon for hostility to persist for so long, and the usual explanations are unsatisfactory.

First of all, it is important to recognise that this is primarily a one-way hostility. Most conflicts between states or people revolve around disputed territory between them – Israel and Palestine, India and Pakistan, India and China, and so forth. That is not the case here. Nor does North Korea challenge the United States in any distinct way, apart from the very fact of its independence. It does not preach world revolution, nor is it the home of some evangelical religion that might disturb the status quo.

Let us take each country in turn.

DPRK US Policy

DPRK policy towards the United States can be summed up as the desire for 'peaceful coexistence'. It wants the United States to drop its policy of 'hostility' and establish normal diplomatic relations. Hostility includes sanctions (physical and financial), the barring of the DPRK from international financial institutions such as the Asian Development Bank, the harassment of foreign trade through the Proliferation Security Initiative (PSI) and actions such as the seizure of a DPRK-contracted cargo plane in Bangkok in December 2009.[3]

There are innumerable official statements documenting this policy.[4] These can be complemented by the assessments of foreign commentators.[5] What states say they want does not, of course, necessarily represent their true desires, but the text of the Agreed Framework does provide some solid evidence. This is the only treaty signed between America and North Korea (the Americans baulked at the word 'treaty' because they dislike treaties – especially with small antagonists). The Agreed Framework, like any negotiated settlement, was a compromise by both sides. The Koreans had to give away something to get what they wanted. We know that the Americans wanted to ensure that North Korea could not develop nuclear weapons and in the Agreed Framework the DPRK bargained that away in exchange for things that were more important to it:[6]

[Clause] II. The two sides will move *toward full normalization of political and economic relations.*
1) Within three months of the date of this Document, both sides will *reduce barriers to trade and investment, including restrictions on telecommunications services and financial transactions.*
2) Each side will open a liaison office in the other's capital following resolution of consular and other technical issues through expert level discussions.
3) As progress is made on issues of concern to each side, the US and the DPRK will *upgrade bilateral relations to the Ambassadorial level.*

[Clause] III. Both sides will work together for peace and security on a nuclear-free Korean peninsula.

1) *The US will provide formal assurances to the DPRK, against the threat or use of nuclear weapons by the US.*[7]

The Agreed Framework does not cover all that the DPRK wants, but it is consistent with what we know from other sources.

It is interesting that there is nothing here that, in theory, should prove problematic for the United States. It is all in compliance with the Charter of the United Nations; it is motherhood and apple pie. Yet, in the end, the United States never delivered on these commitments and others in the Agreed Framework, notably the provision of two light water reactors (LWRs) for electricity generation. There is still no normalisation of political and economic relations; there are still 'barriers to trade' (i.e. sanctions); and the threat against the DPRK persists.

The Bush administration abrogated the Agreed Framework in late 2002 on the grounds that the DPRK had an illicit weapons programme based on heavy enriched uranium (HEU). In recent years the DPRK has announced that it is developing low enriched uranium (LEU) for use in LWRs, and in November 2010 it displayed a laboratory with uranium-enrichment centrifuges to the US nuclear scientist Siegfried S. Hecker.[8] While LEU can be converted to HEU with further processing, there is no evidence that this has been done, or that there are any plans to do it.

The nuclear devices which were tested after the US walked away from the Agreed Framework were based on plutonium. So, more than eight years after the Bush administration declared that it had conclusive evidence of a uranium weapons programme, no such weapons have appeared. Which brings us to a very important, but usually overlooked point about negotiations between the US and the DPRK. Such is their overwhelming disparity in strength that if the US were to cheat – say, by attacking North Korea after giving an assurance that it would not – the results for Korea could be fatal.[9] But if North Korea were to cheat – say, by hiding away some plutonium – the effects would in reality be negligible. For one thing, you cannot develop delivery systems, such as missiles, fully under cover. So, while the DPRK has to be very cautious about negotiating with the United States – hence the emphasis on a mutual sequence of moves called 'commitment for commitment', 'action for action' – this does not hold for the US.[10]

In January 2011 the DPRK Foreign Ministry yet again reiterated its position on denuclearisation, and drew attention once more to the key question of 'simultaneous action' (also described as 'commitment for commitment', 'action for action'):

> The nuclear issue on the peninsula surfaced due to the US threat of a nuclear war and its hostile policy towards the DPRK and it is, therefore, essential to find a modality of dialogue for eliminating its root cause.
>
> The DPRK remains unchanged in its stand to denuclearize the whole peninsula. Invariable is the DPRK's will to comprehensively implement the September 19 Joint Statement in the spirit of equality and according to the principle of simultaneous action.[11]

On top of which we must bear in mind the overwhelming importance to the DPRK of peaceful coexistence with the United States. This is a very minor matter for the US. Even if there were an economic transformation in North Korea, its 24 million people would never be a large market for the US. The US can quite easily live without the DPRK, but North Korea cannot achieve real prosperity without the United States. That is partly because of its importance as a market (think what would happen if we took the US out of China's export profile), source of investment, and so on, but also because of its role 'administering' the global economy. American policy also affects that of its client states, especially South Korea and Japan. North Korea desperately needs normal, and preferably good, relations with the United States, and there would have to be very strong reasons for it to do anything that might prevent it from achieving them.

It is often argued by those opposed to negotiations that, whatever it agrees in talks, North Korea will 'never give up nuclear weapons'.[12] Naturally, we cannot know until it is put to the test; but if there is an agreement on peaceful coexistence, if North Korea no longer feels threatened, and if the economic and political benefits of peace flow through, it seems highly unlikely that North Korea would renege on any agreement.

The media, for its part, often obfuscates the issue, either deliberately or though laziness or incompetence, especially by not picking up mistranslations. Take, for instance, a reported interview with Kim Jong Il's eldest son, Kim Jong Nam:

He also said that North Korea's strength comes from nuclear weapons, and that as long as North Korea *confronts* the United States, it is very unlikely to give up its atomic programs.[13]

This comes from a *Washington Post* article quoting the Japanese newspaper, which conducted the interview with Kim in China. His words have thus been translated, and we do not know whether competent interpreters were used at the interview. It is surely clear that what Kim Jong Nam really said was that North Korea would keep nuclear weapons as long as the United States confronts or threatens it. Perhaps he said 'as long as North Korea is confronted by the United States'. He certainly did not put things the way he was reported as doing.

It is the overriding foreign policy objective of the DPRK to draw the United States into peaceful coexistence. That entails the dropping of sanctions and the establishing of normal diplomatic and economic relations. That in turn opens the way for trade between the two countries (and others within the American imperium who are influenced, in either direction, by perceived US policy). The DPRK wants the removal of the American threat and the withdrawal of US troops from the peninsula, and wants to sign a peace treaty with the United States ending the Korean War (which at the moment is only held at bay by an Armistice Agreement).[14]

It will be clear that, if this analysis is correct – and the documentation and evidence is overwhelming for all those not blinded by preconceptions – then this calls into question, *on the issue of motive alone*, the charges discussed in Part II that the DPRK sank the *Cheonan* and instigated the Yeonpyeong incident as a provocation.

US DPRK Policy

Many commentators claim that North Korean policy is impenetrable, and that its leadership is 'unpredictable'. In fact its policy is really quite straightforward, because it has no satisfactory alternative, and its actions are strategically compatible with that policy.

The same cannot be said of the United States. The United States is a large democracy with a global empire. There are always alternatives and conflicting objectives. Foreign policy is contested not only because of the nature of the system and culture, but also because there is a lot to argue about. Decisions taken by one administration are often overturned by the next. Indeed, they are frequently negated within the term of an administration, as factions come and go. This indeed was an important characteristic of the development and implementation of US policy during the Bush administration (and perhaps since), and this has been well documented by former CNN reporter Mike Chinoy.[15] One example is the collapse of negotiations in late 2008, after the US reneged on a commitment to remove North Korea from the Terrorism List once it had provided a declaration on its nuclear programme:

> North Korea's move to restart its Yongbyon reactor means that one of the Bush administration's few foreign policy achievements – a deal to roll back Kim Jong Il's nuclear program – is on the brink of collapse.
>
> The conventional narrative, put forward by administration officials and unquestioningly accepted by most of the media, is that it is North Korea's fault – an unpredictable rogue state, perhaps thrown into turmoil by Kim's ill health, abruptly breaking a painstakingly negotiated denuclearization deal.
>
> There's only one problem with this account. It's wrong – and failure to understand what's really happening, and the reasons for North Korea's behaviour, guarantees that the crisis will escalate ...
>
> Once Pyongyang provided the declaration, it was supposed to be taken off the terrorism list. The disabling of Yongbyon would then be completed. Talks would then address plans for verification as a first step to the complete dismantling of all of North Korea's nuclear programs.
>
> Whatever its flaws, Bush and Rice accepted the arrangement, as did the other members of the six-party talks. However, Bush administration hardliners pushed back, arguing that the declaration was not credible and that the United States had to insist that Pyongyang accept a verification protocol before the delisting – unilaterally moving the goalposts.
>
> When Washington announced this decision, Pyongyang was predictably furious.
>
> Senior Bush administration officials have acknowledged privately to me that the North Koreans are right when they say that the United States reneged on its commitment to delist.
>
> If Pyongyang has nothing to hide, critics ask, why should it object to verification? But that is not how these things work. Getting North Korea to abandon its nuclear programs is a reciprocal process that requires an understanding of Pyongyang's own strategic thinking rarely displayed in Washington ...

Consequently, the North's pattern has always been tit for tat – if the United States cooperates, it too will be cooperative, but pressure from Washington will be met with even sharper retaliatory moves. Restarting the Yongbyon reactor fits into this pattern. And it isn't the first time.[16]

Squabbles within the elite and a lack of coherent policy-making, as documented by Chinoy and others, explain the minutiae of the US failure to negotiate peaceful coexistence with the DPRK, but they do not account for the unremitting hostility of 60 years. It may be clear why the US feels no great compulsion to come to terms with the DPRK, but that still leaves the basic reason for the enmity unexplained.

Continuity: From Malign Neglect to Strategic Patience

In the early years of the Bush administration, the policy towards North Korea was labelled, by friends and enemies alike, as one of 'malign neglect'.[17] This was followed, until the end of his second term, by a process of fitful negotiation, as chronicled by Chinoy. Obama the candidate promised to negotiate with everyone, including Kim Jong Il, but this promise was soon abandoned, and the North Korea policy settled down to what was called by its supporters one of 'strategic patience'.[18]

In fact it was really a policy of indecision, of muddling through.[19] Worse, some described it a 'strategic passivity'.[20] It might better be described as strategic paralysis, because it is the result not of lethargy, but of conflicting forces – even if those conflicts are not articulated clearly. This, I argue elsewhere, is a characteristic of the Obama administration, trapped between rhetoric and reality, faced with deep-seated problems around the world and at home.

Obama's policy towards North Korea shares this sense of paralysis. The 'military option' of attacking and destroying North Korea has been raised many times over the years and rejected as a matter of policy – though, as we will see in Part III, the US may find itself being sucked into that outcome through the dynamics of South Korean policy. On the other hand, the United States finds it impossible to consummate a negotiated deal with the DPRK, though no great obstacles would be placed in the way of such a goal by the Korean side.

Why this inability to move forward? It is clear that this is not just a failing of the Obama administration, but reflects a continuity stretching back to Bush and beyond. There must be underlying reasons for this failure to engage North Korea and settle the issue.

Failure to Engage

The Korean War was the first war that the US did not win, creating a wound within the US political and military establishment that has yet to heal. That war was the pivot around which the rearmament of the Cold War revolved, so it is no surprise that the enemy – the North Koreans and the Chinese – were much vilified in justification of that rearmament. Since then, unremitting indoctrination at both popular and elite levels has created its own momentum of hostility.

Hostility towards the DPRK is the daily stuff of the media, so there is no need to give any examples. But not everyone is caught up in the hysteria: there are a number of American individuals and groups who call for engagement, and even peace. In some cases this is for moral reasons, and this usually comes from Korean-Americans and/or religious groups.[21] While the mainstream liberal left is probably as antagonistic towards the DPRK as anyone else – which attests to the effectiveness of social indoctrination – those concerned with Korean affairs tend to be pro-engagement.[22]

Then there are those whose motivation, while not devoid of moral imperatives, is primarily pragmatic. One who is well qualified to voice an opinion is former President Jimmy Carter. It was he who forced the Clinton administration into the Agreed Framework in 1994. The administration was not at all keen to conclude negotiations with the DPRK, but Carter gave an interview to CNN from Pyongyang in which he said that Kim Il Sung wanted to do a deal. This gave the administration no option but to proceed with the talks that led to the Agreed Framework. Carter has continued to visit North Korea occasionally, most recently in August 2010.[23] In 2009 he gave an interview to Peter Speilmann of the Associated Press in which he was scathing about the hyperbole of the difficulty of negotiating with the DPRK:

> During Monday's interview, Carter also discussed North Korea's nuclear program, saying he thought the communist nation would be willing to give up its nuclear weapons for US diplomatic recognition, a peace deal with South Korea and America, and if it got new atomic power reactors and free fuel oil.
>
> 'It could be worked out, in my opinion, in half a day,' Carter said.
>
> Last week, North Korea's Foreign Ministry said it would give up its nuclear weapons only if Washington establishes diplomatic

relations with the regime and the US ceases to pose a nuclear threat to the North.

'I went over there in 1994 and I worked out a complete agreement with Kim Il Sung to eliminate all nuclear programs, and to let International Atomic Energy Agency inspectors come in without impediment,' Carter said.

'President Clinton adopted that and put it into effect.' But he said it was later shelved by President George W. Bush.

Carter believes a deal could be accomplished with good will.

'North Koreans, in my opinion, whom I know fairly well, have always been willing to forego their nuclear capability if they have diplomatic relations with the United States, first of all, which is not easy, Carter told the AP.

'And if they have an assurance with the United States that it would not attack them militarily, of course with the proviso that North Korea not attack South Korea,' he said.

Carter said the rest of the solution is as easy as replacing their old dangerous reactors with new, safer designs with guaranteed IAEA inspection access, and giving North Korea fuel oil to run electric generators until its power grid is improved.[24]

Robert Carlin and John W. Lewis, who have made a number of high-profile visits, argue on very pragmatic grounds that peaceful coexistence is workable:

Being realistic about the North makes no moral judgment about its system or policies, nor does it cede anything in terms of our values or goals. US policymakers need to go back to square one. A realistic place to start fresh may be quite simple: accepting the existence of North Korea as it is, a sovereign state with its own interests.[25]

An interesting insight into the difficulties of getting the United States to negotiate with North Korea is provided by Donald Gregg. Gregg is a former CIA operative (he was involved with the Iran-Contra scandal) who was Bush Senior's ambassador to Seoul, and is currently chairman emeritus of the Korea Foundation. In a letter to the *Washington Post* in December 2010, he lamented America's failure to engage:

New Mexico Gov. Bill Richardson (D) ended a five-day visit to North Korea this week, trying to help defuse the crisis between

Washington and Pyongyang.[26] He reported conciliatory gestures on the part of North Korea, but based on my experience eight years ago and what I see from the Obama administration, which apparently is not even interested in debriefing Mr. Richardson, the visit may have been for naught.

I visited North Korea in 2002 at the invitation of First Vice Minister Kim Gye Gwan – Mr Richardson's host this week – with an indication that North Korea would respond to my suggestion that it return the USS *Pueblo*, seized in 1968. As I was about to leave for Pyongyang, the United States accused North Korea of developing a secret, second path to build nuclear weapons with highly enriched uranium.

During my visit, Kang Sok Ju, Kim Jong Il's top foreign policy adviser, delivered a written offer, in blind memo form, for talks with Washington. We were asked to carry it in secret to the White House. Deputy national security adviser Stephen Hadley read the memo and immediately said, checking with no one, that direct talks would 'reward bad behavior.'

Michael Green, a tough National Security Council staffer in the Bush administration, says the Obama administration has been harder on North Korea than he and his colleagues were. But the need for direct talks outweighs any evil acts that the North Koreans may have perpetrated. I wish that President Obama and his advisers would recognize that and listen to the messages Bill Richardson brought back.[27]

Underneath the 60 years of hostile propaganda and the flurry of bureaucratic politics, there are a few underlying factors that should be mentioned.

First of all, as discussed below, the militarisation of American society militates against peace unless there is no alternative. There are also two good realpolitik reasons for refusing to negotiate peaceful coexistence with the DPRK. First, it would give a bad example to other small countries trying to preserve or establish independence. Libya caved in and got little for its pains.[28] Iran, among other countries, will be watching the struggle between Washington and Pyongyang.

Secondly, a state of tension in East Asia keeps South Korea and Japan in the alliance against China. This is of huge, if unstated and unacknowledged, importance. For the United States, Korean policy is a subset of China policy. Peace in Korea would also make it much more difficult to justify its military presence in the region;

or, to put it another way, it would make obvious the fact that the military presence is aimed at China.

This use of the purported 'threat' from North Korea is illustrated by the comments of Pentagon Press Secretary Geoff Morrell regarding Defense Secretary Robert Gates' remark during his visit to China in January 2011 that North Korea is 'becoming a direct threat to the United States':

> [He] also commented on news reports that US President Barack Obama told his Chinese counterpart Hu Jintao that the US would redeploy US troops in Asia unless China applies pressure on the North. 'Over the long-term lay-down of our forces in the Pacific, we are looking at ways to even bolster that, not necessarily in Korea and Japan, but along the Pacific Rim, *particularly in Southeast Asia*,' he said.[29]

If North Korea, in Northeast Asia, is the threat, why build up forces *particularly in Southeast Asia*, other than to contain China?

Globally, the administration gives the impression of strategic paralysis. In East Asia the Obama administration is antagonistic towards China and refuses to negotiate with North Korea. Although there are contraindications, in general it seems that its Korea policy has been captured by Lee Myung-bak.[30] For an administration in strategic paralysis, having someone else show the way must be enticing. And if that way involves displays of military strength and tough talk against North Korea and China, it must be irresistible.

Lee Myung-bak, for his part, sees that the time is ripe to precipitate a collapse of the North and its absorption by the South.[31] In circumstances such as these, a relatively small event could trigger a chain of actions that end up in war.[32]

Part II

Buildup to Crisis: The *Cheonan* Incident and Its Consequences

Part I outlined the context of the events that took place in the Korean peninsula in 2010. This part examines the sinking of the *Cheonan* in March, the official investigation of it, and the controversy surrounding that investigation. The official South Korean government verdict on the *Cheonan* sinking brought about a great increase in tension, which led to the fire-fight at Yeonpyeong Island, off the coast of North Korea, in November. This process can been seen as a series of steps in a build-up of tension that may well lead to war. In 2010, the peninsula, and with it Northeast Asia (within which we must include the United States), was brought closer to war than at any time since the 1950s.

It is relatively easy to see why the danger of war receded after the Korean War armistice of 1953. North Korea and China needed peace for economic reconstruction. For the United States the war had been costly and unpopular; it was the first war it had fought that it had not won. Syngman Rhee had wanted to continue, but could not do so without the Americans. It seems that Kim Il Sung accepted that a military solution was off the agenda, and turned to political initiatives for reunification. The generals in the South who succeeded Syngman Rhee, notably Park Chung-hee, realised their political, economic and military weakness, and were in no position to reignite war. The Americans became involved in Vietnam, and the Chinese had other concerns. Democratisation in the South in the late 1980s led the way to Kim Dae-jung, and then Roh Moo-hyun, with policies of peaceful engagement with the North, and a vision of gradual reunification. This engagement culminated in the summit of 2–4 October 2007.

The situation changed rapidly with the accession to the ROK presidency of Lee Myung-bak in February 2008. North Korea was by then much weaker than the South, its strength sapped away by sanctions and the loss of its relationship with the Soviet Union and the socialist bloc. The balance of power had swung very much in favour of the South, and Lee seems to have decided to utilise the situation in ways that his predecessors had not. An astute politician, he complemented his hard-line policy towards the North with talk of a 'grand bargain'. The British Korea expert and former diplomat Jim Hoare put it well:

> The Lee government has adopted a more aggressive policy towards North Korea. It has not refused assistance outright, but has couched its offers in such a way that rejection is inevitable – the most recent example is the 'grand bargain' proposed in 2009 in which the DPRK must first give up its nuclear program to receive security guarantees and aid. This is then played back as evidence that the North is incorrigible and not deserving of assistance.[1]

The key word here is 'first'. It is a posture the Americans have been wont to adopt in their negotiations with the DPRK: surrender first, and then we will be generous. Not surprisingly, North Korea has not fallen for it – they insist on sequential reciprocity, or 'action for action'.[2] It is always uncertain to what degree US policy is based on rational calculation rather than infighting within the elite, with policies tripping over the obfuscations of their progenitors. When George W. Bush or Barack Obama make such proposals, they might conceivably be serious. It is unlikely that Lee Myung-bak was so deluded. Rather, he must have known he was making an offer that the North neither could nor would accept. However, that was a necessary first step that left the field free for the hard-line policy to come into play. This policy was predicated on the assumption that the North was now so weak and fragile that tightening sanctions and an increase in military political pressure, combined with a build-up of tension, would precipitate a collapse – or at least sufficient disarray for the Americans to be persuaded that an invasion would not be met with much resistance.

Relations between South and North rapidly deteriorated through 2008 and 2009, and 2010 ended with the clash at Yeonpyeong. This was important not because of the casualties themselves – an unknown number in the North and four (two marines, two civilians) were killed in a military base in the South – but rather because of the climate it engendered. By December 2010 Lee Myung-bak was talking openly of a takeover of the North, and urging the people not to be afraid of war.[3] Such admonitions mean one thing when a country is faced by a stronger adversary, but take on quite a different complexion when the other side is so much weaker. Lee couched his war talk in terms of responding to 'provocations' from the North, but an examination of the facts (see especially Chapter 10) shows that the initiatives come from the South. This is scarcely surprising given the disparity in power, but it is quite at variance with the official line promulgated in the media, which portrays the North as belligerent and Lee Myung-bak as showing 'statesmanlike' restraint. That is not uncommon: most wars break out when, according to the stronger power, they have exhausted all avenues towards peace, and must reluctantly face up to their responsibilities by going to war.

It would be a mistake to lay too much importance on Lee Myung-bak himself. He may be the trigger for bringing about a second Korean War, but that trigger is only dangerous because the war was never really ended.

The Armistice which brought the fighting to an end planted the seeds of future conflict – in general because it did not resolve outstanding issues or lead to a peace treaty; specifically because it left an uncertain situation on the West Sea, which the United States exacerbated with its unilateral drawing of the Northern Limit Line (NLL). The NLL became the scene of various clashes over the years, and in 2010 the setting of the *Cheonan* and Yeonpyeong incidents. The relationship between the NNL (which is discussed in more detail in Chapter 9) and the incidents of 2010 is a strong one, especially in the case of Yeonpyeong. The NLL undoubtedly contributed to the sinking of the *Cheonan*, but it was not the proximate cause. The Yeonpyeong incident, by contrast, represented a clash over the NLL itself.

The Timeline in the Appendix may be useful when reading this part of the book.

6
The Mysterious Sinking of the *Cheonan*, and the Official Investigation

THE SINKING OF THE *CHEONAN*

On 26 March 2010 the South Korean Patrol Combat Corvette (PCC) *Cheonan* sank in 'mysterious circumstances' near Baengnyeong Island, adjacent to the NLL, with 46 casualties. In the weeks following the sinking, speculation was rife as to the cause: explanations included a Northern torpedo or mine, Northern suicide squads, an explosion caused by an 'internal act of terror', or some sort of malfunction igniting ammunition or fuel.[1] The right-wing media naturally blamed the North, and was criticised by the liberal press for doing so.[2] Distrust of the military led to rumours that the *Cheonan* had been mistakenly sunk by friendly fire, or that the incident had been fabricated to whip up anti-North sentiment.[3]

President Lee Myung-bak set up a team of enquiry called the Joint Investigation Group (JIG). JIG issued its first interim report on 20 May, in which it decided that

[b]ased on all such relevant facts and classified analysis, we have reached the clear conclusion that ROKS 'Cheonan' was sunk as the result of an external underwater explosion caused by a torpedo made in North Korea. The evidence points overwhelmingly to the conclusion that the torpedo was fired by a North Korean submarine. There is no other plausible explanation.[4]

On 24 May President Lee declared on national television in an address to the nation that

[f]inally, on May 20th, the international joint investigation group released their conclusive findings, backed by definitive evidences. With the release of the final report, no responsible country in the international community will be able to deny the fact that the Cheonan was sunk by North Korea.[5]

In fact it was not until 14 September that the JIG issued its final report. This reiterated the initial conclusion, but in style. The initial report was five pages long. The final report came out in pdf files in Korean and English, and in a handsome hardcover book, the English version of which runs to 313 pages.[6] No expense had been spared, and the final report was replete with pictures, diagrams and mathematical formulae. It is a fine example of what the Americans call a snow job – a technique otherwise described as 'blinding with science'.

At this stage we do not know what caused the sinking of the *Cheonan*, and we may never know. What we can be reasonably certain about is that the official South Korean explanation is false, and, it would appear, deliberately so. The evidence produced by what was essentially the South Korean Ministry of National Defense was very complex in parts, and led to extensive coverage in the media, and particularly in cyberspace. It is important to cut through the details and focus on the key aspects, and this is what I will do in this chapter and the next.

In this chapter I will examine

- setting the stage for the enquiry;
- the composition of the team of official enquiry – the Joint Investigation Group;
- the purported discovery of torpedo remnants – the physical evidence of the assertion of the North's culpability.

The following chapter will consider

- the scepticism of the South Korean public, as well as civic organisations;
- the refutations of the report's conclusions by Korean scientists in the United States;
- the Russian investigation;
- the torpedo and its contradictions;
- implications of the fabrication.

SETTING THE STAGE FOR THE ENQUIRY

In retrospect, it is evident that the reaction to the sinking was stage-managed in a very competent manner. Initial comments from the government in Seoul – as well as that in Washington – said there was no evidence of Northern involvement. Military personnel who asserted that the North had sunk the *Cheonan* were slapped down. President Lee said that he would not jump to a conclusion, but would seek the truth. A seemingly impartial and international team of enquiry was set up. As the weeks passed, it appeared that President Lee was reluctantly coming to the conclusion that the North was responsible. Finally, on 20 May, the initial report was issued, and four days later President Lee made his address to the nation, naming North Korea as guilty and promising stern measures:

> We have always tolerated North Korea's brutality, time and again. We did so because we have always had a genuine longing for peace on the Korean Peninsula. But now things are different. North Korea will pay a price corresponding to its provocative acts. I will continue to take stern measures to hold the North accountable.[7]

In the immediate aftermath of the sinking, military sources – official and retired, identified and anonymous – were naturally quoted extensively in the South Korean media. The officials, perhaps responding to government pressure, initially tended to play down the suggestion of North Korean involvement, but the general tone was one of suspicion, even of certainty, that the North was behind the sinking. Defense Minister Kim Tae-young, a former general who had headed the ROK army, was reprimanded for blaming the North in defiance of presidential policy.[8]

However, what was interesting was swift government action – first by the State Department in Washington, then by the government in Seoul – to assert that there was no evidence of Northern involvement.[9] This set the stage for the Lee Myung-bak government to position itself as an honest seeker after truth. In an interview with Fred Hiatt of *Newsweek* on 12 April, President Lee assured his less-than-critical interviewer of the disinterested nature of the government's approach – it was after the truth, not seeking simply to blame North Korea:

> *Hiatt*: You've said no one should jump to conclusions about the sinking of your naval ship. But if North Korea turns out to be responsible, what options would you have for response?

> *Lee Myung-bak*: The most important thing for us is to determine, of course, the actual cause of the sinking, but also for us to come up with a result, a report, that the international community will find acceptable and approve. So the process must be transparent

and it must yield accurate results, and for that, we have invited experts from our ally the United States to take part in the investigation to determine the cause of the sinking. If need be, we will be inviting other countries or other experts from other institutions and countries. And also we've asked the United Nations for help and assistance in determining the accurate cause, and all of these measures are being carried out so that we can increase the credibility of the report that will be coming out. And for me, as president, I don't attach too much importance on whether we can come up with results as soon as possible, because I attach much more importance on the accuracy of the report.[10]

And indeed, the investigation took quite some time to run its course, and the results were not officially announced until 20 May, which happened fortuitously to mark the beginning of formal campaigning for local and gubernatorial elections on 2 June – a coincidence not overlooked by the liberal press (nor, it transpired later, perhaps by many electors).[11] It was assumed by all sides that a rise in anti-North Korean feeling would bring votes to Lee's ruling party, the Grand National Party (GNP).[12]

LEE MYUNG-BAK: HARNESSING THE NORTH WIND

When the *Cheonan* was sunk, Lee Myung-bak had various options open to him in order to advance his own agenda and also to protect the reputation of the ROK navy. These would have been separate but congruent objectives. However, the necessity of deflecting criticism from the military did constrain his options.

Losing a ship and a large number of sailors in what was the worst disaster in many years potentially exposed the navy, the Joint Chief of Staff, and the Ministry of Defense to serious criticism, and worse. Whatever had happened on 26 March, the ROK military was almost certainly at fault. If the *Cheonan* had run aground, been in collision with another ship or been sunk by friendly fire, then those responsible had to be held accountable. If it had been sunk by a North Korean torpedo, then the ROK was arguably even more culpable. It was, after all, an anti-submarine corvette, on exercises which, during practice for an invasion of the North, must have incorporated defensive measures, of which those against submarines must have had high priority. Clearly, any investigation essentially had to be controlled by the military, but carried out in such a way as to enjoy some credibility; as the *Chosun Ilbo* put it ten days after the sinking,

> this is all the more necessary considering the amount of rumors floating around on the Internet, including claims that the South Korean military mistakenly fired on its own vessel, or that the entire incident was fabricated by the administration to make North Korea appear evil.[13]

So President Lee had a difficult task before him. He had to protect the military, but not be associated with its failings. He needed to 'show firmness to the North' to appease the right, but not appear too belligerent and inflammatory, in order not to frighten the centre and particularly the Americans. He had to take China and Russia into account – they would not want to see anything that threatened instability; though Japan could be ignored as long as the Americans were kept on side.

These contradictory pressures, and the changing position of the military as it tried to evade blame, did erode public confidence. A survey conducted on behalf of the liberal *Hankyoreh* in early April showed that some 60 per cent of South Koreans polled distrusted the military and had little confidence in the government's handling of the situation.[14]

In retrospect, Lee handled the situation well. There were two investigations – by the JIG, whose function was to exonerate the military and blame the North; and by the Board of Audit, which was to demonstrate that the government was in control and would discipline those members of the military who failed to live up to expectations.

Lee acted to distance himself from the military, casting himself as a 'responsible statesman' who was willing to restrain those members of the military, including the Minister of Defense, who jumped to accusing North Korea without waiting for evidence to be assembled. It was, in effect, a version of the good cop/bad cop routine. On 5 April, Minister of Defense Kim Tae-young was 'told off for speculating about the shipwreck'.[15] Hillary Clinton was apparently impressed by Lee's 'statesmanlike' behaviour, as was a *Financial Times* journalist who quoted her approval in a eulogistic article about the South Korean president.[16]

LEE'S DILEMMA: THE TRADE-OFF BETWEEN CREDIBILITY AND VERDICT

The composition of the investigation team – the JIG – illustrated the dilemma facing Lee and the degree of success that he achieved. Although it was called a 'Joint Civilian–Military Investigation Group', it was in fact firmly under the control of the military. Although it claimed to be 'international' and was widely reported as such, its multinationalism consisted in little more than a few friendly foreigners endorsing the military investigation. The obvious way around that would have been to invite China and Russia to join the investigation – an option favoured, for instance, by Tae-Hwan Kwak: 'In retrospect, the ROK should have included Chinese and Russian experts in the multilateral probe team to support the findings.'[17] However, Professor Kwak was overlooking a key consideration: it is highly unlikely that either Russia or China would have supported the findings of 20 May, which found North Korea guilty. Both countries have an overriding interest in preserving the stability of the Korean peninsula, and would be extremely reluctant to support findings that endangered it – even if the *Cheonan* had been sunk by a North Korean torpedo.

So there is a certain Catch-22 quality to the situation. Since Russia and China were not involved in the investigation, they are preventing the UN Security Council from condemning North Korea as Lee has demanded.[18] As a consequence the UNSC has displayed an unusual degree of impartiality:

> Ambassador Claude Heller of Mexico, the current UNSC chair, in a statement said that the UNSC is 'seriously concerned' about the *Cheonan* sinking and its consequences for the peace and stability of the Korean Peninsula. He urged *both Koreas* to refrain from action that could heighten tensions in the region.[19]

The DPRK ambassador was even allowed to make a presentation to the UNSC, although, whether at its own request or by the ruling of the UNSC, he had only half the time of the ROK ambassador.[20]

This was a significant diplomatic setback, since the UNSC has had no compunction about condemning, and sanctioning, North Korea in the past, despite those actions being in flagrant violation of the Charter of the United Nations, and of natural justice.[21] Both Russia and China are reluctant to use their veto, but they use other methods to attempt to restrain the Americans' hegemonic influence

– the convoluted moves over Iran are a case in point. In other words, the UNSC is not a place where justice is dispensed, or truth prevails, but one where politics is played. South Korea has usually been on the winning side, but not quite this time. This is perhaps no more than an embarrassment, and certainly is a long way from the sanctions imposed on North Korea; but one can see from the South Korean press how galling they have found it:

> UN Security Council members appeared to understand the outcome of a multinational probe that found North Korea responsible for the deadly sinking of a South Korean warship ...
>
> France and the United States expressed support for the investigation results and called for a strong punishment of the North. But China and Russia, the North's traditional backers, neither voiced support for the probe nor asked any questions, officials said.
>
> The fate of South Korea's push for a rebuke of the North at the Council hinges on Beijing and Moscow. The two nations, which hold veto power at the 15-member Council, have expressed reservations about the findings of the investigation.[22]

Reservations about a verdict which the JIG had insisted allowed 'no other plausible explanation'?

Lee Myung-bak had been faced with a dilemma. An investigation involving China and Russia would at best have resulted in an inconclusive verdict, but at worst might have thrown up some embarrassing evidence of an accident – or, worse still, friendly fire. A friendly-fire incident involving the US would have been a diplomatic nightmare. President Karzai might grumble about such things, but would not be able to do much about it; the president of South Korea would be in a very different position, and would be expected to do more than lodge an impotent protest.

It may be that Lee tried to resolve this dilemma by inviting the Chinese and Russians not to participate in the investigation as such, but to inspect the evidence assembled by the JIG after the event. As discussed below, the Russians accepted this potentially poisoned chalice and the Chinese did not.

Another option facing Lee Myung-bak in the early days, when governments in both Seoul and Washington were saying there was no indication of North Korean involvement in the sinking, would have been to ask Pyongyang to send investigators. This would have involved the same risks as participation by China and Russia, but with one significant difference: if China and Russia had been asked at the outset, they surely would have agreed. But would the DPRK? It is impossible to say. Pyongyang would have been very suspicious of Seoul, and might have seen a trap. So Lee may have taken a calculated risk, guessing that Kim Jong Il would decline. In which case Pyongyang would have limited reason to complain about the fairness of the investigation. In the event no offer was made, and Seoul seems to have been taken by surprise by Pyongyang's demand to send investigators. The boot is now on the other foot, and Seoul's refusal suggests that South Korea has something to hide.

One obvious complicating factor in all this is the question of military secrets – not only South Korean, but also, ultimately, American. That raises another question. What was the US role in the determination of the composition of the investigation team? They would not have been quite so worried about the North Koreans, but would be concerned at Chinese and Russian involvement.

FRIENDLY FACES: THE COMPOSITION OF THE INVESTIGATION TEAM

Following the sinking of the *Cheonan*, true to his word, Lee had set up an investigation team incorporating experts from the United States and some other countries. The team described itself as follows:

> The Joint Civilian-Military Investigation Group (JIG) conducted its investigation with 25 experts from 10 top Korean expert agencies, 22 military experts, 3 experts recommended by the National Assembly, and 24 foreign experts constituting 4 support teams from the United States, Australia, the United Kingdom and the Kingdom of Sweden.[23]

Although it was called a civilian-military team, it was in fact run out of the Ministry of Defense, which issued all its statements, including the final report.

The inclusion of '3 experts recommended by the National Assembly' must have been an attempt to portray the JIG as independent of the government, at least to some degree. It turned out that one of them indeed was, but he was soon replaced.[24] This was Shin Sang-cheol (also spelled Shin Sang-chul, or abbreviated to Shin SC), who was nominated by the opposition Democratic Party (DP). The other two were presumably chosen by the ruling Grand National Party (GNP). Shin had studied oceanography at the Korea Maritime University, and served in the ROK navy. He subsequently worked seven years for shipbuilders, before setting up the politically progressive Internet magazine Seoprise.[25] In short, he is a man who knows something about ships. Shin came to the conclusion that the *Cheonan* had run aground and that the JIG investigation, and its verdict that the *Cheonan* had been sunk by a torpedo, was a cover-up. He wrote to US Secretary of State Hillary Clinton expressing his admiration for 'my hero Obama', but giving in some detail, with a profusion of photos and illustrations, his argument: 'There was no Explosion. There was No Torpedo'.[26] The State Department website makes no mention of Mr Shin, but his letter did not go unnoticed in South Korea, and he soon came 'under investigation himself for allegedly spreading false rumors about the incident'.[27]

Shin was not the only high-profile sceptic to come under investigation. Park Sun-won, who had served as National Security Strategy Secretary for President Roh, was also charged with defaming the military.[28] Shin and Park were by no means alone in challenging the findings of the government investigation, and the South Korean internet seems to have been awash with rumours. The police were kept busy 'hunting' for those spreading rumours – deemed a criminal offence by the government.[29]

Despite the intensive government-led campaign and the attempts to stifle dissenting voices, according to a poll conducted by the *Hankook Ilbo*,

> [t]wenty-four percent of respondents said they didn't trust the government's evidence, with more skepticism among younger and better-educated people, the *Hankook Ilbo* poll found. Almost 90 percent of people over 60 trusted the findings, while only 70 percent of those in their 40s did.[30]

Other reports put the number of unbelievers as high as 40 percent.[31] On 18 May, according to the same article,

> [t]he leaders of South Korea's four opposition parties – the Democratic, Democratic Labor, Creative Korea and National Participation parties – as well as a handful of civic groups issued a joint statement on Monday saying they cannot trust the results of the investigation into the sinking of the Navy corvette *Cheonan* as long as [the] authorities refuse to reveal information about the incident from the Korean Navy Tactical Data System as well as communications and navigational records of the vessel.[32]

The impotence of opposition politicians, and the disdain of the ROK and American governments, was highlighted when Hillary Clinton offered a copy of the 400-page report on the incident to China, and it was revealed that this had not been released to the National Assembly:

> US Secretary of State Hillary Rodham Clinton, who visited South Korea two days ago, said that China would better understand the situation if it read the 400-page *Cheonan* report, but not a single lawmaker in the National Assembly has laid eyes on this report. If a report provided to a country overseas is not presented to the National Assembly, this demonstrates an unbelievable disregard for the legislature and people of South Korea.[33]

The title of the JIG and its asserted 'international' composition were nice touches giving the impression, at least to the unwary, that this was a disinterested team of experts. The fact that the report was released by the ROK Ministry of Defense, which provided the administrative facilities, and that most – probably almost all – of the members were military might suggest the 'civilian' tag was a decoy. This was angrily denied by the right-wing *Chosun Ilbo*, which pointed out that the team was led by Yoon Duk-yong, an honorary professor at the Korea Advanced Institute of Science and Technology. It contrasted his scientific detachment ('objective lens of a scientist') with the attitude of the 'conspiracy theorists'. Nevertheless, it complained,

> opinion polls still show that some 30 percent of the public are skeptical of the findings. The Internet is seething with posts from self-proclaimed experts posting misinformation regarding the sinking, while so-called intellectuals, celebrities and even lawmakers running for office are fuelling interest in this rumor mongering.[34]

One reason for the profusion of 'conspiracy theorists' was the frequent changing of the official line. The composition of the JIG was one such instance. The report of 20 May quoted above gives a total of 74 'experts'. An earlier report from the *JoongAng Ilbo* said the team was composed of 'up to 130 individuals, including about 30 civilian experts'.[35] The *JoongAng Ilbo* also said that Professor Yoon was only the 'civilian head' of the team, who was joining 'Army Lt. Gen. Park Jung-yi, the military chief of the team'.[36]

Exactly how much of a role the 70-year-old professor played in the investigation is unknown.

The precise meaning of 'civilian' is also unclear. The JIG report implies that the Korean civilians are government officials: '25 experts from 10 top Korean expert agencies'. The *JoongAng Ilbo* article says 'of the seven Americans, three are active servicemen and the rest are civilians working in the navy'.[37] We know that the Australian team came from the Australian navy, and it seems likely that all the other foreign experts were service personnel. If any of them had been independent civilians from, say, a university, then that surely would have been trumpeted.

A 'military commentator' from Pyongyang, apparently drawing on reports on South Korean blogs, suggested that the token civilians were kept under close supervision by the military:

> As for the 'civilian-military joint investigation team', there is enough ground for controversy as to how significant the role played by some civilians in the investigation was.
>
> The carefully selected civilians were not allowed to use their mobile phones but compelled to make a written pledge to observe secrecy and stay in warship 'Tokdo' until the end of the investigation.[38]

These articles by the 'Military Commentator' constitute the most detailed critique of the investigation from the North.

If 'civilian' in 'Joint Civilian-Military Investigation Group' is problematic, then calling it international, or multinational, as is invariably done (in his address to the national assembly on 20 May President Lee mentioned that 'the international joint investigation group released their conclusive findings') is also deceptive. 'International' has connotations of neutrality, beyond the interests of any particular nation. But in this case that was not so: the foreigners came from the hegemonic power, the United States, and its close allies Australia and Britain.

Sweden, the other country represented, is somewhat different. It is formally described as a neutral country and did not, for instance, participate in the Korean War. North Korea, for its part, does not regard Sweden as neutral, but as a US puppet.[39] However, there is little doubt that Sweden is widely perceived as neutral. The right-wing and mainstream press naturally made some mileage out of Sweden's 'neutrality'. Thus, the *Chosun Ilbo*, countering

Pyongyang's claims that the international members of the JIG came from the US and its allies, put it as follows:

> But the team said besides experts from the US, the UK and Australia, there was also a contingent from neutral Sweden – a fact the North chose to ignore although the experts all signed their names in support of the findings.[40]

To cite another example, the US magazine *Businessweek* expanded on this 'neutrality': 'The commission included experts from Sweden, which has an embassy in Pyongyang and isn't aligned with South Korea and the US.'[41] Sweden does indeed have an embassy in Pyongyang where, among other things, it represents the United States and its citizens (such as the journalists Euna Lee and Laura Ling, who were apprehended after illegally crossing into the DPRK in 2009); Sweden is, in diplomatic parlance, the 'protecting power' of the United States in North Korea.[42] There is no indication that Sweden plays the same role for the DPRK in the United States.

In reality, though the Kingdom of Sweden is formally neutral, it is certainly part of the 'Western camp'. Sweden has troops in the Balkans, as well as troops supporting the US-led invasion in Afghanistan. The Swedish Ministry of Foreign Affairs states that Sweden's cooperation with NATO is based on 'our policy of military non-alignment'.[43] The Ministry does not quite explain how cooperation with a military alliance is consistent with non-alignment.

The Tokyo-based freelance journalist John McGlynn, in an excellent dissection of the JIG statement, very plausibly suggests that the Swedes did baulk: 'However, the section of the 5-page statement that blames North Korea for the *Cheonan* sinking suggests that Sweden did not endorse this conclusion, and in absenting itself, required that a new group be constituted.'[44] The JIG was certainly not international in the sense of having representation from countries that would challenge the position of the ROK military. The Russian official international broadcaster, Voice of Russia, accurately described it as a 'South Korean investigative commission, with the involvement of western experts'. [45] As the liberal Seoul paper *Hankyoreh* put it after the release of the report,

> It is also necessary to form an international investigation team with the participation of both North Korea and South Korea in addition to the US, China and Russia. The South Korean government loses credibility when it conducts an investigation

without including relevant parties and then instructs everyone to simply follow along.[46]

The deputy chairman of the DPRK's National Defense Commission, Kim Yong Chun, demanded to be able to send investigators, as it is entitled to do under the Basic Agreement signed with Roh Tae-Woo's government in the early 1990s. The agreement was signed on 13 December 1991, but came into force on 19 February 1992. The DPRK dates it as 1991, and the ROK usually as 1992:

> Kim said in a statement sent to Seoul, 'There is no reason for the South not to allow in our inspectors if the findings of its probe are objective and scientific. It is also justified based on Chapter 2 Article 10 of the Basic Agreement and Chapter 2 Article 8 of the Annex.'
>
> Chapter 2 Article 10 stipulates that North and South Korea must resolve confrontation and disputes through dialogue. Meanwhile, Chapter 2 Article 8 of the Annex states that North and South Korea will conduct a joint investigation if the agreement is violated to find out who is responsible for the violation and seek ways to prevent a recurrence.[47]

There was a certain irony in this, because Lee Myung-bak, in his statement of 24 May, had accused the DPRK of violating the Basic Agreement by sinking the *Cheonan*. The liberal *Hankyoreh*, for one, called on the government to accede to the North Korean request, noting 'the necessity for a joint North Korea–South Korea investigation'.[48]

Alexander Vorontsov and Oleg Revenko, writing in *International Affairs*, the journal of the Russian Foreign Ministry, stress the value of the South agreeing to the North's proposal both in terms of ensuring credibility and also as a means of defusing the situation:

> Pyongyang's offer to delegate representatives to review South Korea's 'evidence' is a timely and rational initiative. This form of cooperation should keep the inter-Korean dialog afloat during the crisis and, if both sides approach the problem honestly, help defuse the conflict. A lot depends on how Seoul reacts to the proposal but, sadly, initial reports seem to indicate that the [South] Korean leadership is under various pretexts trying to dodge the issue. South Korea's stonewalling [of] Pyongyang would further diminish the credibility of the evidence.[49]

So far, Seoul has rejected the demand from Pyongyang.

The Russians, reportedly unhappy that they had been excluded from the 'international investigation', declared that they would have to have '100% proof' before they committed themselves to any course of action, and sent their own small team of investigators.[50] It seems likely that they will publicly declare the evidence inconclusive and seek methods to defuse the situation.[51] Clearly, Moscow does not want any escalation of tension around the Korean peninsula.[52]

Although the Russian Defence Ministry said that its report would not be issued until July, by early June the South Korean press was reporting that the Russians were 'unconvinced' about the JIG verdict.[53] In the event the Russians never published their report, but details were leaked to the South Korean press (see Chapter 7).

China has followed much the same course, although it has not sent investigators. Premier Wen Jiabao has constantly stressed the need to defuse tensions. After his meeting with Lee Myung-bak and Yukio Hatoyama on South Korea's Jeju Island on 30 May, his words were reported in the *Washington Post*:

> 'The urgent task for the moment is to properly handle the serious impact caused by the *Cheonan* incident, gradually defuse tensions over it and avoid possible conflicts,' Wen said at a joint news conference with his South Korean and Japanese counterparts.
>
> 'China will continue to work with every country through aggressive negotiations and cooperation to fulfil our mission of maintaining peace and stability in the region.'[54]

The skewed composition of the investigation group, and particularly the exclusion of China and Russia – not to mention North Korea itself – inevitably affected its credibility, and laid the foundation for doubts about its report. This in turn made the Russian investigation even more important, because the Russian team was the only reasonably impartial group of experts to gain access, however limited, to the evidence. The Russian conclusion was very different to that of the JIG.

SEARCH FOR THE SMOKING GUN

It was virtually two months after the sinking of the *Cheonan*, on 26 March, that the initial JIG report was released, and by that time what it had to say had become a foregone conclusion.

During that period the South Korean press churned out a continual flow of rumours, leaks, assertions and various other titbits to excite the imagination.[55] One of the more interesting of these was the claim that residue in the hull of the *Cheonan* indicated that it had been sunk by a German torpedo – which was rather awkward, because it would have been extremely difficult for the North to get hold of one, whereas they were standard issue in the South Korean and US navies.[56]

Underlying everything was the need to produce a 'smoking gun' that would tie North Korea to the sinking. That did not appear until virtually the last moment, by which time the Americans had apparently finished their part of the investigation; in other words they came to a verdict before having access to the evidence.[57]

While rumours about North Korea's guilt flooded the South Korean media in the week preceding the release of the report, making its verdict predictable, there was a noticeable lack of evidence. As the release date for the report approached there was still no substantial evidence, no 'smoking gun'. Then, on Wednesday 19 May, the *Chosun Ilbo* exulted:

> Investigators have … at the 11th hour found a desperately needed smoking gun linking North Korea to the sinking of the Navy corvette *Cheonan*, a government official claimed Tuesday. Investigators apparently discovered a propeller from the torpedo that likely sank the ship in relatively good condition in waters where it sank and the serial number handwritten on it is North Korean.
>
> 'US, Australian and other foreign experts who took part in the investigation agree that a North Korean torpedo caused the *Cheonan* to sink and that this is the smoking gun following various pieces of the torpedo and traces of gun powder that had been gathered so far,' the official said.[58]

It was later claimed in the report that the discovery had taken place on Saturday 15 May, and consisted of more than just a propeller:

> The torpedo parts recovered at the site of the explosion by a dredging ship on May 15th, which include the 5x5 bladed contra-rotating propellers, propulsion motor and a steering section, perfectly match the schematics of the CHT-02D torpedo included in introductory brochures provided to foreign countries by North Korea for export purposes.[59]

Not merely was the timing of the discovery fortuitous, but so also was the method. According to the South Korean media, it was not dredged up by the naval salvage ships, where it might have been observed by the international experts and the civilians, but by a pair of trawlers on one of which were 'some navy and investigation team members':

> Kim Cheol-an, 51, the caption [sic] of one of the trawlers, said that some navy and investigation team members were aboard the trawler when they found the evidence.
>
> 'Initially, I was skeptical about finding any decisive evidence. But the moment we lifted the parts, we were sure that they were the parts of a torpedo. I think it was luck from heaven,' said Kim, who was present at the press conference.[60]

This version, which is probably true, is in conflict with a BBC report which credited the navy with the find:

> The *Cheonan* was lifted from the sea bed in April. It was crucial to find direct evidence of the type of weapon involved.
>
> To that end the South Korean navy even designed its own special nets and they have been dragging them, up to eight times a day, across the seabed close to the site of the sinking.
>
> Just five days ago, they found what they were looking for – the propellers, a propulsion motor and a steering section of a torpedo, a perfect match for a model known to be manufactured and exported by North Korea.[61]

This 'luck from heaven', this 'smoking gun' was quickly asserted to be 'conclusive evidence', and became the centre-piece of the South Korean government's case.

7
From 'Smoking Gun' to Rusty Torpedo

THE SCEPTICISM OF THE SOUTH KOREAN PUBLIC, AND CIVIC ORGANISATIONS

Governments around the world, with the important exception of China and Russia, accepted the South Korean government's verdict on the sinking of the *Cheonan* without demur, and without checking to see if there might – possibly – be some doubt.[1] The same was true of the Western media and much of academia; when it comes to North Korea, those standards of impartiality and scrutiny we hear so much about are so often absent. However, the one place the South Korean government had trouble selling its story was at home. Poll after poll showed that a substantial proportion of the population did not believe the government's explanations. This scepticism was reflected in the gubernatorial and local elections. Abraham Lincoln's aphorism about fooling the people comes to mind.

Barbara Demick and John M. Glionna, writing in the *Los Angeles Times* were slightly puzzled by this:

The way US officials see it, there's little mystery behind the most notorious shipwreck in recent Korean history.

Secretary of State Hillary Rodham Clinton calls the evidence 'overwhelming' that the *Cheonan*, a South Korean warship that sank in March, was hit by a North Korean torpedo. Vice President Joe Biden has cited the South Korean–led panel investigating the sinking as a model of transparency.

But challenges to the official version of events are coming from an unlikely place: within South Korea ...

Armed with dossiers of their own scientific studies and bolstered by conspiracy theories, critics dispute the findings announced May 20 by South Korean President Lee Myung-bak, which pointed a finger at Pyongyang.

They also question why Lee made the announcement nearly two months after the ship's sinking, on the very day campaigning opened for fiercely contested local elections. Many accuse the conservative leader of using the deaths of 46 sailors to stir up anti-communist sentiment and sway the vote.

The critics, mostly but not all from the opposition, say it is unlikely that the impoverished North Korean regime could have pulled off a perfectly executed hit against a superior military power, sneaking a submarine into the area and slipping away without detection. They also wonder whether the evidence of a torpedo attack was misinterpreted, or even fabricated.[2]

It was really not surprising that the South Korean public expressed scepticism while the public pronouncements, at least, of US politicians and officials were suffused with certainty. How much Secretary Clinton actually knew about the investigation she called 'overwhelming' is uncertain, and perhaps will ever remain so.

Neither was it surprising that scepticism varied with demographics as well as with political persuasion.[3] The young, and the better-educated, tended to be less ready to accept the government line than their elders, who had had a lot more practice:

> Although 70 percent of the South Korean public believe North Korea was behind the sinking of the Navy corvette *Cheonan*, the proportion is only 60 percent among people between the ages of 20 and 40, a survey suggests ...
>
> The poll shows that younger Koreans, especially those in their 20s, are suspicious of accusations against North Korea. When asked which country they did think attacked the ship, only 64 percent of them said it was North Korea. Some 5.6 percent said the US and some even pointed to Japan (3.3 percent) and China (1.9 percent). Twenty-five percent said they didn't know.[4]

This poll was taken by a government agency; a later one, conducted by Seoul National University, put the proportion of non-believers much higher: 'Only *three out of 10* South Koreans *trust* the findings of an international inquiry into the sinking of the Navy corvette *Cheonan* that blamed a North Korean torpedo attack.'[5] Scepticism also varied with education, which is a comforting thought for those of us in the business:

> Twenty-four percent of respondents said they didn't trust the government's evidence, with more skepticism among younger and better-educated people, the *Hankook Ilbo* poll found. Almost

90 percent of people over 60 trusted the findings, while only 70 percent of those in their 40s did.[6]

President Lee was disconcerted about the lack of credibility, and also that 'some young Koreans' were not as fearful of the North as he would like:

> President Lee Myung-bak expressed regret over the allegations that the sinking of the South Korean Navy vessel *Cheonan* in March was not the result of a North Korean attack, saying it is not understandable that some fellow South Koreans don't trust their government ...

Lee said he was worried about some young Koreans who are not afraid of North Korea.[7]

Things reached a pretty pass the next month, when even the state media found the official report wanting and called for a reinvestigation. The mainstream/conservative *Korea Times* noted that '[t]he state-run broadcaster KBS aired an investigative program that refutes the latest governmental report on the cause of the sinking of the frigate *Cheonan* in March'.[8] Shortly afterwards the Yeonpyeong incident, discussed below, caused a lot of anger among South Koreans, pushing doubts about the *Cheonan* into the background, as perhaps was the intention.

The polls reflected a passive public response, but there has been a considerable degree of activism from citizen groups. Perhaps the leading group has been the People's Solidarity for Participatory Democracy (PSPD), which raised many doubts about the investigation.[9] The PSPD went so far as to take its campaign to the United Nations Security Council during the deliberations on the *Cheonan*.[10] Unfortunately, but not surprisingly, the UNSC seems to have taken no notice:

> None of the diplomats raised the issue of a letter from South Korean civic group People's Solidarity for Participatory Democracy that questioned the veracity of South Korea's investigation. The letter to the council last week said the probe report had 'many loopholes' and 'lacks convincing rationale.' 'The matters raised by the PSPD were never mentioned,' said the Seoul official.[11]

The only reason the UNSC did not condemn North Korea was not doubts about the evidence, but opposition from China and Russia.[12]

The South Korean government condemned the PSPD action and there were subsequent reports that the group was being hounded.[13]

Why was there such scepticism among the South Korean public, especially the younger and better educated? We have seen in the previous chapter that the JIG, because of its composition, was not credible as an impartial investigator. When we look at the evidence as presented by the JIG, we see that it too is not credible. To this day we do not know why the *Cheonan* sank, but we can be pretty sure that the claim by the South Korean government that it was sunk by a North Korean torpedo is fabricated.

DISSECTING THE *CHEONAN* INCIDENT

As any reader of detective stories knows, there are three elements in a forensic investigation: means, motive and opportunity. In this case the JIG report can be considered to cover the means (essentially the torpedo parts) and the opportunity (the alleged movement of North Korean submarines). The JIG report does not speculate as to motive. Leaving aside means for the moment, let us briefly look at motive and opportunity.

Motive: *cui bono*?

For those who saw the sinking of the *Cheonan* as a deliberate act by Pyongyang, the question of motive was, or should have been, a very troublesome issue. We know that the Americans benefited: they got their base at Futenma and got rid of the Hatayama government at a stroke:[14]

> Yukio Hatoyama resigned as Japanese prime minister on June 1 because he said he had broken his campaign promise to remove the US Marine base [at] Okinawa. Mr Hatoyama reversed his position after the South Korean report into the *Cheonan* incident raised concerns about North Korean aggression in the region.[15]

For William F. Engdahl, the answer to the question 'Cui bono?' was obvious:

> In 1999 this writer spoke with a former US Ambassador to Beijing, a career CIA officer and close friend of the Bush family. The former diplomat stated, in an incautious moment, 'If North Korea did not exist, we would have to create it. They allow us to keep our fleet in the Japanese waters despite the end of the

Cold War.' Perhaps the sudden heating up of Korea tensions is also related to a longer-term Pentagon agenda for the region. If we ask Cui Bono, the clear reply is Washington.[16]

Lee Myung-bak did not get as much as he would have liked. In the lead-up to the election it was assumed that the *Cheonan* incident would swing voters behind the government. The *New York Times*, in an article reminiscent to the *Chicago Tribune*'s headline about Dewey beating Truman in the 1948 election (he didn't, but the Republican paper was certain that he would, and jumped the gun), declared: 'Ship Sinking Aids Ruling Party in S. Korean Vote':

> Politicians and political analysts agree that voters decisively turned to the Grand National Party after the announcement on May 20 of the results of an international inquiry into the sinking that found North Korea responsible. Political analysts said the results were enough to persuade many undecided voters to swing to the conservatives, who are seen as stronger on defense.[17]

That was before the election. On the actual day, in an Abraham Lincoln moment, it was found that the electorate had decided otherwise: 'Main opposition heading for stunning victory in local elections.'[18] The opposition romped home, and the election defeat '[cast] gloom over Lee administration, ruling party'.[19] It may well have been that the government would have done worse without the *Cheonan* sinking, but it certainly did not reap the benefit that it hoped. None of this means that either the US or the South Korean government sank the *Cheonan* – merely that they both benefited from its sinking.[20]

That was not the case with North Korea. It faced predictable economic damage and an increase in the military threat against it. It greatly set back its goal of negotiating peaceful coexistence with the United States. As discussed previously, the DPRK's 'utmost foreign policy objective is to establish better relations with the US, particularly via the conclusion of a peace agreement'.[21] Sinking the *Cheonan* would hardly advance that objective.

Needless to say, these realities did not prevent many commentators from ascribing all sorts of motives to Pyongyang. For some, this was just standard anti–North Korean propaganda. For others, who were convinced by the South Korean investigation, it was a matter of casting about to explain the inexplicable.

Der Spiegel, in a survey of the German press, reported that the conservative *Die Welt*, finding it all too confusing, pronounced that 'North Korea Seems To Have a Sort of Death Wish' – a conclusion perhaps not representing the best of German journalism (though, to be fair, the other papers quoted in *Spiegel* were not much better).[22]

Christian Oliver of the *Financial Times* is made of sterner stuff, and came up with his 'top seven theories':

1. Revenge
2. To smooth the succession
3. An internal power struggle
4. A reversion to hardline ideology
5. Breakdown of command in North Korea
6. To distract from economic woes at home
7. Bitterness about G20 meeting in Seoul[23]

The 'succession hypothesis' is discussed in Chapter 8. Revenge – 'North Korea wanted revenge for a sea battle in November, when one of its ships was badly damaged' – has a fair number of advocates.[24] But to suggest that Kim Jong Il would sacrifice strategic objectives for a little local victory in this way is not plausible. So then people came up with the idea that it was some sort of maverick action, not sanctioned by the leadership.[25] Others countered that that is not the way North Korea works.[26]

All in all, a barrel with very meagre scrapings.

The problem is further compounded by the fact that North Korea has made an unprecedented number of denials and refutations. It has demanded to join in the investigation of the sinking and had offered to provide evidence about its torpedoes. Not conclusive in itself of course – countries, like individuals, may protest innocence while being guilty. However, most of the explanations for motive lose a lot of what little explanatory power they have if the deed is not acknowledged.

Opportunity

The question of opportunity is governed by whether any North Korean submarines were detected in the vicinity of the *Cheonan*. The short answer is no. The European parliament, in its condemnation of North Korea, skirted around this problem by asserting that 'all submarines from other neighbouring countries were either in or near their bases at the time of the incident'.[27] This is a undeniably a curious argument; even though no North Korean submarines were discovered in the vicinity, North Korea must be guilty because no other submarines were found there either.

Actually, the European parliament made at least a couple of other mistakes. US and South Korean submarines were in the area conducting military exercises.[28] That is where the possibility of friendly fire comes into play. Beyond that, there is the problem that the basic advantage of submarines is that they are impossible to detect from a distance:

> 'Satellite and communications coverage of sub bases can tell when subs have left base,' adds Bruce Bechtol, Jr, professor of international relations at the Marine Corps Command and Staff College. 'It cannot tell locations of submarines once they are at sea – unless they surface or communicate.'[29]

Soon after the sinking, there were a number of reports that discounted the idea of a North Korean submarine.[30] But the interim JIG report of 20 May stated:

> [W]e assess that a small submarine is an underwater weapon system that operates in these operational environment conditions. We confirmed that a few small submarines and a mother ship supporting them left a North Korean naval base in the West Sea 2–3 days prior to the attack and returned to port 2–3 days after the attack.[31]

So, no evidence that any North Korean submarines had been anywhere near the *Cheonan*, merely an assertion that some had been absent from base at the time. A further problem is that this is merely an assertion by the South Korean Ministry of National Defense (or perhaps the US; South Korea appears to be dependent on the United States for this sort of intelligence). There is no corroboration from any outside sources. The Chinese might know, but would not divulge their intelligence capabilities.

Then, in October, it was reported that the submarines were probably undergoing trials in the harbour:

> It has been revealed that the Joint Chiefs of Staff judged it a low possibility that a North Korean Yono-class submarine, which the Military-Civilian Joint Investigation Group (MCJIG) into the sinking of the *Cheonan* named as the vessel that sunk the

South Korean warship, would infiltrate the West Sea as it was still undergoing trials prior to operational deployment

Lawmaker Song Young-sun of the Future Hope Alliance said the Joint Chiefs of Staff believed that the Yono-class submarine that disappeared on March 26, the day of the sinking, was undergoing trials, and asked how a submarine undergoing trials could take on torpedoes on March 26 and attack the *Cheonan*.[32]

Another difficulty with the submarine scenario was that many experts judged that a successful North Korean submarine attack on the *Cheonan* was just not feasible given the technological differences between the two navies.[33]

The *Cheonan* was no *Belgrano* – an ancient ship easy prey for a modern submarine. On the contrary, the *Cheonan* was a modern ship with other top-class ships, American and South Korean, in the vicinity:

A joint South Korean–US naval exercise involving several Aegis warships was underway at the time, and the *Cheonan* was a patrol combat corvette (PCC) that specialized in anti-submarine warfare. The question remains whether it would be possible for a North Korean submarine to infiltrate the maritime cordon at a time when security reached its tightest level and without detection by the *Cheonan*.[34]

With motive and opportunity looking decidedly thin, the JIG must have been very relieved to be able produce a 'smoking gun'.

Means

There has been a huge amount of debate and discussion about the torpedo remnant, much of it very technical.

On the technical side, the South Korean military did not have it all its own way. Shin Sang-cheol, the Democratic Party nominee to the JIG who was fired for expressing dissenting opinions, used his technical expertise in shipbuilding to counter the official verdict.[35] Shin concluded that the *Cheonan* sank after running aground and that there was neither an explosion nor a torpedo.[36] Korean scientists in the United States and Canada have been very active in challenging the official verdict, and conducting their own scientific tests.[37]

However, much of this debate became redundant with the Russian investigation. If neither China nor Russia would have declined to take part in the *Cheonan* investigation at the beginning – when they would have been in a position to influence, and if necessary veto, the outcome – it seems unlikely that either welcomed the opportunity to scrutinise the evidence after the verdict had been delivered. It would have been difficult to avoid offending at least one, and probably both, of the Koreas. In the event, Russia accepted and China declined. Russia is in a much weaker position vis-à-vis South Korea than China. It still has a sizeable debt to South Korea (about $1.6 billion in 2003), which dates back to a deal to support South Korea's entry into the United Nations in 1991.[38] Relations have been strained recently by mutual recriminations over the failure of the South Korean space rocket Naro, which uses a Russian first stage.[39]

According to one report, the discussion on a Russian investigation did not occur until 21 May, the day after the JIG statement:

On May 21, Russia's foreign minister S. Lavrov talked over the phone to his Korean counterpart Yu Myung-hwan. The latter reiterated that the evidence obtained by the investigation pointed to Pyongyang, but the reply of the former – as the official account posted by the Russian foreign ministry shows – was diplomatically cautious. Lavrov said Moscow would carefully review the pertinent materials, both those from South Korea and 'from other sources'. Thus he made it clear that Moscow had reservations about the S. Korean version of the incident and deemed further verification necessary. Lavrov also urged restraint on both sides of the conflict to prevent escalation on the Korean Peninsula. This is exactly the responsible type of behavior required under the current circumstances, and hopefully Moscow's position will remain unchanged.[40]

According to another Russian report, 'Russian President Dmitry Medvedev accepted Seoul's offer to send specialists at the end of May'.[41] As Leonid Petrov, the Russian-born Australian Korea specialist, pointed out,

The invitation of Russian and Chinese experts into the team of foreign investigators should have been done from the outset. It was strange to see the investigation team composed only of ROK's allies (US, Australia, Canada, UK and neutral Sweden). This can only be explained by the sensitivity of joint ROK–US military and naval exercises which were going on in the area where *Cheonan* sank.

Now, two months after the incident, inviting Russian experts does not make much sense because they will get access only to the second-hand evidence and convenient answers rather than the crime scene. I doubt that they will be allowed to inspect the incident site and examine the seabed as thoroughly as it was done by their predecessors.[42]

So why did President Medvedev accept this invitation to a warmed-over meal of 'second-hand evidence'? Perhaps because it was second-hand, he would be able to declare the Russian investigation inconclusive, implying that they had done their best but were not there at the beginning, as they should have been. Not an entirely satisfactory solution, but face would be saved in both Seoul and Pyongyang.

The Russian navy team arrived in Seoul on 30 May and returned home on 7 June.[43] Reports on the Russian investigation illustrated how different Seoul's relations are with Moscow and Washington. It seems that the Russians were kept at arm's length:

The Russian experts inspected the ship, watched computer simulations that showed how a torpedo destroyed it, and Seoul officials also offered them the computer file that detailed how the simulation was created.

The South Korean team also offered the Russians detailed records of the 2000 suicide bombing of the US Navy destroyer USS *Cole* in the waters off of Yemen. Al Qaeda claimed responsibility for that bombing.

During their investigation, the Russians also asked to see the combat information center of a South Korean warship similar to the *Cheonan*. *The military refused that request because of security protocols, but offered a tour of the captain's cabin.*[44]

It appears that the Russian team was made up of 'submersible and torpedo experts', and were sceptical about North Korea's technological capability in that area:

'The Russian investigation team's primary interest was in whether North Korea, which had been unable to produce its own torpedoes until 1995, suddenly was able to attack the *Cheonan* with a state-of-the-art bubble jet torpedo', said a South Korean diplomatic source.

Indeed, the technology for bubble jet torpedoes, which are capable of splitting a vessel in two through the expansion and contraction of a bubble resulting from a powerful explosion, is possessed only by the US and a small number of other countries, and has only been successful to date in experiments on stationary ships rather than actual fighting. The joint civilian–military investigation team also acknowledged in its June 29 briefing to media groups that North Korea was the first to have succeeded in using a bubble jet torpedo in the field.[45]

Figure 7.1   The Corroded Torpedo

It seems that their scepticism was justified.

The Russians refused to make their report public, but it was said that they gave copies to the United States and China – though not to South Korea, much to Seoul's chagrin.[46] On 26 July the South Korean Liberal paper *Hankyoreh* acquired a document titled 'Data from the Russian Naval Expert Group's Investigation into the Cause of the South Korean Naval Vessel *Cheonan*'s Sinking'.[47] Descriptions of this Russian document were published in the English edition on 28 July,[48] and what appears to be a translation of it on 29 July.[49] The *Hankyoreh*'s description of the Russian findings seems to be genuine. The South Korean government attacked the Russian conclusions, but did not challenge the validity of the report itself.[50] The *Hankyoreh* itself admitted: 'Of course, there is also no reason to believe that the results of the Russian consideration are close to the truth',[51] and continued by saying, not for the first time, that an objective reinvestigation of the sinking was necessary: 'The only thing that is clear is that the need for a complete reinvestigation of the cause of the sinking of the *Cheonan* has grown more pressing.'[52]

Since it became apparent that the JIG was hopelessly compromised, there have been frequent calls in South Korea for a credible reinvestigation.[53] North Korea has called for a reinvestigation with the involvement of its own experts, and China has suggested reconvening the UN Military Armistice Commission.[54]

There is no possibility of the present South Korean government agreeing to a reinvestigation, especially one over which it would not have control. We are therefore left with unofficial reports of the Russian investigation as the next best thing. How much credence should we give to the Russian conclusions?

Firstly, as the *Hankyoreh* points out: 'This report is significant, as it comes from the only outside group allowed access to the investigation results from the South Korean government.'[55] In addition, it is surely safe to assume that the Russian navy team were experts in their field; they knew what to look for and what questions to ask. We can also assume that they would have no incentive to lie or cover up information in a non-public report to their own government.

The Russian investigation was limited in a number of ways. In addition to the fact that, as we have seen, it was cold meal by the time they got to it, they were denied access to information, about which they complained publicly.[56] Donald Gregg, former US ambassador to Seoul, was reported as regretting that the South Korean government had impeded the Russian investigation.[57]

Impeded they might have been, but they had sufficient access to the evidence to draw very different conclusions from that of the JIG. The very fact that the report was kept under wraps suggests that it was credible. We know that the Russians were in an awkward position, not wanting to offend either Korea (or the United States) or to exacerbate tensions on the peninsula. An anodyne report that offended no one would equally have satisfied no one – and it would not have been convincing.

The Russians seem to have extricated themselves from an impossible situation pretty well. By not publishing their report they gave no opportunity for a formal objection, though the South Koreans did berate the Russian ambassador.[58] Non-publication also suggested that they had in fact discovered an inconvenient truth. Donald Gregg commented: 'When I asked a well-placed Russian friend why the report has not been made public, he replied, "Because it would do much political damage to President Lee Myung-bak and would embarrass President Obama.'"[59] By subsequently leaking the report to the South Korean press (and we do not know at what level that was authorised), they made it known that their conclusions contradicted the JIG report and that they knew the evidence had been fabricated.

The Russian report challenged the JIG on various points, including the timing of the incident.[60] It agreed that there had been a 'non-contact explosion below the ship', but suggested that this was probably due to a mine rather than a torpedo. It did not absolutely rule out a torpedo, but suggested that 'it might have been exploded by [an ROK] torpedo'.[61] According to the *Hankyoreh*, the Russians

> conjectured that the accident occurred when 'the vessel's propeller happened to get caught in a net as it was sailing through shallow waters near the coast, and as the vessel was trying to extricate itself to deep waters, its lower part struck a [mine] antenna and set off the triggering device.'[62]

This was conjecture, not proof. That might have been attainable if the Russians had been brought into the original investigation, but no longer. However, what actually caused the sinking is of less consequence than what did not – and the Russians were adamant on that.

Firstly, they were sceptical about the writing on the torpedo that the JIG had claimed proved it was North Korean: 'It may be possible that the presented torpedo part was made in North Korea, but the ink mark is inconsistent with the normal standards of marking (the location and the method of the mark).'[63] There has been an extensive debate about the writing on the torpedo remnant, regarding both its orthography and whether it would have survived an explosion.[64] However the final sentence was unambiguous: 'The torpedo part that ROK presented seems to be an electronic torpedo with a radius of 533mm. *However, we do not conclude that this particular torpedo was launched to and impacted on the* Cheonan *ship*.'[65] They do not say at that point in the report what led them to that conclusion. There is an implication that they consider that, for technical reasons, it could not have sunk the *Cheonan*. But a few paragraphs above that, there is something explosive: 'Visual examination of the torpedo part indicates that the torpedo had been in the water *for more than 6 months*.'[66] Since the *Cheonan* was sunk on 26 March, and this torpedo was 'recovered' less than two months later, it could not have been responsible for the sinking.

That the amount of corrosion on the torpedo was considerably greater than it should have been had it only been under water for two months was much commented upon right from the beginning.[67] For instance, Jung Sung-ki in the *Korea Times* raised the issue with Yoon Duk-yong, the nominal head of the JIG, on 20 May:

> But it seemed that the collected parts had been corroding at least for several months.
>
> Yoon Duk-yong, co-head of the investigative group, denied the suspicion.
>
> 'The corrosion status of the fragments and wreckage of the *Cheonan* is almost identical', Yoon said.[68]

The JIG continued to deny that the corrosion was more than could be expected from two months under water, but, curiously, there is no mention in the final report that scientific tests were undertaken to ascertain how long the torpedo had been submerged[69] – despite a claim when it released the interim report that it would be conducting accelerated experimentation to determine the precise corrosion time.[70] The Russians judged that the torpedo had been in the water for much more than two months, and since they are the only outside experts who have been able to examine the torpedo, their assessment is difficult to contest. However, the Russian verdict is corroborated by an unlikely source: the International Crisis Group (ICG). The ICG claims to be impartial, but it would be difficult to discern any difference between its reports and those of Western government agencies, certainly on Korea matters. It does have good contacts, it would seem, in the intelligence community, though whether these are Korean or American, or both, is unknown. In any case, its reports are liberally footnoted with references to interviews with anonymous sources, which is usually code for intelligence operatives.

> Critics cite the Russian investigation as evidence of a mine having sunk the [*Cheonan*], although the findings from the investigative team that visited the ROK from 31 May to 7 June 2010 have not been released ... A puzzling finding is that they estimated it must have been in the water for about six months because of the amount of corrosion (Crisis Group interview). The part was retrieved 50 days after the attack, but another source told Crisis

Group that *corrosion could have begun well before the attack depending how and where the torpedo was stored* (Crisis Group interview, Seoul).[71]

The intelligence source seems to be agreeing that there was more than two month's worth of corrosion on the recovered torpedo, but that that was because it was corroded before it was fired. This is an astounding claim: not only had the North Koreans knocked off a modern anti-submarine corvette with a world first bubble-effect torpedo shot, but they had done it with a rusty torpedo.[72] In reality, the North Koreans surely take care of their torpedoes like everyone else. Indeed, the North Korean counter-report of 2 November 2010 specifically mentioned the issue:

> When one looks at the back part of the propelling body and the rudder of the torpedo shown by the puppet 'investigation team', one can judge that their surfaces are heavily corroded.
> A torpedo is painted to prevent it from corrosion before its use. Its paint is burnt up due to high heat caused during its explosion and its remains are bound to be corroded under the sea.[73]

To double-check this point, I contacted Rob Green, a former Royal Navy Commander now resident in New Zealand and a high-profile peace campaigner.[74] I put the following question to Rob: 'Do you have any comment on the argument that "corrosion could have begun well before the attack depending how and where the torpedo was stored"? It doesn't sound plausible to me.' His reply came straight back:

> Agreed. My comment would be: 'The only plausible way for corrosion to have occurred would be if it had been on the seabed for far longer than was the case. Stored torpedoes, like all munitions, are never allowed to corrode, because of the obvious risk of malfunction.'[75]

So it would appear that, on the basis of corrosion alone, the torpedo remnant produced by the JIG did not sink the *Cheonan*.

Where does that take us?

Firstly, the South Korean government had no evidence to connect North Korea with the sinking of the *Cheonan*. The No. 1 torpedo, as it came to be called (because No. 1 was written on it in Korean) was not responsible. It may be that another North Korean torpedo was responsible, but the South Koreans have no evidence of that. With the discrediting of No. 1 torpedo, the South Korean case falls apart.

But there is more to it than that.

Where did No. 1 torpedo come from? It surely stretches credulity too far to suggest that it had been lurking on the seabed near where the *Cheonan* was struck by another torpedo, yet unfound (or by a mine). By far the most plausible explanation in the circumstances is that it was planted. It was found, it will be recalled, not by the South Korean navy, but by a trawler under contract. There were no international observers present. It was found just on the eve of the self-imposed deadline for the interim report; the deadline was the beginning of the local election campaign. We know that the South Koreans have at least one North Korean training torpedo.[76] Seunghun Lee, a professor of physics at the University of Virginia and a leading critic of the JIG investigation, was acerbic:

> Lee called the discovery of the propeller fragment five days before the government's news conference suspicious. The salvaged part had more corrosion than would have been expected after just 50 days in the water, yet the blue writing was surprisingly clear, he said.
>
> 'The government is lying when they said this was found underwater. I think this is something that was pulled out of a warehouse of old materials to show to the press', Lee said.[77]

The debate over whether the *Cheonan* was sunk by grounding, by a mine, or by a torpedo could be construed to reflect differences of opinion in good faith. But the fabrication of evidence takes us into different territory.

The next question is how far up the chain of command knowledge of the fabrication extended. Was it something concocted by members of the JIG without the knowledge or approval of superiors? In particular, was President Lee Myung-bak privy to the deception? Ironically, this mirrors the debate among those that hold that North Korea sank the *Cheonan* but disagree whether it was ordered from the top or was the initiative of a local commander.[78] We don't know, but it does seem unlikely that Lee was not involved. After all, it was not a spur-of-the moment affair. It must have taken some time – and resources – to locate a suitable torpedo and surreptitiously position it where it would be found.

Then there is the question of the Americans. If the Russians could see that there was much more corrosion than could have occurred in just two months under water, surely Rear Admiral Thomas J. Eccles, the senior US representative on the JIG, could do so too? Apparently he did not work directly on the torpedo, but he did sign the report.[79] This is especially intriguing, because he appears to be something of an expert on the management of corrosion in the US navy.[80]

He must surely have realised that the evidence had been fabricated, and he must have reported this back to Washington. Given the importance of the subject, and his rank, it seems implausible that this did not go to a high level – perhaps not to Obama, but would the navy have kept Secretary Clinton unaware? Perhaps, but a good working assumption is that, at the minimum, she knew that there were serious doubts about the investigation, and the conclusion that North Korea had sunk the *Cheonan*.

The 2003 invasion of Iraq perhaps offers a guide to the problem of ascertaining guilty knowledge. Did Bush and Blair know that there were no weapons of mass destruction? Surely they did, but it is unlikely we will ever know for certain, and no inquiry – especially not the Chilcot inquiry – is going to tell us. However, they are guilty because they should have known. The same is true of Lee Myung-bak and Hillary Clinton: they have a duty to determine the truth before proceeding on a path that might lead to war.

If Lee Myung-bak (and perhaps Hillary Clinton) knew that North Korea did not sink the *Cheonan*, then all of their words and actions since May 2010 take on a new complexion. The huge military exercises are not carried out to deter a belligerent North Korea; they can be seen, rather, as a deliberate escalation of tension against the North (and China), and perhaps a preparation for war. The refusal to return to the Six-Party Talks may thus be interpreted in a new way; and the sinking of the *Cheonan* can be seen as a pretext for that refusal, rather than its cause.

And what about China? The government presumably is well aware of all this and is assessing the American actions (the South Koreans are less significant) with great care and caution.

North Korea, for its part, would have little difficulty in interpreting what is going on. Its concern that the South Korean government has deliberately utilised the accidental sinking of the *Cheonan* to lay false charges against it, and to escalate tension, feeds through to its active diplomacy to disprove the charges, and to its frequent overtures to the United States, as exemplified by the Carter and Richardson visits in 2010. The other component of that strategy is the policy of zero-tolerance towards infringements of its territory and threats against it.

This strategy was demonstrated in the Yeonpyeong Incident of November 2010.[81] On 22 November there was an exchange of artillery fire between ROK marines on the island of Yeonpyeong, close to the Northern Limit Line, and DPRK units on the nearby North Korean mainland. Although the South Korean government claimed that the firing from the North was unexpected and unprovoked, it did follow a live-fire exercise by the marines on Yeonpyeong into contested waters, which the North had warned would be met with retaliation. The artillery fire from the North killed two marines and two civilian contractors working on the base, and wounded a disputed number of marines and a couple of civilians. It is not known where the civilians were, but satellite photos did indicate that houses in the town had been hit by stray fire. The South Korean government, anxious to present the incident as an attack on civilians, refused to accept the military status of the contractors, thereby depriving their families of full compensation.[82]

It remains unclear whether this incident was an act of deliberate provocation by the South Korean government – and, if so, at what level. In the event, North Korea was roundly criticised internationally, and within South Korea. One result was that Lee Myung-bak recovered some of the anti-North momentum he had lost due to the widespread scepticism in the South about the *Cheonan*.[83]

Although the North had vowed that any further live-fire exercises from Yeonpyeong would be met with even greater retaliation, they did not, in fact, respond when the South carried out another drill on 20 December. The Southern exercise was a toned-down affair, only using up the ammunition left over from 23 November. There was a suggestion in a communiqué from the North that this time they had not fired into what the DPRK considered its territorial waters.[84]

These nuances aside, it seemed that a more important reason for the North to show restraint on 20 December was that Arizona Governor Bill Richardson was visiting Pyongyang at the time. Richardson is a former presidential candidate and a leading member of the Democratic Party.[85] He was in the DPRK for a short visit, at the invitation of Vice Premier Kim Kye Gwan, the chief nuclear negotiator.[86] Clearly, Pyongyang saw him as a conduit for yet another peace overture to Washington, so any flare-up of fighting was to be avoided.[87] Any hopes they may have had that his visit would initiate effective dialogue were, it seems, to be dashed in the familiar manner. In an angry letter to the *Washington Post*, Donald Gregg wrote:

New Mexico Gov. Bill Richardson (D) ended a five-day visit to North Korea this week, trying to help defuse the crisis between Washington and Pyongyang. He reported conciliatory gestures on the part of North Korea, but based on my experience eight years ago and what I see from the Obama administration, which apparently is not even interested in debriefing Mr Richardson, the visit may have been for naught.

However much North Korea might want peace, the powerful forces arrayed against it have other ideas. It is unlikely we will see any real moves towards peace from Seoul, or Washington, any time soon. Whether that circumstance leads to war is as yet unknown, but the danger is clear.

Lee Myung-bak was quoted as having said, on 9 December 2010: 'I feel reunification is now not far off.'[88] He was not thinking of peaceful reunification.

Part III

Collapse and Takeover

Part I set the wider geopolitical scene, and Part II analysed the key events on the Korean peninsula in 2010 – the *Cheonan* and Yeonpyeong incidents. Although these two were very different in many ways, they shared a common function in pushing the peninsula further towards crisis. Part III will examine six interrelated aspects of that looming crisis, under the following headings:

- the collapse scenario
- the Northern Limit Line: keeping the war alive
- military exercises: precursors to collapse and invasion
- the siege: sanctions, their role and effect
- the costs and consequences of invasion
- the China factor: into the abyss?

THE COLLAPSE SCENARIO

Just as people have been talking about the decline of the United States for a long time, so too have the pundits for two or more decades been predicting the collapse of the DPRK. In Chapter 3 I discussed the collapse of the Soviet Union and how this inflicted huge, and continuing damage on the North Korean economy and security. Many at the time thought the days of the DPRK were numbered.

One such was Aidan Foster-Carter, who, writing in the early 1990s, confidently predicted:

> In a nutshell: the North Korean system is in terminal crisis …
> I expect continued failure to embrace serious reform while Kim Il Sung lives (whether or not Kim Jong Il takes over), leading to an elite coup and/or a Timisoara-style popular arising [*sic*]: certainly after Kim dies, and possibly even before if things (and people) get desperate enough. Such a prospect carries obvious risks.
> Equally, my conclusion is that collapse will lead to absorption.[1]

As recently as 2009, Foster-Carter repeated his prediction in an interview in the Seoul *Korea Times*:

> Foster-Carter points to two main factors to support his argument: Firstly, he said, the possibility of a popular uprising is ever-increasing.
>
> 'Just because they haven't done it before doesn't mean they won't do it in the future', he said ...
>
> For this, he quoted the lyrics of reggae artist Bob Marley: 'A hungry man is an angry man.'
>
> The second factor, said Foster-Carter, was the imminent succession of North Korea's leadership, presenting it as a crucial point with regards to the continuity of the reclusive state.
>
> 'I don't see how anyone, this time, can say [North Korea] can survive. Successions are the Achilles heel of dictatorships', he said.[2]

Just because he was not right in 1993 does not mean he will not be right now, or in the future; for in reality the collapse of regimes is a very complex matter that defies simple predictions. If poverty, deprivation and declining living standards were sufficient, then there would be few governments left.

However, what is perhaps more important in the present context is not whether the DPRK will collapse, but that Lee Myung-bak thinks it will if the pressure is increased. Towards the end of 2010, in the aftermath of the *Cheonan* and Yeonpyeong incidents he claimed, 'I feel reunification is now not far off.'

THE NORTHERN LIMIT LINE: KEEPING THE WAR ALIVE

The NLL was an important part of the background to the previous two chapters, and here we look at it in some detail. Both the sinking of the *Cheonan* and the firefight at Yeonpyeong took place in disputed waters off the North Korean coast. Whatever its origins, the NLL is maintained by the present South Korean government mainly in order to increase tension with the North. The Yeonpyeong incident led to various suggestions from outside that the NLL situation be defused, and I will address those suggestions and the likelihood of Lee Myung-bak responding to them.

MILITARY EXERCISES: PRECIPITATING COLLAPSE AND PREPARING FOR INVASION

The fondness of the Americans, and of the South Korean government and military, for frequent and threatening military exercises has come up repeatedly in the previous chapters. Here we document the main exercises and discuss their role. We know that military exercises are big business, but exactly how big is uncertain. There appear to be no comprehensive sources of information, but only snippets here and there. For instance, the Federation of American Scientists, one of the main sources of information in this area, says that '[t]he Navy participates in about 175 unit exercises annually. Ninety percent of these exercises involve operations with other US or multinational forces.[4] No further information is given; the number of ships and personnel, the cost, details of other participants, location, and so on, are all missing.

The US navy, for its part, does publish media releases, and so we know, for instance, that Rim of the Pacific (RIMPAC) 2010 is the biggest RIMPAC ever:

> The US Pacific Fleet-event includes participating units and personnel from Australia, Canada, Chile, Colombia, France, Indonesia, Japan, Malaysia, Netherlands, Peru, Republic of Korea, Singapore, Thailand and the United States.
>
> RIMPAC is the world's largest multinational maritime exercise, with more than 20,000 personnel participating in this year's event.[5]

So while it is clear that 'war games' have a major *political* function in the exercise of US hegemony, there is a big gap in our knowledge about them. We can see them being used as statements of power or threat, and this has been marked since the *Cheonan* incident; but the available metrics are limited. One of the interesting aspects of military exercises as a political instrument is that their real target is often not stated, and is sometimes denied. This, again, was noticeable during the post-*Cheonan* escalation, when it was clear – certainly to the Chinese – that although its stated purpose was to 'deter North Korea', its real object was China. China also uses military exercises – though on a far smaller scale than the Americans – to make a statement. China conducted 'unusually large' exercises in July, presumably prompted by Hillary Clinton's speech to the ARF in Hanoi, and by escalating US–ROK exercises. This interpretation was denied, so it is almost certainly true:

> China's military has condemned a US intervention in the long dispute over maritime borders in the South China Sea, less than a day after Beijing said it had conducted a large naval exercise in the area …
>
> The scale of the People's Liberation Army's naval manoeuvres in the South China Sea this week [was] unusually large, according to state media reports …
>
> Chinese military analysts said, however, that the exercises were unlikely to be related directly to Mrs Clinton's remarks or to a joint US–South Korean naval drill earlier this week, which was also criticised by Beijing.[6]

Military exercises are a major instrument of geopolitics, and nowhere more so than around the Korean peninsula, so it is important to understand them.

THE SIEGE: SANCTIONS, THEIR ROLE AND EFFECT

We hear a lot about weapons of mass destruction, but one that comes in under the radar is the use of economic warfare. This has a long history. If the wall of a castle were impregnable and the boiling oil a bit too hot, the preferred option – circumstances permitting – was to lay siege to it and starve the defenders into submission. Not surprisingly, the modern version of the this – sanctions – is very popular with the United States. Like the use of drones, it does not fill American body bags. It deploys America's huge economic strength against weaker adversaries and, to cap off the advantages, the effects – say, malnourished children – can be blamed on the other side. North Korea has been the victim of sanctions longer than any other country in modern times.

Jennifer Rubin, who has a column entitled 'Right Turn' in the *Washington Post* waxed lyrical in a eulogy for retiring head of the US Treasury Department's sanctions programme, Stuart Levey, calling him an American hero who has given the United States a marvellous new weapon – economic sanctions:

> What Stuart has done is totally transformational. He basically rewrote the book on sanctions and economic warfare – discovering

that the US had massively more leverage than anyone before imagined. It's not just Iran. It's North Korea and Al Qaeda too.[7]

Ms Rubin also assures us that '[t]he point of sanctions was not to inflict pain on the Iranian people; it was to force the country's despots to change their behavior'. In reality, things are rather different. In most cases – and Iran, North Korea, and probably Al Qaeda are examples – sanctions do not change the policy of the target government (because the consequences of surrender are worse than the sanctions), but do inflict pain on ordinary people, and not on the leaders. Indeed, Levey's sanctions against North Korea, particularly over the Banco Delta Asia (BDA) affair, if anything, strengthened the resolve of the North Korean government. Levey, as assistant secretary of state for the Office of Terrorism and Financial Intelligence, had the US Treasury take action against this small Macau bank on charges of laundering North Korean drug-dealing money. The charges were subsequently disproved, but the action derailed the Six-Party Talks. If the BDA action was intended to stall negotiations until the liberal Roh Moo-hyun administration was about to be replaced by the conservative Lee Myung-bak, as seems likely, it was successful, but it certainly did not change Pyongyang's policies.[8]

One of the prime purposes of sanctions – more important than any supposed attempt to change government policy – is subversion and the erosion of the will to resist military intervention. The 2003 invasion of Iraq would not have been so easy had it not been preceded by 13 years of sanctions that had eroded military capacity and public resilience.[9] Sanctions also killed some 1.5 million Iraqis – perhaps 500,000 of whom were children.[10] Physical and financial sanctions are a part of a wider range of weapons in what could be called 'subcritical warfare' – war that stops short of hot war, the use of bombs and troops, but which shares the same objectives. That embraces economic warfare (physical, technology, financial and tourism sanctions, military threat and arms race), psychological warfare (travel bans, propaganda), cyberwar, and subversion.

THE COSTS AND CONSEQUENCES OF INVASION

A somewhat similar scenario is being played out in North Korea. However, while we know that many have died, and many surviving children have suffered stunted growth through malnutrition, we do not know what has happened to the will to resist.

Lee Myung-bak's assumption seems to be that resilience is now so depleted that a relatively minor incident – such as the death or incapacitation of Kim Jong Il – will trigger a crisis during which a ROK/US military intervention would not meet with much resistance. Others disagree, about both the possibility of collapse and the resistance to invasion that might be expected.

Even leaving the Americans aside, we know that the South is far superior to the North in terms of military equipment, as is partly indicated by the amount of military equipment imported. By definition, this will be superior to anything produced at home. Even the Chinese, who are rapidly developing an indigenous weapons capability, still tend to buy advanced weaponry from abroad.[11] As Fig. III.1 shows, between 2000 and 2008 South Korea bought one hundred times more foreign arms than did the North.

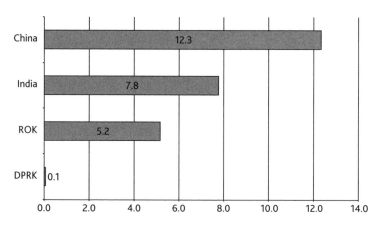

Figure III.1   Share of World Imports of Arms, 2000–2008 (Source: World Bank/SIPRI; for details see online Statistical Appendix)

But equipment isn't everything, especially against popular resistance, as the Americans and many others can attest. It is important, therefore, to canvas various estimates of the likely costs and consequences of an invasion

THE CHINA FACTOR: INTO THE ABYSS?

One of the immediate consequences of a US/ROK invasion of North Korea is the likely intervention of China. This is much discussed, and in the introduction to Part I I examined what seemed a deliberate attempt by the South Korean government to persuade the American ambassador to Seoul that the Chinese would not intervene, but would accept a Southern takeover of the North.

A second Sino-American war carries with it far more danger than the first. China is now much stronger militarily than it was in 1950, and while it is still far weaker than the US, the balance has shifted in its direction. Then there are the economic implications. In 1950 China was a minor economy, and what foreign economic engagement it had was primarily with the Soviet Union. Now it is a major economy with deep connections to the United States, to both Koreas, to Japan and the world at large.

All this would seem to make thought of war unimaginable. And yet, as Hugh White put it, war in Asia remains 'thinkable'.[12] Underlying everything else is the challenge to American hegemony from the rise of China. If, as I argued in Part II, the United States is attempting to halt its decline increasingly through militaristic means (which in turn exacerbate its problems), then a clash with China, by accident or design, becomes frighteningly possible. The pseudonymous China Hand, writing on the US attempts to contain China, comments:

> Also, I expect the fact that the Chinese military is a paper tiger figured into US calculations.
>
> The PLA has not fought a war since the border conflict with Vietnam in 1979. It didn't do particularly well then, and the current generation of officers has never been 'blooded' (experienced the routine chaos and catastrophe of actual battle) and is unlikely to seek out on-the-job training by engaging the world's biggest and most experienced military in a genuine conflict.[13]

A possible corollary of this is that there are those in the 'world's biggest and most experienced military' who think that now is the time to give China a bloody nose – and what better place to do it than in Korea?

8
Scenario Building:
Failed Succession and Collapse

Kim Jong Il has long attracted writers of a certain sort. You can write anything you like, as long as it is uncomplimentary and preferably lurid, and you will not be contradicted, taken to task, or asked to provide meaningful evidence. He has been variously described as a playboy, sex maniac and drunkard, who lives a life of lavish excess, and a workaholic who only takes four hours of sleep a night.[1] There is also an inbuilt tendency towards personalisation in the imperial mindset which mirrors and reinforces 'personality cults' in targeted countries. Historically, countries have tended to elevate leaders to a ridiculous degree (the divine right of kings, and so forth). This has its roots in the vanity of the leaders themselves, the currying of favour by subordinates, and a rational mechanism to inculcate national integrity and purpose. Fortunately this is becoming less common, but it does persist – and of course North Korea is an example (although the situation is much more nuanced than commonly described). But it is interesting to see how this personalisation also operates in international politics as a mechanism to disguise real objectives and the reality of struggle between states. Thus Saddam Hussein became the personification of Iraq, and the country itself became somehow disembodied – something to be possessed and owned as legitimately by Americans as by Iraqis. The Republic of Iraq (with its oil) was not invaded and conquered by the American republic; it was divested of Saddam Hussein, and became organically part of America in a sort of religious transubstantiation whereby America becomes the true embodiment of Iraq. Thus, in describing a battle with Iraqi resistance in 2004, it could be reported with no hint of irony that 'Captain Carrie Batson, a [US] marine spokeswoman, said: "We estimate we've killed 300 anti-Iraqi forces in the past two days of fighting."'[2] The same process obtains in respect of North Korea. Instead of being represented as a state with natural desires, aspirations and functions, as well as rights, as represented by the United Nations charter, it becomes personalised. If Kim Jong Il dies, or is removed, then what is left is not the North Korean state (under whatever title) but a *terra nullius*, as bereft of national rights as pre-European Australia.

Two recent articles illustrate this process of personalisation. A *Chosun Ilbo* article of November 2009 headlined 'US at Work on Strangling Kim Jong-il's Cash Flow' described how the US was active in attempting to block DPRK exports around the world.[3] By identifying the revenue from exports as accruing personally to Kim, it is made less likely that anyone would draw the connection between the stifling of exports and economic deprivation in North Korea. Sanctions are effectively sanitised.

A similar device was used in a recent *Daily Telegraph* story headed 'Kim Jong-il Keeps $4bn "Emergency Fund" in European Banks'.[4] Kim, we are told, keeps this $4 billion in Europe so that he can 'continue his lavish way of life if he is forced to flee the country'. This would happen 'in the event of a military invasion by a foreign power, with China his most likely destination'. The foreign power was not identified. Exactly why he would keep this money in Europe, where presumably he would not be able to access it from exile in China, was not mentioned.

North Korea is not unusual in being demonised through the vilification of its leader, but it is perhaps taken further here than elsewhere. This leads to inordinate attention being paid to the individual leader, and undue importance being placed on him and the state of his health. Hitler apparently thought that the death of Roosevelt would remove America from the war; he was mistaken.[5]

Kim Jong Il's Health Problems

Rumours about Kim Jong Il's health started circulating in August 2008, and there was a quickening flurry of speculation about his imminent death or incapacitation, and who would succeed him. We were told that he had suffered strokes and convulsions, that he had been treated by French doctors, German doctors, and Chinese doctors.[6] Kim's non-appearance was pounced upon, and any photos issued by the Korea Central News Agency (KCNA), the official news outlet, were minutely scrutinised for clues.[7] Many expressed scepticism about the photos, and thought the Koreans were covering up: 'Amid continuing speculation that Kim Jong-il is gravely ill – or even dead – North Korean state media have stepped up reports about purported appearances by the dictator, most recently [at] a reported public classic[al] music event.'[8]

Whatever the state of his health had been beforehand, during 2009 it became impossible to deny that he was fit and in control – impossible for all except those such the Japanese professor Toshimitsu Shigemura, who consider that the Koreans are using a double, and that the real Kim Jong Il died in 2003.[9] The Russian Oleg Ovsyannikov, who was introduced to Kim Jong Il at a concert in Pyongyang in September 2009, reported that his 'memories and speech were clear':

> Looking at Ovsyannikov, who is 2m tall, Kim greeted him with a smile saying 'You are very tall indeed.' Then Kim introduced the North Korean singers on stage to Ovsyannikov without any trouble, and showed off his good memory by reeling off a list of names of Russian lieder composers.[10]

But the clincher had been Bill Clinton's meeting with Kim on 4 August that year. Clinton, who had gone to Pyongyang at the Koreans' invitation in respect of the two US journalists who had been held following their illegal crossing of the China–DPRK border in March, had taken along one of his doctors, Roger Band. This was apparently at the suggestion of the administration, which had asked 'Band to look closely at Kim's teeth, facial color, hair, scalp, speech, movements of hands and feet, and weight'.[11] Band, it was reported, judged that Kim's condition had 'significantly improved'. The Clinton visit led to US national security adviser Jim Jones admitting that Kim 'still appears to be in "full control" of his government'.[12]

The Succession Issue

There were basically two sorts of responses to reports of Kim's illness – coming from factions we might conveniently divide into the 'negotiators' and the 'conquerors'. The negotiators are those who genuinely, if naively, want the United States (and, appropriately, the ROK) to conduct genuine negotiations with the DPRK. That would involve Pyongyang relinquishing its nuclear deterrent and Washington providing compensation, such as light water reactors and oil; lifting sanctions, including unblocking access to international financial institutions; and removing its military threat.[13] For the negotiators, a sick or incapacitated Kim Jong Il, or a weak and insecure successor, was a great problem. The weak find it difficult to negotiate because they do not have the authority to carry through the concessions that their side has to make. This is true irrespective of the strength of the two negotiating countries.

Indeed, the big problem in US foreign policy, not least in respect of North Korea, is that although the US has always been stronger, and usually immensely stronger, than its adversary, presidents and their delegates have usually been very vulnerable to attacks from domestic critics for being 'too soft'. Nixon was able to pull off a deal with China in the 1970s because no one could accuse him of being 'soft on Communism'. Obama's vulnerability to domestic pressure is all too evident.[14] So, argue the negotiators, if negotiations with the DPRK are to succeed they require a firm leader in Pyongyang. As Joel Wit, a former Clinton staffer, put it in late 2009, the 'US government should seize the opportunity [of 'dialogue'] while Kim is still powerful'. [15]

The conquerors, on the other hand, while they might agree to negotiations as a stalling tactic, have no intention of allowing North Korea to remain as an independent entity. They are by far the majority and have varying tactical positions, but share the same strategic objectives. Victor Cha, who served under the Bush administration from 2004 to 2007 as director for Asian Affairs on the National Security Council and as deputy head of the US delegation to the Six-Party Talks from 2006 to 2007, expressed it succinctly in advice to the incoming Obama administration:

> Keep an eye on the prize: Remember that the ultimate prize is not denuclearization but managing an eventual 'inheritance' process where a united Korea, free and democratic, is an engine of peace and economic growth in Asia and a global partner of the US in world affairs.[16]

Succinct, but of course coded. Stripped of the euphemisms and cant ('engine of peace', 'global partner'), Cha sees the South taking over the North, delivering a unified Korean peninsula under US hegemony, extending the American empire to the banks of the Yalu. But would it stop there?

Although reports of Kim's death, like that of Mark Twain, have been much exaggerated, it seems certain that his health has been bad – and even if he is much recovered, it is unlikely that he will live very much longer. Exactly how long is a matter of speculation, much of it based on wishful thinking. Assistant US Secretary of State for East Asian and Pacific Affairs Kurt Campbell visited Seoul in March 2010, and in an interesting version of Delphic methodology invited three North Korean defectors to a meeting and then concluded that Kim had three years to live.[17]

So the key question is, when Kim Jong Il dies (or is incapacitated), what happens then? Again, wishful thinking comes into play, and it is frequently asserted that there will be a succession crisis.[18] Not everyone buys the disputed succession-collapse theory. Significantly, Yang Sang-hoon, a columnist for the right-wing Seoul newspaper *Chosun Ilbo*, discounts it:

> Chances are that Kim Jong-il, in view of his age, will die once the North is publicly recognized as a nuclear power and has opened the gate to a great, prosperous and powerful nation. No outside strength can sway a nuclear power. Accordingly, the often raised equation of Kim Jong-il's death with the North's collapse is unlikely.[19]

In fact, a real collapse or succession crisis is unlikely, but that is not the issue. It is not necessary. More to the point is whether outside forces – some mixture of the ROK and US military/political establishments – will utilise a *reported* crisis to invade the DPRK.

The succession issue is frequently brought up by those who blame North Korea for the sinking of the *Cheonan* but have to tackle the awkward problem of motive. The argument is that Kim Jong Il expressly ordered the sinking of the *Cheonan* and the shelling of Yeonpyeong Island in order to facilitate the succession of his youngest son, Kim Jong Un.

The American liberal commenter John Feffer, struggling with the motive issue in an article irreverently entitled 'Kim Jong-Il: Right-Wing Mole?', brings this up as one possible explanation. Feffer is in a bind. For some reason he accepts that North Korea sank the *Cheonan*, but he is very knowledgeable about Korean affairs and realises that none of the motives really fit:

> If the Dear Leader didn't receive under-the-table payments from John Bolton and friends, what on earth motivated such a self-destructive act? Perhaps Kim wanted to rally nationalist sentiment in the country on the eve of his son's succession to the top spot.[20]

Others are less aware of the inherent contradiction in the argument. At the top of his top seven 'Theories why Pyongyang sank warship', Christian Oliver, in the *Financial Times*, puts 'To smooth the succession':

Kim Jong-il, North Korea's dictator, is almost certainly transferring power to his third son, Kim Jong-eun [Kim Jong Un]. Some defectors have said he is trying to associate Jong-eun's name with *major successes* in domestic propaganda. One civic group with contacts in North Korea says celebrations at a naval base directly honoured Jong-eun for the sinking.[21]

Some go further, asserting that Kim Jong Un himself ordered the attacks to display his credentials: 'Some experts have also speculated that the recent acts were ordered by the younger Kim to establish his leadership credentials with the military, arguably the most powerful institution in North Korea.'[22]

The problem with all these explanations, which only Feffer has the wit to recognise, is that being accused of the sinking of the *Cheonan* was a great setback for North Korea. Predictably, it led to devastating sanctions from the South – the immediate annual loss in cash revenue is estimated to exceed US$300 million, or about 10 percent of the North's 2008 income of $3.47 billion – and increased military threats from US and South Korea.[23] Scarcely a good way to introduce your son to the people, or for him to display his credentials to the military. Miscalculation can of course never be ruled out, but as a deliberate act of policy, sinking the *Cheonan* to facilitate the succession is really very implausible.

What is more plausible is to see the rushed succession of Kim Jong Un as *a response* to the *Cheonan* crisis. In this reading, the North is not responsible for the sinking of the *Cheonan* but is under increased pressure because of the accusation and the resulting sanctions. Kim Jong Il and the leadership are well aware that Lee Myung-bak has been talking up the possibility of collapse and his hopes for a takeover of the North. One way to counter that is to demonstrate that there is unity within the leadership, and that the succession issue has been resolved.

This reading was given further credence by a report of an interview with Kim Jong Il's eldest son, Kim Jong Nam. The *Washington Post* article articulated the standard story:

Kim Jong Il is preparing his country for a leadership change, apparently to his youngest son Kim Jong Un, and some analysts have linked two violent incidents last year to an attempt to display the younger Kim's bravery to North Korea's military and bolster his legitimacy as the next leader.[24]

But the interview with Kim Jong Nam gave quite a contrary, and far more plausible, explanation:

> North Korean leader Kim Jong Il's eldest son said in an interview published Friday that his father opposed continuing the family dynasty into a third generation but ended up naming his youngest son as heir to keep the country stable …
>
> Hereditary succession 'does not fit with socialism, and my father was against it as well', the *Tokyo Shimbun* quoted Kim Jong Nam as saying in an interview in a southern Chinese city in mid-January. 'My understanding is that (succession) was to stabilize the internal system. An unstable North Korea leads to instability in the region.'[25]

Or, in other words, an unstable North Korea invites invasion, so the regime goes through with formalising a succession within the Kim family to prevent South Korea from attempting to use schisms, real or imagined, within the elite. The corollary of this is that, if there had been no outside threat, then succession might naturally have moved outside the family in some sort of political process, probably resembling the Chinese one.

It is curious what contradictory attitudes we have towards inherited succession. It is at the core of the monarchical system that still plays an important role in nominally democratic societies such as Britain, Thailand and Spain. And so the liberal London *Observer* agonises not over whether monarchy is compatible with contemporary democracy, but rather on the unfairness of giving men precedence over women in the line of succession.[26] Succession by inheritance is very common in business, and family businesses are much eulogised. Attitudes towards political inheritance are ambivalent. Political dynasties in the United States – the Kennedys, the Bushes, and so on – are commented upon and often criticised, but without any great indignation. Similarly, in many countries the role of political families, whereby leadership is handed down from one generation to another, sometimes with an interim caretaker, is common, and seldom condemned – the Bhuttos in Pakistan and the Gandhis in India. It was planned that son Gamal would follow father Egypt's Hosni Mubarak, and few American commentators thought that a problem until the riots of January 2011. One interesting case is that of Singapore, which is quite similar in some ways to North Korea, both being autocratic Confucian societies where the streets are kept clean. In Singapore the current prime minister, Lee Hsien Loong, is the son of founding prime minister, Lee Kuan Yew, just as Kim Jong Il is the son of founding President Kim Il Sung.

Generally speaking, inheritance of political (or business) power is seen to be sub-optimal and an indication of an underdeveloped political system. One of the curiosities of the North Korean case is that Marxism, coming out of the nineteenth-century anti-monarchist and anti-military traditions, was set against inheritance. The Soviet Union, China and Vietnam were all successful in avoiding family rule. Whether dynastic succession in North Korea is a case of Confucianism trumping Marxism, the particular ambitions of the Kim family, or the exigencies of the situation, is a matter of dispute. However, it seems clear that it is an expression of the vulnerability and weakness of the DPRK which, if it is to survive, needs to professionalise and democratise political power.

COLLAPSE

Failed succession is by far the most popular trigger for the collapse scenario.

Scott Snyder, director of the Center for US–Korea Policy of the Asia Foundation (a nominally non-government entity based in Washington), at a symposium in March 2010, said that US intelligence predicted that Kim Jong Il had between three and five years of life left. When he died, predicted Snyder, there would be disorder and chaos, and this would 'bring an overall crisis to North Korea and its neighboring states as well'.[27] This might be considered as representative of 'Trans-Pacific' (US/ROK) mainstream opinion.

The symposium at which Snyder was speaking was entitled 'OpCon Transfer and Its Implications for the US–ROK Alliance'. OpCon is Pentagon-speak for 'operational control', and it refers to the US relinquishing its control of the ROK military and handing it back to the government in Seoul. This is a very involved and contentious issue, and one of the functions of the 'collapse scenario' and of the general ratcheting up of tension is to delay that handover. As discussed in Chapter 10, a collapse of the DPRK, and intervention/invasion (OPLAN 5029) would require US military leadership. The argument then goes that Kim Jong Il will die soon, chaos and collapse will ensue, and intervention will be necessary – but that necessitates the US military retaining operation control.

As Ruediger Frank has pointed out, the demise of the DPRK has been predicted from various quarters ever since the collapse of the Soviet Union two decades ago.[28] Why the resurgence of such predictions at this time? Is it merely a reflection of Kim Jong Il's health? The short answer is that a growing number of this trans-Pacific elite think that sanctions have destabilised the DPRK to such an extent that Kim's death, and uncertain or contested succession, will trigger its collapse.

In other words, it is not succession in itself that is the issue, but its context. Obviously, succession is an issue in all political systems, but usually – if the system itself is in reasonable health and not under undue stress, such as economic crisis or external military threat – then this does not lead to collapse. Yet, for all that, the tea leaves are difficult to read.

Hwang Jang-yop, former secretary of the Korean Workers' Party who defected to the South in 1997 after reputedly falling out with Kim Jong Il, was reported in 2010 as discounting either a succession crisis or a military coup:

'In North Korea, the influence of the late leader Kim Il Sung remains strong. So even if Kim Jong Il has health problems, North Korea will see no major upheaval as long as Kim Kyong Hui, Kim Jong Il's younger sister and a Workers' Party director, remains in power', Hwang said.

He added that a coup d'état by North Korea's military is unlikely since it has been indoctrinated by ideology.

Last week at a lecture hosted by the Center for Strategic and International Studies in Washington, Hwang said, 'Since no major force can possibly challenge Kim Jong Il in North Korea, we cannot predict a crack in North Korea's political system. There is also little chance for an immediate major change within North Korea as long as it has China's support.'[29]

The position of China is obviously very important, and explains the clutching at straws about differences between China and North Korea revealed in some of the WikiLeaks cables. Some of this was, as we have seen, the result of what seems like the South Korean government's attempt to manipulate the American government; in other cases the Americans were probably reading too much into China's irritation with North Korea.[30] In any case, relations between China and the DPRK have become much warmer since the *Cheonan* incident.[31] Lee Myung-bak's fabrication of the investigation into the sinking, and the escalation of US confrontation with China, has pushed Pyongyang and Beijing closer together.[32]

Some argue that the economic crisis strengthens the regime because the people see the difficulties as the product of hostile outside forces. The view of Karin Janz, country director in North Korea for the German NGO Welthungerhilfe, was reported as follows:

> Economic sanctions by the United States and other western countries [are] actually strengthening the Kim Jong-il's regime, a German social worker involved with a non-government organization told reporters here this morning.
>
> 'The leaders are using the sanctions as a justification. People believe the country is in a bad condition because of outside forces'.
>
> Patriotism runs high among the people and most have full faith in their leaders.[33]

Others, such as Alexandre Mansourov, see the economy coming out of crisis, stabilising and growing. Political 'instability' remains a possibility, but he makes no mention of collapse:

> In spite of recent speculation in the *New York Times* and other Western media about North Korea's growing economic desperation and political instability, Pyongyang is, in fact, on a path of economic stabilization. Last year's harvest was relatively good – the second in a row – thanks to a raft of developments including favorable weather conditions, no pest infestations, increased fertilizer imports from China, double-cropping, and the refurbishment of the obsolete irrigation system. Thanks to the commissioning of several large-scale hydro-power plants which supply electricity to major urban residential areas and industrial zones, North Korea generated more electricity in 2009 than the year before, although losses in the transmission system remain significant.
>
> How [the new economic development strategies] will all work out remains to be seen. Whether the new equilibrium will facilitate economic growth and contribute to increasing production, trade, and consumption, or end up in economic failure causing social chaos and political instability is obviously the core question. Contrary to the rampant, often inaccurate speculation in the Western media, it's much too soon to tell.

Certainly, on my most recent visit to Pyongyang, in November 2010, I was struck by the signs of economic recovery compared with my previous visit, in 2008. There are many more vehicles on the road – trucks, buses, cars, and bicycles; but the most noticeable improvement was in the electricity supply. Whereas just a few years ago lighting was very limited and public buildings were only illuminated on special occasions, now Pyongyang at night looked more like a normal city. And the traffic-light system, closed down in the 1990s, had been restored – and the beautiful female traffic police who had previously directed traffic, and were often remarked upon by foreign visitors, were now relegated to the side of the road.

However, the reality on the ground is not so important as the perception, in the security industry and among politicians in Washington and Seoul, that collapse, or something approaching it, is imminent and can be brought about with a little more pressure.[34] 'Collapse' and 'instability' tend to be used somewhat interchangeably, although they are conceptually distinct. In international law neither offers an excuse for intervention; but since international law does not hold that much sway in world affairs, the difference between the two might be important. 'Collapse' would be portrayed as affording more justification and legitimacy for intervention than 'instability'. However, any categorisation will be based not on reality but on the decision of the political and military leadership in Washington and Seoul. That, in turn, will revolve around a judgement about how much resistance could be expected from the North Koreans, as well as about the Chinese reaction. We hear this from the US military:

> US Forces Korea Commander Gen. Walter Sharp has warned of sudden regime collapse in North Korea and called for urgent preparation for such an eventuality. Sharp was speaking at a subcommittee hearing of the US House Appropriations Committee on Wednesday.
>
> 'We would also be mindful of the potential for instability in North Korea', he said. 'Combined with the country's disastrous centralized economy, dilapidated industrial sector, insufficient agricultural base, malnourished military and populace, and developing nuclear programs, the possibility of a sudden leadership change in the North could be destabilizing and unpredictable.'[35]

American security industry pundits tend to be confident that collapse, if not imminent, is virtually inevitable. They vary on its timing and on what its consequences might be – and on how they should be handled; but what they all have in common is a lack of any recognition that the United States might have some responsibility for bringing it about. After all, if the DPRK were to collapse it would be primarily because of outside forces, and that ultimately means the United States. If the US made peace with the DPRK, lifted sanctions and allowed trade and investment, then there would be no 'dilapidated industrial sector, insufficient agricultural base, malnourished military and populace'. These are essentially consequences of American policy, as I argue in Chapters 10 and 11. It will be noted that General Sharp makes no mention of sanctions, so we have effects without causes – and this dislocation is not uncommon. There is a strange detachment in American political thought, which on the one hand sees the US as the world's hyper-power and at the same time accepts no responsibility for the effects of its actions, and sees no connections, for instance, between it and the rise of Islamist militancy, or a possible disintegration of a state of 24 million people in Northeast Asia that was at one stage a star of the developing world, and in some respects still is.[36]

There is a parallel here with the invasion of Iraq. That invasion did not just happen, and it certainly was not caused by the government of Iraq. Perhaps all victims, whether of rape, burglary or invasion, contribute to their fate, but that does not absolve the perpetrator of ultimate responsibility. The United States did not have to invade Iraq – it chose to do so. That invasion may have been morally reprehensible or morally correct (as Tony Blair would have us believe); it may have been foolish or wise (as Donald Rumsfeld still contends); but whatever it was, it was a war of choice.[37] The same is true with North Korea. The US policy of hostility, of seeking to destroy the DPRK, is a matter of choice. It follows that its consequences – probably war, perhaps a war with China – are also matters of choice and responsibility.

Bonnie Glasser and Scott Snyder, writing in the *PacNet Newsletter*, in an article entitled 'Preparations Needed for North Korean Collapse', hedged their bets on timing but were confident enough that collapse would happen to advocate detailed planning. They seemed to have a strangely sanguine approach to the Chinese reaction, and ignored the possibility that the North Koreans might object to foreign troops:

It is premature to predict near-term regime collapse in North Korea, but it is not too early for major regional parties to plan for the effects of instability, potentially including massive refugee flows and unsecure nuclear weapons, materials, facilities, and knowhow that could be smuggled out of the North and into the hands of the highest bidder. Responses to instability could include decisions by China, South Korea and the US to dispatch troops into North Korea to restore order and to locate and secure weapons of mass destruction facilities. Absent advance coordination, these forces could come into conflict with each other.[38]

Also in *PacNet Newsletter*, Michael J. Finnegan, discussing 'Preparing for the Inevitable in North Korea', took a similar line. Actually he admitted that the only thing that was inevitable was the death of Kim Jong Il, but cautioned that preparations were necessary to cope with 'the potential instability that will arise'. Finnegan is unusual in being one of the few commentators to acknowledge the challenge the demise of the DPRK would pose to the US military presence in South Korea, and by extension, in East Asia:

> Kim's death as well as the potential end to the North Korean state and the threat it poses would also challenge the existence of the alliance: if the primary purpose of the alliance is to defend against North Korea, and the North is no longer a threat, then what?[39]

The further away from Korea the commentator is, the more confident is the predication of collapse. Fareed Zakaria, formerly of *Newsweek International* but here writing in its sister-publication the *Washington Post*, has no doubts about collapse ('When North Korea falls ...'). He is more aware of the possible consequences than others, but he does share the sanguine assumption of some, such as Bonnie Glasser and Scott Snyder, that some sort of deal can be stitched together with China:

> In geopolitics there is one [event] that should have us all thinking hard – the collapse of North Korea.
>
> Most of Washington's attention has been devoted to the Pyongyang regime's small nuclear arsenal. But perhaps a more likely scenario, and possibly one that would be even more disruptive, is a meltdown of the regime.
>
> And at that point, unless there is careful planning among South Korea, China and the United States, all hell will break loose.
>
> There are big issues at stake. Does a unified Korea retain its close alliance with the United States? Does it keep the North's

nuclear arsenal? Do American troops stay in the country? If the answer to all three questions is 'yes', then a unified Korea will be an American ally, with American troops, and nuclear weapons – sitting on China's border. How is Beijing likely to react to that? Would it move troops in to shore up the regime? What would South Korean and American forces do then?

When North Korea collapses, it is easy to imagine chaos on the Korean peninsula that triggers a series of reactions from Beijing and Washington that are competing and hostile.[40]

John Bolton does not agonise over the dangers, but rather embraces them, although from a safe distance:

Our objective should be to increase pressure on Kim Jong Il's regime, hopefully leading to its collapse.

We should thoroughly isolate North Korea by denying it access to international financial markets, ramping up efforts to prevent trade in weapons-related materials and pressuring China to adhere to existing UN sanctions resolutions. Opening North Korea to foreign commerce to benefit its near-starving population, as some advocate, is utterly fanciful. If the regime had ever cared about its people, they wouldn't be in such dire straits.

We should also dramatically expand preparations for Kim's inevitable demise. It is a self-fulfilling prophecy for Washington to see his death only as a risk, rather than an opportunity. We should take every advantage of the inevitable rivalry and confusion that will accompany the transition, and use whatever levers are available to undermine the regime. We must also plan to meet the North's evident humanitarian needs, whether or not there are massive refugee flows. Even if the population stayed put after a regime collapse, the North's misery would still require urgent attention. And we must ensure that the North's weapons of mass destruction do not fall into the wrong hands ...

After 10 years of error, we should recognize, better late than never, that unifying Korea is key to Asian peace and stability.[41]

Bolton does, at least, display a certain recognition of agency, as is appropriate in a man of action rather than a commentator. Unfortunately, Bolton's actions are seldom moral and never wise: 'Although their elders may be hopeless on the subject, the rising policy makers [in China] must hear from us that peacefully reunifying Korea is in Beijing's long-term interests.'[42] Whether

Chinese policy-makers of whatever age would happily accept that the United States acquiring more prime real estate on their border as being in their country's long-term interest is debatable.

It could well be argued that China must take some responsibility for America's aggressiveness in respect of North Korea. There seems to be a certain air of wishful thinking in Beijing that frequent calls for peace and stability will dampen hostilities. Ding Gang, writing in *Global Times*, addresses the same issue as Bolton – long-term interest – but comes up with a very different answer:

> The US should be aware that strengthening military alliances exclusively with Japan and South Korea will not solve the problem nor foster peace on the Korean Peninsula.
>
> It is short-sighted to depend on its military power to maintain its position in Asia. Such a policy is bound to fail …
>
> Effective Sino-US coordination on the Korean Peninsula issue, which will improve US relations with a rising China, is more in line with long-term US interests in Asia.[43]

The problem with Ding's analysis is that the US does not want peace based on the status-quo, as China does. Does that mean that the United States wants war? General Luo Yuan, interviewed in the *Global Times*, is sanguine:

> Neither [Korean] side is showing a will for war. South Korea's backer, the US, would forbid South Korea to begin a war. The US cannot afford another war when it is still bogged down in Afghanistan and Iraq. China is going to actively mediate between the two sides to settle them down by using its international influence to encourage a restrained and peaceful way to settle the dispute.[44]

He is right in saying that South Korea cannot go to war without American permission, and that the US has some other wars on its plate. However, while neither Seoul nor Washington want war, they do want victory, and that is a different matter. Of the two, Seoul has a much stronger desire for victory than Washington. Indeed, a victory in the sense of a Korea united by a Southern absorption of the North, even without Chinese intervention, presents the United States with the problem of how to justify its military presence in Northeast Asia. That is presumably not a matter of such concern for Lee Myung-bak, who would adjust to the new situation by balancing China against the US:

> People generally regard Lee Myung-bak as pro-US and pro-Japan. To my mind, it's also very possible for Lee to take a pro-China attitude because what he considers the most is South Korea's national interests. Lee might change his attitudes as the international situation develops.[45]

If a Southern takeover of the North might be a Pyrrhic victory for the United States, it would certainly not be welcomed in Japan, except of course in public statements.[46]

While the Americans would, on balance, approve of a Southern takeover of the North, the real driver is Lee Myung-bak. In 2010 a marked change could be observed in at least the public position of the Lee government towards the North. Although talk of a 'grand bargain' has always been bogus because of its preconditions, and measures had been taken to clamp down on North–South economic linkages – especially through tourism – on the face of it engagement was still the official policy. At the beginning of the year there was talk of a summit; by the end of the year Lee was talking of a 'unification tax' to pay for the absorption of the North:[47]

> The government is to start fully fledged preparations for reunification with North Korea next year [2011], in a signal shift from the traditional emphasis on stability and cross-border exchanges to a more aggressive vision for the future.
>
> A senior official on Sunday said the Unification Ministry will brief President Lee Myung-bak on Wednesday on its objectives for next year, which will be focused on preparations for reunification.
>
> Following North Korea's artillery attack on Yeonpyeong Island, Lee has made a series of comments hinting at signs that [the] North Korean regime is cracking. At a meeting with Korean residents in Malaysia on [December] 9, Lee said, 'I feel reunification is now not far off' and called it an 'important change that nobody can stop.' And in a speech at a government meeting on [December] 3 he said, 'No power in history has been able to resist the changes sought by the public.'
>
> Another government official said, 'The focus of next year's North Korea policy has shifted to bolstering our capacity to handle reunification rather than on communicating with the North.' ...

This marks a U-turn in North Korea policy, given that Unification Minister Hyun In-taek only told Lee in his New Year's briefing early this year that an inter-Korean summit could be possible in 2010.[48]

We see here suggestions that collapse is on its way ('signs that North Korean regime is cracking'), with the preparation of public opinion through the unification tax, and the move towards 'bolstering our capacity to handle reunification'. And yet there are many uncertainties. Lee is a pragmatist who will only move if he thinks the conditions are ripe. But he is also an activist – 'the bulldozer' – and it is unlikely that he will just sit back and hope, or pray, for a crisis in the North that will provide the opportunity for intervention.

Indeed, one intriguing explanation for the escalation of military tension by Lee Myung-bak, especially following the fabrication of the *Cheonan* investigation, is that the North Korean economy is recovering, and collapse because of economic stress is less likely than before. Time is running out – his term comes to an end in 2012 – and, short of a crisis that might produce the equivalent of Roosevelt's third term, he will be out of office.[49]

Crisis, and war, are by no means foregone conclusions. There is much opposition to Lee Myung-bak in South Korea, and while that has receded because of the Yeonpyeong incident (a lesson that surely will not be lost on either Lee or Kim Jong Il), it may gather force once again. Opposition politician Kwon Young-ghil, founder of South Korea's left-wing Democratic Labor Party, is perhaps overly optimistic when he tells the Beijing *Global Times*:

> In my opinion, every Korean, whether in the North or South, yearns for reunification, even in their poems or songs.
>
> Without reunification, there is no future for Korea ...
>
> The second point is that I believe almost every Korean believes reunification must be achieved through a peaceful resolution, not by force.[50]

One South Korean who does not believe that reunification must be by peaceful resolution is Lee Myung-bak. Kwon Young-ghil's party holds only five of the 295 seats in the National Assembly. Lee Myung-bak holds power, and has the ear of the Obama administration.

9
The Northern Limit Line: Keeping the War Alive

The land barrier between the two Koreas, the Demilitarised Zone (DMZ), drawn up in the Armistice negotiations between the Chinese and North Koreans on the one side, and the Americans (nominally the United Nations) on the other, is accepted by both Koreas and is not in itself an issue. The maritime boundary on the east coast does not seem to have caused any problems. The boundary to the west is different. Good maps of the Northern Limit Line, claimed by South Korea, showing it in relation to the DMZ and the Military Demarcation Line (MDL), claimed by North Korea, are hard to come by. Fig 9.1 suggests why that may be so. Whereas the MDL is effectively a continuation of the DMZ, the NLL skirts the North Korean coast. The NLL comes between some five offshore islands and the coast of North Korea, while the MDL heads straight out to sea, away from the coast and away from the islands. So when clashes occur around the NLL, the suspicious may wonder about its strange configuration. Surely the location of the NLL is conducive to clashes between the two side which would be avoided if the MDL were accepted by both?

There are historical reasons for the drawing of the NLL, but its continued existence is a matter of politics. During the Korean War the United States had control of the sea (as well as virtual control of the air), so when the fighting came to an end the five offshore islands were under the control of the Americans, or formally the United Nations Command. In retrospect it was unfortunate that the matter was not better resolved at the time:

Within ten (10) days after this armistice agreement becomes effective, withdraw all of their military forces, supplies, and equipment from the rear and the coastal islands and waters of Korea of the other side. If such military forces are not withdrawn within the stated time limit, and there is no mutually agreed and valid reason for the delay, the other side shall have the right to take any action which it deems necessary for the maintenance of

140

security and order. The term 'coastal islands', as used above, refers to those islands, which, though occupied by one side at the time when this armistice agreement becomes effective, were controlled by the other side on 24 June 1950; provided, however, that all the islands lying to the north and west of the provincial boundary line between HWANGHAE-DO and KYONGGI-DO shall be under the military control of the Supreme Commander of the Korean People's Army and the Commander of the Chinese People's volunteers, except the island groups of PAENGYONG-DO (37° 58' N, 124° 40' E), TAECHONG-DO (37° 50' N, 124° 42' E), SOCHONG-DO (37° 46' N, 124° 46' E), YONPYONG-DO [Yeonpyeong Island] (37° 38' N, 125° 40' E), and U-DO (37° 36' N, 125° 58' E), which shall remain under the military control of the Commander-in-Chief, United Nations Command. All the island [sic] on the west coast of Korea lying south of the above-mentioned boundary line shall remain under the military control of the Commander-in-Chief, United Nations Command.[1]

The North Koreans accepted US control, which in time came to mean ROK control, of the islands, but not the sea around them. Why they acquiesced to the US demand, and indeed why the US wanted those islands, is unclear. If other islands could be restored to pre-war ownership, why not these? Perhaps the islands were useful for mounting commando raids into North Korea, or for supporting guerrilla units there.[2]

The nationality of the signatories to the Armistice Agreement is significant. On one side there was Nam Il, a general in the Korea People's Army and senior delegate in the Delegation of the Korean People's Army and the Chinese People's Volunteers; and on the other, William K. Harrison, Jr, a lieutenant-general in the United States army and senior delegate in the United Nations Command Delegation. It is as if the Chinese were saying to the North Koreans: 'It's your country, you sign,' and the Americans were saying, 'It's our world, we'll sign.'

The NLL was unilaterally established by the Americans in August 1953, and has since been claimed by the US and ROK.[3] Whatever the original reasons for the establishment of the NLL, by the 1990s commando raids were a thing of the past, yet the ROK refused to negotiate a settlement that would be more peace-friendly. This was despite two major incidents, in 1999 and 2002, which presented a distinct threat to the 'Sunshine Policy' of then President Kim Dae-jung.[4] A further clash occurred in November 2009, under

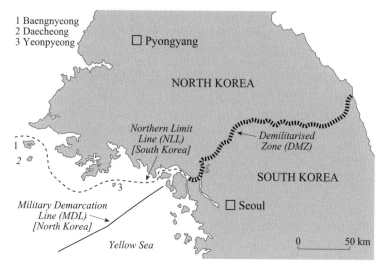

Figure 9.1   Northern Limit Line, Military Demarcation Line and the Demilitarised Zone (Map by Catherine Lawrence)

the presidency of Lee Myung-bak.[5] This 2009 incident may have owed something to the more assertive North Korea policy of the Lee administration.[6]

The NLL did not receive much international attention until the *Cheonan* incident of March 2010. There were a number of reasons for this. Most of the casualties in previous incidents had been Northern and so, in the eyes of most of the international media, warranted less attention. The *Cheonan* was the largest single disaster for the ROK navy.

Many commentators were quick to point out what a dangerous situation the sinking of the *Cheonan* represented. Typical was Nicole Finnegan of the Washington-based Korea Economic Institute: 'Regardless of what we learn the true cause of the tragedy to be, the sinking of the *Cheonan* has revived fear and debates on how easily North and South Korea could lurch into war unexpectedly.'[7]

There is nothing new in these concerns. The NLL, by its unilateral nature, its configuration close to the North Korean coast and running through highly prized crab grounds, is a recipe for conflict. Fishing boats from both South and North sometimes ignore the NLL during the crab season, and their respective navies tend to follow them. The NLL is also at variance with the now-standard territorial sea limit of 12 nautical miles.[8] Writing in 2002, after the clash of June that year, John Barry Kotch and Michael Abbey, point out that

[i]f the two Koreas are genuinely committed to reconciliation, these differences can be resolved through negotiation, thereby preventing future incidents. A line that was drawn more than a half-century ago for an entirely different purpose should no longer be allowed to fester as a source of conflict, thereby retarding the peace process.[9]

The differences were not resolved – but why? If this failure to negotiate a resolution had occurred during the Lee Myung-bak administration it might not have been surprising. But this was during the time of Kim Dae-jung and Roh Moo-hyun. It is clear that a resolution would have meant the South abandoning the NLL in whole or in part, and agreeing to something more closely approximating to the North's line. Whatever the role of Americans behind the scenes, it seems clear that resolution of the NLL was opposed, successfully, by the ROK military. The logical conclusion is that there were strong forces in the ROK political elite, revolving around the military, that wanted to keep the NLL precisely because it would 'fester as a source of conflict, thereby retarding the peace process'.

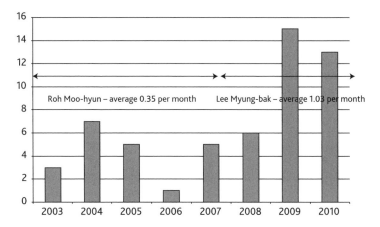

Figure 9.2 Measuring Policy Change: KCNA Mentions of the NLL over Two Administrations

All of the previous conflicts around the NLL had been at sea, and the artillery duel at Yeonpyeong was the first one on land. To understand how that came about, we must return to the map. It appears that the DPRK acknowledges ROK control over the islands, but claims they are in its territorial waters, except for the access channels.[10]

While the NLL has long been a bone of contention, the situation has greatly worsened since the Lee Myung-bak administration came into office. One rough way of measuring that is to calculate the number of times the official KCNA news agency mentions the NLL. Roh Moo-hyun was in office from 25 February 2003 to 25 February 2008, when Lee Myung-bak took over. Fig. 9.2 shows the monthly average of NLL stories over those two administrations. This is admittedly an imperfect metric, but the difference between the two administrations is compelling: under Lee Myung-bak, the number of North Korean complaints rose nearly three-fold. In March 2008, for instance, the KPA navy warned:

> Combined firepower drills for 'striking and destroying' warships of the Navy of the Korean People's Army and drills for tactical naval maneuvers are staged on Paekryong, Taechong and Yonphyong Islets and in waters around them almost [every day].
>
> A situation in which an armed conflict may break out any moment is prevailing in the frontline waters in the West Sea due to the reckless military provocations of the south Korean military warmongers.
>
> Any attempt on the part of the south Korean military authorities to 'protect' the 'northern limit line' at any cost would only spark off a clash in the said waters.[11]

The following year, as the Lee administration moved to join the US-led Proliferation Security Initiative (PSI), the KPA navy issued another warning:

> For the present, we will not guarantee the legal status of the five islands under the south side's control (Paekryong, Taechong, Sochong, Yonphyong [Yeonpyeong] and U islands) in our side's territorial waters northwest of the extension of the Military Demarcation Line in the West Sea of Korea and safe sailing of warships of the US imperialist aggression forces and the south Korean puppet navy and civilian ships operating in the waters around there.[12]

The PSI is in many ways similar to the NLL. It is unilateral, and has no legal standing. The PSI claims that the US and its clients are above international law, and may stop and search ships on the high seas. Ostensibly this is to stop the shipping of weapons of mass destruction which, given US pre-eminence in the international arms trade, smacks of a certain degree of chutzpah.[13] Indeed, as Hazel Smith has observed, 'There is little hard evidence that the government of North Korea is involved in the illicit shipping of WMD or components of WMD.'[14] The real purpose of the PSI seems to be to harass the DPRK and stoke tension, and that also holds for the NLL.

ATTEMPTS AT RESOLUTION

The DPRK made many complaints about the NLL over the years.[15] In 1999, after the 'first battle of Yeonpyeong', in June, the DPRK proposed its Military Demarcation Line, which would separate the two sides and provide a logical solution:

> The serious lesson from the west sea incident proves that future conflict is inevitable unless both sides reach a clear-out agreement on the Military Demarcation Line at the west sea and battleships of the sides are set apart from each other under such an agreement, [said Senior colonel Pak Rim Su, delegate of the Korean People's Army].
> He clarified which was more appropriate and reasonable from a legal and logical point of view of the two kinds of the Military Demarcation Lines at the west sea proposed by the KPA side and the US forces side and where this issue should be handled, the main issues over which the two sides [disagreed] at the meeting.
> He said that to fix the line the KPA side extended the provincial boundary line between Hwanghae-do [Province] and Kyonggi-do [Province] (a–b line) stipulated in paragraph 13b of the Armistice Agreement, and applied the principle of equidistance according to the international maritime law.[16]

The following year the KPA navy proposed a series of measures that would ensure navigation rights to the ROK-held islands (such as Yeonpyeong), but without accepting the NLL.[17] However, the South would not recognise the maritime MDL and the North did not accept the NLL.

There was an attempt to resolve the issue during the summit between Roh Moo-hyun and Kim Jong Il in October 2007:

The declaration issued on October 4, 2007, after President Roh met with North Korean leader Kim Jong Il in Pyongyang, tried to address this dispute by stating: 'The South and the North have agreed to create a "special peace and cooperation zone in the West Sea" encompassing Haeju and vicinity in a bid to proactively push ahead with the creation of a joint fishing zone and maritime peace zone, establishment of a special economic zone, utilization of Haeju harbor, passage of civilian vessels via direct routes in Haeju and the joint use of the Han River estuary.'[18]

However, Roh's term of office was to end shortly after that, and incoming president Lee Myung-bak had no time for peace zones. He is reported by the US scholar Jon van Dyke as declaring that the NLL was a 'critical border that contributes to keeping peace on our land.'[19] Van Dyke continues by offering this justification for Lee's obduracy: 'It is hard for any political leader to take action that is perceived as making a territorial concession, especially one that may create additional security concerns.'[20] He is right to say that 'territorial concessions' are a problem for any political leader. In addition, a joint fishing zone would imply sharing some of the crab fishing with the North Koreans, though that might be offset by joint efforts to keep illegal Chinese fishing boats at bay. However, talk of 'additional security concerns' does not hold water. A move that would separate the two navies would enhance security and avoid clashes. Perhaps, for Lee, that was the problem.

Even more bizarre is the rationale against moving the boundary offered by Michael J. Green, a former Bush official now heading the Japan Program at the Center for Strategic and International Studies in Washington. It would make it easier for North Korea 'to smuggle out military equipment and drugs, and smuggle in things that are part of their nuke program ... Nothing good comes from it.'[21]

The Korean-American activist Paul Liem is closer to reality when he writes: 'The [NNL] has no legal basis in the Korean War Armistice Agreement, and the West Sea has been the most likely site for outbreaks of fighting with loss of life.'[22]

RAMIFICATIONS OF THE YEONPYEONG INCIDENT

One of the interesting consequences of the Yeonpyeong incident, and the awareness about the NLL that it raised, was an article on Bloomberg.com entitled 'Defending Korea Line Seen Contrary to Law by Kissinger Remains US Policy'.[23] This provided a good overview of the NLL and its origins:

> The border was drawn by Army General Mark Clark and his aides in 1953 to stop South Korea from disrupting the fragile armistice he oversaw at the end of the Korean War, according to Narushige Michishita, an associate professor at the National Graduate Institute for Policy Studies in Tokyo.
>
> The line snakes around the Ongjin peninsula, creating a buffer for five island groups that South Korea kept under the armistice that ended the 1950–1953 Korean War, in which US-led forces fought under a UN mandate against North Korean and Chinese troops. The agreement doesn't mention a sea border, which isn't on UN maps drawn up at the time.
>
> The 3-nautical mile (3.5-statute mile) territorial limit used to devise the line was standard then. Today almost all countries, including both Koreas, use a 12-mile rule, and the islands are within 12 miles of the North Korean mainland. The furthest is about 100 miles (160 kilometers) from the closest major South Korean port at Incheon.
>
> 'If it ever went to arbitration, the decision would likely move the line further south,' said Mark J. Valencia, a maritime lawyer and senior research fellow with the National Bureau of Asian Research, who has written extensively on the dispute …
>
> 'There was concern over President Rhee and what he might do,' said Larry Niksch, a former Asian affairs specialist at the US Congress's research arm. 'There was a lot of concern he might try to open hostilities again.'
>
> So Clark and his aides drew the line to restrain Rhee and prevent clashes, said Michishita, author of the 2010 book *North Korea's Military–Diplomatic Campaigns, 1966–2008*. 'North Korea was not notified of the line,' he said.[24]

However, what was most important about the Bloomberg article was that the journalists turned up a number of embarrassing cables – from Henry Kissinger, from the State and Defense Departments, and from the US ambassador to Seoul. A Joint State/Defense message sent to the US embassy in Seoul in 1973 expressed American concern about Seoul's 'territory creep':

> WE HAVE RESERVATIONS ABOUT MOFA'S [ROK Ministry of Foreign Affairs] ATTEMPT TO GIVE NLL VALIDITY AS A

'RESPECTED' ELEMENT OF 'ARMISTICE REGIME' WHICH HAS DEVELOPED OVER PAST 20 YEARS. WE ARE AWARE OF NO EVIDENCE THAT NLL HAS EVER BEEN OFFICIALLY PRESENTED TO NORTH KOREAS [sic]. WE WOULD BE IN AN EXTREMELY VULNERABLE POSITION OF CHARGING THEM WITH PENETRATIONS BEYOND A LINE THEY HAVE NEVER ACCEPTED OR ACKNOWLEDGED. ROKG [ROK Government] IS WRONG IN ASSUMING WE WILL JOIN IN ATTEMPT TO IMPOSE NLL ON NK ...

THE ROKG SHOULD UNDERSTAND THAT OUR POSITION WILL BE DETERMINED SOLELY BY THE TERMS OF THE ARMISTICE AGREEMENT WHICH MAKES NO REFERENCE TO NLL.[25]

Another cable, from the US ambassador, Francis Underhill, back to Washington in December that year expressed further concern about South Korea's belligerence:

THE ROK POSITION HAS BEEN FIRM IN ITS RESOLUTION TO MAINTAIN ITS CONTROL OF THE ISLANDS, BUT THE TONE OF PUBLIC STATEMENTS HAS BEEN IN OUR JUDEGEMENT [sic] SOMEWHAT OVERLY BELLIGERENT. THERE IS A DANGER THAT THE ROKG MIGHT APPEAR TO BE ACTIVELY SEEKING A SHOWDOWN ...

WHILE MAINTAINING RIGHT OF ACCESS AND SAFEGUARDING ALL OF OUR BASIC INTERESTS UNDER THE ARMISTICE AGREEMENT, IT WAS VITAL THAT WE AVOID THE NORTH KOREAN TRAP AND NOT LET OURSELVES APPEAR TO HAVE PRECIPITATED OR INCITED AN INCIDENT ...

THE CHARGE SAID THE RIGHT OF ACCESS TO THE ISLANDS WAS ACKNOWLEDGED, BUT THAT THERE WERE A NUMBER OF OTHER COMPLEX QUESTIONS ON WHICH WE WERE SEEKING GUIDANCE. THE CENTRAL OBJECTIVE WAS AVOIDANCE OF AN UNNECESSARY INCIDENT.[26]

It seems there was no problem with 'right of access to the islands'; rather, the government in Seoul was 'actively seeking a showdown'. In 1975 there is a secret cable from Henry Kissinger which accepts that the NLL is illegal: 'The line "was unilaterally established and not accepted by NK," Kissinger wrote in a confidential

February 1975 cable. "Insofar as it purports unilaterally to divide international waters, it is clearly contrary to international law."' The main thrust of the Bloomberg article was that in 1973 the United States was trying to restrain South Korean belligerence, and in 2010 was supporting it. Moreover, the State Department seemed to be handing over leadership to Defense:

> State Department spokesman P. J. Crowley referred questions about the current American view of the line's justification to the US military in South Korea. Colonel Jonathan Withington, a spokesman for the US-led United Nations Command in Seoul, said the NLL should not be renegotiated.[27]

Nevertheless, the obvious illegality of the NLL cannot be completely ignored. Nor can its role in fomenting crises. The solution is fairly obvious: to draw a line which would separate the two sides, acceptable to both. The modalities are another matter. Selig Harrison takes a no-nonsense, unilateralist approach:

> Can anything be done to put an end to the simmering conflict in the Yellow Sea? Yes, and the solution could be quite straightforward: the United States should redraw the disputed sea boundary, called the Northern Limit Line, moving it slightly to the south ...
>
> If the boundary were refashioned in a more equitable way, tensions would undoubtedly ease.
>
> And, fortunately, President Obama has the authority to redraw the line. On July 7, 1950, a United Nations Security Council resolution established the United Nations Command for Korea and designated the United States as the executive agent, with authority to name its commander. That original command is still with us today in vestigial form. It is commanded by Gen. Walter Sharp, who is thus the current successor to Gen. Mark Clark, who signed the 1953 armistice.
>
> The Obama administration would do well to consult with both Seoul and Pyongyang on where to best set the new boundary, get an agreement from both governments to abide by it, and put it on the map. South Korea should not be given a veto over the redrawing.[28]

The International Crisis Group came up with something far less muscular. In its report on the Yeonpyeong incident, it produced recommendations to the four main governments concerned (the two Koreas, China and the US). In respect of the NLL, its recommendations are:

To the Government of the Republic of Korea:
1. Abandon claims that the NLL is an inter-Korean maritime boundary and offer to accept international arbitration, overturning previous rejections of such mechanisms.

To the Government of the Democratic People's Republic of Korea:
...
5. Ratify the UN Law of the Sea Convention and accept an arbitration under international law – under the framework of UNCLOS – to establish an inter-Korean maritime boundary in the Yellow Sea.

To the Government of the People's Republic of China:
...
9. Encourage the DPRK to ratify the UN Law of the Sea Convention and both the DPRK and ROK to accept an arbitration under international law to establish an inter-Korean maritime boundary in the Yellow Sea.

To the Government of the United States:
...
10. Encourage the ROK to accept an arbitration under international law in the establishment of an inter-Korean maritime boundary in the Yellow Sea.[29]

It is really very difficult in the current climate to see any international arbitration that would be acceptable to both Koreas.

The onus clearly lies with Seoul and Washington. If either one of them wants to defuse the situation caused by the Northern Limit Line, they can. Despite what Harrison writes, the ROK is in de facto control of the area, and can negotiate the boundary if it wants. The Lee government could, in fact, resuscitate the 4 October 2007 summit agreement between Roh and Kim, and establish that special peace and cooperation zone in the West Sea. If the ROK does not want to negotiate, the US could override their objections.

At the time of writing, neither South Korea nor America show any sign of wanting to remove this flashpoint in the West Sea. The implications of that are surely obvious.

10
Military Exercises: Precipitating Collapse, Preparing for Invasion

Joint US/ROK military exercises have been a feature of the Korean peninsula for decades. It is usually forgotten what an anomalous situation obtains. The last Chinese forces left the North in the late 1950s, and there have been no substantial Soviet forces there since the aftermath of the Japanese surrender. Not merely do US forces still remain in South Korea (and neighbouring Japan), they have wartime control (OPCON) of the ROK military – a situation that seems likely to persist despite the efforts of the Kim Dae-Jung and Roh Moo-hyun administrations to regain full control.[1]

This chapter focuses on joint US/ROK military exercises. There are exercises which, at least nominally, are entirely ROK affairs;[2] and there are others that are primarily conducted by the South Koreans, but which have an American component. The Hoguk exercise, which contributed to the Yeonpyeong incident, is an example of the latter. The US military writer Joe Bermudez put the usual gloss on things:

> On November 16, 2010 the ROK Joint Chiefs of Staff (JCS) announced that it planned to conduct the annual Hoguk training exercise during November 22–30. As is routine for these exercises, the DPRK denounced them as 'simulating an invasion of the North' and demanded that they be cancelled. The ROK rejected these demands since the Hoguk exercise had been held annually since 1996.

It is a common but quite erroneous argument to suggest that something becomes acceptable just because it occurs frequently; the woman who complains that her husband routinely beats her up is no less a victim because the violence is routine.

Hoguk was a huge exercise, and one can see why the North Koreans might not take it in good spirit. It involved:

70,000 South Korean and American military troops engaged in an annual military drill, called 'Hoguk [Defend the State],' involving 50 warships, 90 helicopters, 500 warplanes, and 600 tanks mobilized for war simulation exercises scheduled for a period of 9 days, until Nov. 30th.[3]

The Americans were represented by the 31st Marine Expeditionary Unit, which, as was mentioned in Chapter 2, is training to seize nuclear and other assets in the event of an invasion of North Korea.[4]

Actual participation of troops aside, it is unclear whether the ROK military can in fact conduct substantial exercises, let alone engage in real war, without US intelligence support and oversight. One indication of this was the move back to overt US control, both of exercises and the military as a whole, in 2010. In June it was announced that the Americans were taking back control of the joint military exercises that had been handed over, at least nominally, to the South Korean military in 2008.[5] This was part of the process whereby OPCON was deferred from 2012 to 2015.[6] The liberal newspaper *Hankyoreh* lamented:

> It is completely illogical that South Korea, which cries 'Global Korea' with the national strength to host even a G20 summit, is volunteering to remain the only nation in the world to entrust operational command to a foreign military.[7]

No plausible reasons for the change were given. The move to ROK control of exercises, and then OPCON, had been an initiative of the Roh administration which Lee Myung-bak was happy to reverse. One can only speculate. The US military may have decided that, if things were going to get serious, and they were going to war, they needed full control, and the window-dressing of ROK sovereignty was an impediment to that. Lee might have considered that US military control would enhance his political leverage over Washington.

Let us now turn to a survey of the main joint military exercises and what they tell us about war plans.

COMPONENTS

Currently there are three sets of joint exercises, though two of them – Key Resolve and Foal Eagle – have been combined.

Key Resolve

This was formerly known as RSOI (Reception, Staging, Onward Movement and Integration), and is essentially a practice for bringing additional US troops into the peninsula in the case of an emergency. This is clearly a complicated matter, and one official manual runs to 173 pages.[8] Just as the Romans built all those straight roads to get their troops around the empire, so too does the US pay increasing attention to moving forces quickly either from the United States itself, or from bases elsewhere (of which, by one recent count, there are 1,000 around the world; the Pentagon admits to 713).[9] Indeed, one of the issues in the ROK–US relationship has been the Americans' desire for 'strategic flexibility', according to which US forces in South Korea, ostensibly there to prevent a North Korean invasion, would be sent off to other theatres, leading to concerns that 'intervention by the USFK in other regional conflicts, such as the China–Taiwan sovereignty dispute, or the US wars in Iraq and Afghanistan, could have the nation tangled in hostilities with other countries against its will'.[10] However, Key Resolve is primarily about bringing US reinforcements into South Korea – and that, in theory, would be a massive operation: 'Under the current contingency plan, codenamed OPLAN 5027, the United States is committed to dispatching about 690,000 troops with 1,600 aircraft and 160 ships, including five aircraft carriers, within 90 days after an outbreak of war.'[11] However well the US practises bringing in reinforcements, there remains the question of where they are to be conjured from.[12]

Foal Eagle

This was described in 2007 by the American security company and think tank GlobalSecurity as follows:

> Foal Eagle counter-infiltration exercises are large combined annual field training exercises for US and ROK forces. FOAL EAGLE is the Combined Forces' Command's primary FTX. It's [sic] primary training audience is tactical units and functions. It is a multifaceted Joint and Combined Exercise that trains in all aspects of CFC's mission: Rear Battle Area Protection, RSOI, Special Operations, and conventional Multi-Service Force-on-Force. Selected CONUS based US units with OPLAN taskings are brought to Korea to participate in this exercise. The Foal Eagle Exercise is an annual ROK–US combined field maneuver conducted since 1961. Its purposes are to demonstrate ROK–US

military resolve to deter war on the Korean peninsula and to improve the combined and joint operational posture.

FOAL EAGLE is a purely defensive exercise which tests the ability of the Republic of Korea to defend itself, assisted by US armed forces. It is primarily a rear-area exercise in which troops defend against invading forces, hostile special forces and commando attacks, or sabotage operations on critical rear-area targets.[13]

Decoded, this would seem to mean not merely combating North Korean special forces sent South, but also social unrest and rebellion in the South itself. Syngman Rhee spent the later 1940s suppressing rebellion, and it took some ten years after the end of the Korean war to extinguish the last guerrilla group in the South.[14] If today there can be massive protests in South Korea about minor matters such as the importation of American beef, then who knows what might happen in the event of a second Korean War?

Ulchi Freedom Guardian

Formerly known as Ulchi Focus, this seems to be the main 'invasion preparation' exercise. It is a mixture of computer game-playing and actual, physical movement of troops and materiel, involving about 50,000 ROK troops and 10,000 American ones. Just before the 2009 exercise, in August of that year, there was a revealing report in the *Korea Times*. Because negotiations were at a difficult stage, it was reported, the exercises were being 'toned down' so they were not so provocative:

'In the upcoming war games, troops from the Combined Forces Command (CFC) will end their counterattacks in Gaeseong [Kaesong], before reaching Pyongyang,' a JCS official said on condition of anonymity.

Previously, CFC troops often advanced into Pyongyang or the Amnokgang (Yalu River) in their simulated training exercises, the official said.[15]

Curious that the Korean People's Army has over the years misconstrued any of this as training for an invasion of the North.

So, the joint military exercises have three components – training for the massive reinforcement of US military in Korea, for the securing of the 'rear area' of South Korea, and for the invasion of North Korea.

Functions

The joint US–ROK military exercises can be seen to have three functions:

1) No doubt such exercises are seen as fun, a relief from ordinary peacetime activities, and preferable to actual fighting. They must be to soldiers what conventions are to businesspeople and conferences to academics.
2) They serve to inculcate fear in the population and justify the existence of a large and expensive ROK military, which imposes a huge burden on the country; males have to serve for 21 months. Why would the South Korean and American governments go to so much trouble twice a year if there were no danger of an invasion from the North?
3) Another objective is to wear down the DPRK military, who go on a higher level of alert just in case the exercises are the beginning of the real thing.

The North Koreans complain that the continuing large-scale exercises force them to waste scarce aviation fuel, and that keeping the army, and the civilian reserve, on high alert is costly.[16] In a situation where one side has huge resources (the US spends nearly as much on its military as the rest of the world put together) and the other extremely limited resources, this attrition is an effective form of subcritical warfare, and there is no doubt that this is intended.[17]

Finally, there is preparation for real conflict. Real conflict could conceivably come about in seven ways, either on its own or in some combination with the others.

1) Genuine accidental incident
   In a heavily armed part of the world this is always a possibility, which is why, if states do want to reduce the risk of it happening, they attempt to introduce military confidence-building measures (CBM), and communications systems ('hotlines') so that escalation can be halted.[18]
2) Pretext
   Both North and South accused the other of precipitating the Korean War in June 1950 under the pretext that they were responding to an invasion. The contingency scenarios discussed

below could be considered a pretext since, in all likelihood, they would not be of sufficient gravity to justify intervention.

3) Pre-emptive strike

The word 'pre-emptive' is often used loosely now for a surprise attack without a formal declaration of war, but it is important to consider it in its original meaning. It was famously misused by the Bush administration as a euphemism and excuse for invasion. The invasion of Iraq was not pre-emptive, because there was no plausible reason to suppose that Iraq would attack the United States (the fact that Germany lost 27,000 troops invading France, the Netherlands and Belgium in 1940 while the US lost only 161 in conquering Iraq seems to be conclusive evidence of that[19]). The situation on the Korea peninsula is different, and both sides might conceivably consider such an action in the true meaning of the word – that is, to gain some advantage when faced with perceived imminent attack. In January 2010, ROK Defense Minister Kim Tae-young talked of a 'pre-emptive strike against NK nuclear attack'.[20] However, since the balance of power is so overwhelmingly against the DPRK, it is not feasible that Pyongyang would attempt an invasion of the South, nor that military planners in Seoul or Washington would consider that likely.[21] As Hillary Clinton has admitted, 'North Korea Does Not Pose a Threat'.[22] It follows that a (true) pre-emptive attack against the DPRK is virtually inconceivable.[23] But the disparity of power, and the frequent discussion of OPLAN 5029, does make a pre-emptive strike by the DPRK much more plausible. If the leadership in Pyongyang believes an invasion is imminent, they might reasonably calculate that pre-emptive action would be advantageous. At best, it might forestall the invasion or make it so painful that the enemy would not continue; and at the worst it would at least inflict more damage on the invader than a mere counter-attack would. Clearly, such a decision would not be taken lightly, because the consequences of war would be disastrous.

If the DPRK did launch a pre-emptive strike, then logically there could have been two scenarios – though which one actually happened we might never know. An invasion might have been imminent, but there would be no need to admit that, and the blame for the war could be laid on the DPRK. The invasion would go ahead, with suitable variation, as a counterattack. On the other hand, Pyongyang could have been mistaken, and misinterpreted signals. In either case, the consequence for the South, and for American troops and civilians in the South (and for other nationalities as well, of course), would be devastating. Japan also would be considered a legitimate target, since it hosts American bases, including units specifically training for an assault on the DPRK.[24]

The DPRK invariably talks in terms of a counterattack; for instance, in February 2010, in an article on the military exercises, the KPA General Staff were quoted as warning that, in the event of an invasion, 'we will react to them with our powerful military counteraction, and if necessary, mercilessly destroy the bulwark of aggression by mobilising all the offensive and defensive means including nuclear deterrent.[25]

Nevertheless, a pre-emptive strike cannot be ruled out.

4) Overreaction to symbolic gesture

The DPRK often uses symbolic gestures as a negotiating tool, or to convey a message of defiance when threatened. At the upper end of the scale, there have been attempted satellite launches, long-range missile tests, and nuclear tests. But the symbolism continues down the scale. When tension rises, Kim Jong Il is reported as visiting KPA bases.[26] If the situation deteriorates further, or if it is considered there is a need to prod Washington back to negotiations, then there are tests of missiles and artillery. Even when these primarily defensive systems, such as shore-to-sea or air-defence missiles, are tested they can be portrayed as provocative, and could conceivably lead to an incident and ignite a crisis.[27] For instance, a day after North Korea test-fired four short-range missiles in July 2009 (and one wonders how many missiles were tested around the world that week), a poll conducted by CNN/Opinion Research Corporation in the United States found that Americans saw the DPRK as the 'biggest threat' to the United States.[28]

5) Maverick action

There is perhaps always the danger that unauthorised action by junior officers against the wishes and strategies of higher command, or by the military independent of the political leadership, can precipitate war; the incidents instigated by the Japanese Kwantung Army in China in the 1930s come to mind. Before that, much of the growth of the British Empire resulted from local initiatives rather than directives from Whitehall. However, contemporary armies have strict rules of engagement and much better communications, so the freebooting warmongering of the past is probably no longer possible,

> Economically, Pyongyang is not in a position to close off the possibility of future economic aid from Seoul by launching a reckless attack. However, the North Korean military, while loyal to Kim Jong-il, has occasionally [shown] independent actions not necessarily in compliance with Pyongyang's political gestures toward Seoul. A regional commander could have sent a mini-sub or floated mines aiming at South Korean craft, with or without the backing of the high command in Pyongyang.[29]

This is not very plausible, and probably owes more to the dilemma of trying to attach blame to the North in the absence of any credible explanation than anything else. The director of the ROK National Intelligence Service (NIS), Won Sei-hoon, has also discounted any idea of maverick action;[30] for at least two reasons – a looser political structure and greater incentive derived from the South's position of strength – maverick action by the ROK military seems more likely. But this would not necessarily lead to war because the North, being weaker, would show restraint and only respond with rhetoric.

6) Situational probability: the role of the Northern Limit Line
The Northern Limit Line (NLL), as I discussed in the previous chapter, seems to have been preserved, despite its legality, as a venue where clashes are likely to occur.

7) Collapse 'contingency'
As I argued in Chapter 8, the idea of a collapse of the DPRK has become a centrepiece of Lee Myung-bak's strategy. The next section will consider the military modalities of this possibility.

FROM CONPLAN 5027 TO OPLAN 5029

The United States has long contemplated, and frequently threatened, various forms of military action against the DPRK, including nuclear attack. North Korea is of course not alone in this – there is a very long list of countries America has attacked, or threatened, especially since the Second World War – but it is arguably the most threatened nation of our times.[31] Much of the talk about military action remains just that, because the likely consequences, as discussed below, cause second thoughts. However, the rhetoric creates a climate of opinion in which awful possibilities become palatable through repetition, and there is great danger in that. And fantasising about war, in the manner of military bureaucracies, does in some cases lead to detailed planning.

The United States military has developed a large number of plans, ranging from conceptual or contingency plans (CONPLAN) to operational plans (OPLAN). The plans are classified, but we know their general outlines from media reports. The best-structured source of information is the website GlobalSecurity.org, and it is the source for what follows in this section, unless otherwise specified.[32] A number of CONPLANs have been reported. CONPLAN 2052, for example, is aimed at containing 'civil disturbances' in the United States itself.[33] In 2003 the Bush administration completed CONPLAN 8022-02, which was reportedly designed to counter an 'imminent nuclear threat' from Iran or North Korea, or to launch a pre-emptive attack if 'the US intelligence network detected evidence of preparations for such an attack'. CONPLAN 8022-02 incorporated nuclear weapons, and was not primarily about 'boots on the ground', though there was provision for 'commandos operating deep in enemy territory, perhaps even to take possession of the nuclear device'.[34] Since Iran does not even have nuclear weapons and North Korea has no strike capacity to attack the United States, it seems that CONPLAN 8022 has not morphed into an OPLAN, although Pyongyang has on numerous occasions referred to it as OPLAN 8022.[35]

The major plans relating to the DPRK are OPLAN 5026, OPLAN 5027, OPLAN 5030, and OPLAN 5029

OPLAN 5026

This has been described as constituting 'surgical' air strikes against nuclear, government, and military targets in North Korea.[36] It does not appear, in itself, to involve any land operations. 'Surgical' is used in distinction to general or carpet-bombing of the type employed in the Korean War. There is of course a considerable amount of spin in this term. Bombing is an act of war, irrespective of its being concentrated on specific targets. Precision bombing is never as precise as its advocates claim and there is invariably collateral damage. Indeed, when it comes to bombing nuclear plants, the risks are enormous: a study commissioned by the South Korean military in 2005 reported: 'bombing of North Korea's nuclear facilities could in the worst case make the whole of Korea uninhabitable for a decade, it has been revealed'.[37] The word 'surgical' itself, with it implications that although it might be a bit painful for the recipient country, it is really for its own good is quite dishonest.

The use of air power alone has great attraction for the US military, in ways that offer some parallels to the use of sanctions. It minimizes American casualties, and does not require much in the way of additional resources; the US has plenty of bases in South Korea, Japan and Guam, as well as aircraft carriers and cruisers, destroyers and submarines, that could launch land-strike missiles, at just a few days' notice. But there are drawbacks, some more compelling than others. Using air strikes as a way of 'dealing with North Korea's nuclear program' would be an egregious violation of international law. There are no general legal constraints against nuclear programs as such (if so, the US would be the pre-eminent offender), so the DPRK's programme does not represent a *casus belli*. But it is doubtful that such legal niceties would weigh too heavily on US decision-making; more pertinent are the practical drawbacks. Many of the targets would be difficult to identify, and much of the DPRK infrastructure is located deep underground as a protection against such a strike. The Americans would also have to counter DPRK air defences. According to GlobalSecurity, 'This presents an additional problem of creating a target list so large that it might be just as simple for the United States to aim for the liberation of North Korea rather than the more limited strikes.'[38] Yet another country, apparently, that is to be liberated from itself.

Then there is the possibility that bombing of nuclear facilities 'could release radiation that could have negative consequences on the region as a whole'. Others have put those 'negative consequences' in stronger terms, especially a South Korean report of 2005:

> Simulations secretly commissioned by the South Korean military suggest bombing of North Korea's nuclear facilities could in the worst case make the whole of Korea uninhabitable for a decade, it has been revealed. The military commissioned the simulations amid rising tension following North Korea's launch of a Taepodong missile over Japan in 1998 and when suspicions surfaced a year later that the North was operating underground nuclear facilities.
>
> The simulation revealed that destruction of the Yongbyon nuclear plant could cause enormous destruction, with nuclear fallout as far away as China and Japan.[39]

Finally, there is the issue of North Korean retaliation, which is discussed below under 'counteroffensive'. Pyongyang has frequently made it clear that it would respond fiercely to a US attack:

> The Korean People's Army and people are fully ready to react with merciless retaliation of our own style and with all-out war of justice if the US imperialists and the south Korean warmongers invade our inviolable territory even an inch.[40]

GlobalSecuriy gravely informs us that 'the North Korean leadership is already acutely paranoid and sensitive to US military actions and might be predisposed to respond to any air strikes by initiating a full-scale war'.

Although OPLAN 5026, and air strikes in general, have often been discussed, it seems that the combination of limited gains, dangerous consequences and opposition from Seoul has succeeded in keeping that particular genie in the bottle.

OPLAN 5027

This is, in effect, the American mirror-image of the 'retaliation' that the North Koreans have threatened, though it goes much further. The Koreans talk of annihilating the aggressors but do not specify what comes next; there is no public mention of what one might expect – a call to liberate and unify the country. The Americans claim that '[t]he primary objective of North Korea's military strategy is to reunify the Korean Peninsula under North Korean control within 30 days of beginning hostilities. A secondary objective is the defense of North Korea.'[41] This claim is highly implausible. The US has a long list of intelligence failures in respect of North Korea, so there is no reason to think this is any more solid than the others.[42] It is certainly reasonable to suppose that the KPA leadership would like to be able to force the foreigners out of the peninsula and reunify the country, but it is not reasonable to suppose that anyone in authority believes it can be done. Apart from the huge power of the United States, there is also the formidable strength of the Japanese military, which might be more than happy to use a war on the Korean peninsula to legitimise its role and growth – even though its own constitution, in theory, bans its existence.[43] If that were not daunting enough, South Korea on its own is militarily much stronger than the North. Its military is numerically smaller, but its equipment is far superior and its military expenditure is about ten times that of the North.[44]

The Americans are much more publicly ambitious. OPLAN 5027 has undergone various iterations over the years, as the relative military power of the DPRK has declined:

> Further revisions to the concept of operations were elaborated in OPLAN 5027-98, which was adopted in late 1998. Previous versions of OPLAN 5027 had called for stopping a North Korean invasion and pushing them back across the Demilitarized Zone. The new version of the plan was more clearly focused on offensive operations into North Korea. A senior US official was reported to have said: 'When we're done, they will not be able to mount any military activity of any kind. We will kill them all.' The goal of the revised plan was to 'abolish North Korea as a functioning state, end the rule of its leader, Kim Jong Il, and reorganize the country under South Korean control.'[45]

Exactly where OPLAN 5027 stands now is unclear. How, for instance, is it envisaged that China would react? Ironically, it may be that the KPA knows more about OPLAN 5027 than anyone other than the US and ROK military planners; it was reported in December 2009 that North Korean hackers had penetrated its security and accessed parts of the plan. This led to the rightwing *Chosun Ilbo* editorialising: 'Is Our Military Up to the Job of Protecting the Country?' Whether the plan was hacked – and, if so, whether the hackers were North Koreans (it was reported that the hacker had a Chinese IP address) – remains unknown. However, as *Chosun Ilbo* made clear, OPLAN 5027 was not really about 'defending' South Korea, but was, rather, a plan for the invasion of the North:

> OPLAN 5027 is a highly-classified military plan detailing troop deployment, strategic targets in North Korea, plans of attack and amphibious landing scenarios in case of a war with North Korea and even contains information on how to establish military control over the North's key cities following occupation.[46]

OPLAN 5027 is, in theory at least, a reactive plan – in the words, again, of *Chosun Ilbo*, 'formulated in preparation for a pre-emptive strike or provocation by North Korea'. This is rather different from the formulation in the GlobalSecurity description, which talks of three phases: DPRK attack, ROK defense, and US counter-attack.[47]

The word 'provocation' in respect of North Korea is widely misused, especially in the South. For instance, the North Korean satellite launch of 2009 was widely described as provocative, although, as Selig Harrison has pointed out, perhaps the major reason behind it was to get into space before the South's own satellite. Neither launch, as it turned out, was successful.[48] It is worrying when language is used so loosely, and with such double standards. The ongoing discussion about the sinking of the *Cheonan* will put stress on the meaning of the word provocation: if it can be proved to neutral opinion that the sinking was due a deliberate action by the North, that would constitute provocation. But if there is no proof, but only allegation, what then?

OPLAN 5030

OPLAN 5027 is billed as a counteroffensive that would require some North Korean action to trigger it. OPLAN 5030 is different in that it is pro-active and does not require a specific North Korean move as a prerequisite. It seems to have two functions: one is attrition, the depletion of North Korean military resources through feints; and the other is to provoke a North Korean reaction which could then trigger OPLAN 5027. There is very little information on this plan, which seems to have originated from the fertile brain of then Defense Secretary Donald Rumsfeld in 2003. The main source of information on it is a story that appeared in *US News and World Report* that year:

> One scenario in the draft involves flying RC-135 surveillance flights even closer to North Korean airspace, forcing Pyongyang to scramble aircraft and burn scarce jet fuel. Another option: US commanders might stage a weeks-long surprise military exercise, designed to force North Koreans to head for bunkers and deplete valuable stores of food, water, and other resources. The current draft of 5030 also calls for the Pentagon to pursue a range of tactical operations that are not traditionally included in war plans, such as disrupting financial networks and sowing disinformation.[49]

The plan seems to have been leaked by 'some senior Bush administration officials' who were concerned that it contained elements 'so aggressive that they could provoke a war'.[50] In other words, it represents a real provocation, consisting not just of a satellite launch or the routine testing of a missile – both of which the US, among others, carries out in abundance – but of actions that might lead the North Korean military to unleash a pre-emptive strike. Pyongyang complained that it was 'a more concrete and outrageous war plan to invade the DPRK than the preceding "operation plan 5027"'.[51]

Fortunately the more extreme scenarios were never implemented, although 'disrupting financial networks' has been employed.

OPLAN 5029

OPLAN 5027 was predicated on a North Korean invasion, or some action outside the borders of the DPRK, perhaps provoked by OPLAN 5030 or OPLAN 5026, that could be portrayed as a *casus belli*. OPLAN 5029 is different: it relates to events *within* the DPRK which would not, in the normal course of international relations, be construed as a reason for invasion.

When reports of Kim Jong Il's ill health surfaced in August/ September 2008, the invasion plans that had been shelved, or at least kept to some extent under wraps, during the progressive administrations of Kim Dae-jung and Roh Moo-hyun, were revived.[52] Though this was mentioned little in the American press, it was frequently reported in South Korea. Although the health of Kim Jong Il was the trigger, the essential prerequisite was the new conservative administration of Lee Myung-bak. President Roh had forced the suspension of talks on OPLAN 5029 in 2005; with Lee now in the Blue House, the time was ripe to reactivate the plan. As former Bush staffer Victor Cha put it, the 'US and South Korea need to reengage fully in discussions on a "concept plan" that includes agreement on the division of labor in tasks if the two governments were to encounter signs of a collapsing North'.[53]

The invasion plans are defined under the innocuous title of 'contingency plans'. They are not, it should be reiterated, described as actions to repulse a North Korean invasion, or to counter-attack; rather, they are justifications for a military intervention in the North, or in plain terms, an invasion. They have gone through various iterations, from 'Concept Operational Plan' (CONPLAN) to the more concrete 'Operations Plan' (OPLAN). Some reports date CONPLAN 5029 back to 1999:

The South Korea–US Combined Forces Command drew up a conceptual action plan, codenamed CONPLAN 5029, in 1999 to respond to various types of internal instability in the North, including sudden regime collapse and mass influx of North Korean refugees.

Other contingency situations include a civil war provoked by revolt or coup, South Korean hostages being held in the North, natural disasters, and insurgents' seizure of weapons of mass destruction if the regime is involved in a domestic crisis or suddenly collapses.[54]

It was reported in 2005 that the Roh Moo-hyun administration had blocked the transformation of CONPLAN 5029 into an Operations Plan.[55] However, since 2009 there have been frequent references to it as an OPLAN, emanating from the South, the North and the United States.[56] Not surprisingly, Pyongyang has reacted with concern and anger. It has issued a number of warnings, such as:

It is a ridiculous and rash action for the warmongers at home and abroad to make desperate efforts to dare do harm to the DPRK. This only brings to light who is chiefly to blame for disturbing peace on the Korean Peninsula and pursuing confrontation and war.

The bellicose forces of the US and the south Korean military had better roll back their dangerous 'OPLAN 5029' at once, bearing in mind that their hostile policies towards the DPRK will only bring self-destruction.[57]

It seems that much of the planning for OPLAN 5029 relies on OPLAN 5027, and the war games than fed into it. However, OPLAN 5029 also incorporates offensive actions that could not be rehearsed in the usual military exercises, which were portrayed as essentially a counteroffensive. This has presented the planners with problems, for which they have come up with two possible solutions:

Military authorities are considering two options. The first envisages staging the drill as inconspicuously as possible as part of one of the existing annual joint exercises. The other is a drill ostensibly for humanitarian relief in case of a massive natural disaster in a hypothetical neighboring state.[58]

SEIZURE OF NUCLEAR WEAPONS

A key element of OPLAN 5029, and something which is increasingly touted as a justification for it, is the American desire to seize North

Korea's nuclear assets. It has parallels with American plans for intervention in Pakistan.[59] The issue of nuclear weapons has turned rather sour for the United States, which has led to talk over the last few years by such unlikely advocates as George Shultz, William Perry, Henry Kissinger and Sam Nunn[60] of nuclear disarmament. Though there may have been no real moves in that direction, this same area of concern has become a hallmark of the Obama administration.[61] The reason for this disillusionment is not difficult to find. The United States has long since lost the monopoly of nuclear weapons that it had in 1945, and even small and poor countries, notably the DPRK, have been able to develop nuclear weapons (if perhaps not yet the necessary delivery systems). Nuclear weapons are a great equaliser: the United States, for the moment at least, has a virtually unassailable dominance in military technology – demonstrated in the rapid defeat of Iraq – so it is able to devastate adversaries at no immediate cost to itself. The military casualties usually occur only when there are boots on the ground. However, nuclear weapons challenge this invulnerable dominance, at least in theory. A nuclear-armed small country – and perhaps only a nuclear-armed one – could deter an American attack. Hence, of course, the development of Missile Defense, to remove that deterrent capability. However, for all countries, except perhaps the United States, nuclear weapons can only be a deterrent, and a weapon of last resort. Despite all the loose talk, North Korea cannot threaten the United States with nuclear weapons (even if it had effective delivery systems) because of the certainty of massive retaliation. All this changes with non-state actors, who can deliver nuclear weapons without fear of retaliation that would destroy their country. When terrorists – mainly Saudis, led by an Egyptian – attacked the Twin Towers on 11 September 2001, the United States responded by invading Afghanistan, and then Iraq, even though no Afghans or Iraqis were among the militants. However, the United States was unable to wreak revenge on its client states of Saudi Arabia and Egypt. And so 'nuclear terrorism' has become the ultimate nightmare of the United States, and of many countries around the world. This is potentially a very big chink in the behemoth's armour. Fearful things in the dark are particularly frightening, and it is the combination of uncertainty with awesome consequences that lends discussions of nuclear terrorism, in the American media and think tanks at least, an edge of hysteria and irrationality. The American government so often acts in a way that is likely to produce the horror it fears the most; but precisely because it is so horrible, there is a paralysis of appraisal. It is like an animal caught in the headlights of an approaching car, unable to move. In this case, the United States is moving, but increasingly into danger. Pakistan is currently the major instance of the United States exacerbating the dangers of nuclear terrorism; but the pursuit of policy without due consideration of its dangers as well as its merits – a strange courting of self-destruction – also infects policy towards North Korea, and in particular in respect of OPLAN 5029.

The seizure of nuclear weapons has become a driver of America's interest in OPLAN 5029 even though the chaos and anger following an invasion is the only credible scenario in which DPRK nuclear weapons or materials might find their way in terrorist hands.[62] One feature of the March 2010 Key Resolve/Foal Eagle was the public identification of a special US unit with 'responsibility for locating, securing and eliminating any weapons of mass destruction' in the DPRK. Although terrorists might be the main worry, they are not the only one. It had already been agreed in October 2009 that the US would have control of 'removing Pyongyang's weapons of mass destruction and joint marine landing operations'.[63] Although the ostensible reason for plans despatching 'elite forces into the North via US nuclear-powered submarines and special warfare transport aircraft and helicopters' is 'a possibility of weapons or technology being stolen by insurgents and smuggled overseas', the United States clearly does not want the South to acquire the nuclear capability of the North.[64] This is partly because a nuclear (and expanded) Republic of Korea would give added impetus to Japan developing its own nuclear weapons. This has never been a technical problem, but rather a political one. There is much domestic opposition in Japan to nuclear weapons, and other countries, especially China, would react strongly. The acquisition by the ROK of nuclear weapons might embolden the Japanese government to follow suit.[65] Although some Americans have advocated a nuclear-armed Japan, the prevailing opinion seems to be that it would be undesirable, with the added force that could be used against China unnecessary, and the political ramifications too uncertain.[66] The same concerns would apply to Korea. One key difference between the ROK and Japan, ostensibly at least, is that the latter has a 'peace constitution' – though apparently this is not the impediment it might seem. The Congressional Research Service report notes:

> There are several legal factors that could restrict Japan's ability to develop nuclear weapons. The most prominent is Article 9 of

the Japanese constitution, drafted by American officials during the post-war occupation, that outlaws war as a 'sovereign right' of Japan and prohibits 'the right of belligerency.' However, Japan maintains a well-funded and well-equipped military for self defense purposes, and the current interpretation of the constitution would allow, in theory, the development of nuclear weapons for defensive purposes.[67]

One wonders what those American officials would have thought of such sophistry.

The fear of the DPRK's nuclear capabilities getting into 'the wrong hands', whether of Muslims or Koreans, is only part of the impetus behind the reactivation of OPLAN 5029. An increasing number of Americans and South Koreans think that the DPRK is about to collapse, or is at least becoming more vulnerable, and that the time is approaching for what many have yearned for and dreamed of for close to 60 years: the destruction of the DPRK and a Korean peninsula united under the stewardship of Seoul and the supervision of Washington. The underlying reason for that is the assumption that the siege of North Korea – especially the sanctions that have afflicted it – are having the desired effect.

11
The Siege:
Sanctions, Their Role and Effect

'Sanctions' is used here as shorthand for the whole range of instruments that the United States employs against the DPRK. They include physical constraints on the import and export of goods, either bilateral (Trading with the Enemy Act, Terrorism List) or multilateral (UN sanctions – UNSC resolutions 1718 and 1874; the Wassenaar Arrangement), and financial sanctions, such as over Banco Delta Asia affairs, and the blocking of DPRK access to international financial institutions. Also included is the harassment of DPRK ships on the high seas, again either bilaterally (the interception of a cargo of missiles to the Yemen) or multilaterally through the Proliferation Security Initiative (PSI). In addition, I should also add the constant military threat, from invasion-simulation exercises to surveillance and the types of provocations covered by OPLAN 5030. Many of these sanctions are not applied directly by the United States, but are to a large extent the result of pressure on client states – sometimes very gentle pressure, including the long-term establishment of a climate of opinion among the bureaucracy and politicians. That is complemented by a general media and educational campaign to mould public opinion, The whole process is very complex and little understood. Sometimes the sanctions are very petty. New Zealand forbids the export of fountain pens to the DPRK as part of its implementation of UNSC Resolution 1718.[1] The effects can be subtle and obscure. For example, I understand that DPRK citizens resident in Japan are frightened to take holidays abroad for fear that they might not be allowed home again.

In general, however, sanctions, are definite in intent and effect. They kill and maim people, and impoverish them, and are designed to do so.

THE ROLE OF SANCTIONS

Sanctions have two functions: changing the policy of the target government, and destabilisation. The first is openly admitted and discussed, but the second tends to be disguised, though it is none the less real for that.

Instrument of Policy Change

Sanctions as instruments of influence are much misunderstood, certainly in the context of the DPRK. When Pyongyang makes conciliatory gestures – peace overtures to Washington (or Seoul) – this is taken as an indication that sanctions 'work', and the screw is tightened, with predictable results. Thus Hillary Clinton endorsed, as did her predecessors, dual strategy of negotiation and sanctions, in this case financial ones against DPRK overseas enterprises:

> The US envoy charged with UN sanctions, Philip Goldberg, is still trying to block North Korean leader Kim Jong-il's cash flow, even as Washington has agreed to talks with Pyongyang aimed at persuading it to return to nuclear negotiations ...
>
> US Secretary of State Hillary Clinton apparently believes Golberg's efforts have been successful, saying Monday that North Korea now wants dialogue because nations of the six-party talks are taking concerted action in implementing sanctions against the North.[2]

In reality, as the DBA affair showed, such a combination does not work.[3] Washington can have sanctions (for destabilisation) or negotiations, but it cannot successfully have both, because Pyongyang regards sanctions and other warlike measures as showing insincerity – as talking peace while waging war. As Leon Sigal put it when discussing what subsequently turned out to be a false report of North Korea supplying uranium to Libya, 'Instead, [Pyongyang] was playing tit for tat – cooperating whenever Washington cooperated and retaliating when Washington reneged, in an effort to end hostile relations. It still is.'[4]

In other words, sanctions make Pyongyang more distrustful and less likely to make concessions. Appeasement appears not to be a popular word in Pyongyang, which has, with justification, described American strategy as 'gunboat diplomacy':

> This reminds one of the 'gunboat diplomacy' pursued by big countries to occupy smaller countries in the past 18th–19th centuries.
>
> It is foolish of the US to calculate that the DPRK will come out to the [Six Party] talks and yield to it under its military pressure.[5]

The history of US–DPRK negotiations has been long (dating back in some respects to the late 1940s) and tortuous.[6] In such circumstances both sides spar – making feints and offering concessions. Because of the huge disparity in the strength of the two protagonists, and the importance of the outcome to them, the sparring takes different forms. Kim Jong Il might be compared to a fisherman seeking to land a fish so large that it could easily break the line if not handled carefully. There are overtures from Pyongyang, but these are not signs of weakness or diminishing resolve, and interpreting them as such is a mistake that is frequently made, exasperating the more perceptive American observers. Joel Wit, for instance, notes the squandering of opportunities for progress on negotiation:

> But then American officials neglected to re-engage Pyongyang. Instead of using last summer's extraordinary meeting between former President Clinton and Kim Jong-il to jump-start dialogue, they lashed themselves to a set of hard and fast preconditions for talks, demanding that Pyongyang pledge to give up its nuclear arsenal and return to multilateral nuclear negotiations.[7]

Apart from the misinterpretation of signals, there is also a fundamental misunderstanding in the United States, and elsewhere, of Pyongyang's position. However bad sanctions might be (see below), the consequences of relinquishing the nuclear deterrent without confidence that the United States would abandon its 'hostile policy' are seen to be much worse. Hence, of course, Pyongyang's stress on 'action for action', a proper sequence of actions that would provide that confidence. So sanctions are counterproductive in negotiations and, in DPRK eyes, they can never inflict as much damage, especially given the position of China, as succumbing to US pressure.

Destabilisation

The other function of sanctions – that of destabilising the DPRK – is seldom discussed. There is certainly overt destabilisation from the South, especially since Lee Myung-bak came to power.[8] However, when US officials mention 'instability', as they increasingly do, it is couched in terms that have nothing to do with American actions.[9]

Not everyone fails to make the connection. Professor Suk Kim, for the University of Detroit Mercy, observed in discussing UN sanctions in 2006:

The world recently watched as the United States and North Korea approached the brink of war as their leaders played a dangerous and delicate game of checks and balances. The United States tries to show its muscle, while North Korea tries to show that it cannot be bullied. Since the end of the Korean War, the United States has consistently applied sanctions on North Korea. The US and the UN have done so on numerous occasions in at least twenty-three different years since 1950, in an attempt to destabilize and manipulate the North Korean regime.[10]

A very clear description of the process was given in a article from Voice of America with the blunt title, 'Sanctions Expected to Harm North Korean Economy':

> Seoul-based research fellow Cho Boo Hyung of the IBK Economic Research Institute agrees with the negative forecast for North Korea. He says the sanctions and restrictions imposed on North Korea's trade are causing a shortage of raw materials. That has reduced output. Consequently, he says, decreased food production will certainly lead to negative economic growth in the North.
>
> Cho is among those warning this could cause famine similar to the 1990s when hundreds of thousands of North Koreans apparently succumbed to starvation or disease.
>
> Intense famine, he warns, will cause people to fend for themselves and the North Korean government to respond with harsher restrictions. That, he says, could lead to open conflict between the people and the authorities.[11]

Curiously, and ironically, 'destabilisation' is often applied to the DPRK nuclear deterrent – 'its role as a destabilizing regional influence'[12] – although in reality it is difficult to discern any sign of destabilisation that could possibly be attributed to it, apart from possible Japanese remilitarisation.[13]

Perhaps the leading authority on sanctions as an instrument of foreign policy is Gary Hufbauer who leads a team of researchers at the Peterson Institute for International Economics (PIIE), a Washington think tank. His colleague, and deputy-director of PIIE, Marcus Noland, frequently writes about North Korea, and often about sanctions.[14] The latest (third) volume of the Hufbauer team's major work, *Economic Sanctions Reconsidered*, surveys 170 cases of economic sanctions imposed since the First World War.[15] The DPRK features twice, firstly in respect of the sanctions imposed in

1950 during the Korean War, and secondly in respect of the more recent US (and UN) sanctions imposed in relation to the nuclear programme. Hufbauer gives two 'goals' for the ongoing sanctions since 1950: 1) impair military potential, and 2) destabilise communist government.[16] Elsewhere he notes that 'Regime change remains an unstated goal in two other nuclear cases: North Korea and Iran.'[17] How are destabilisation and regime change to be brought about? For that, we have to have to examine the effect of sanctions.

THE EFFECT OF SANCTIONS

Although there has been talk in recent years of 'smart sanctions' that target leaders, the reality is that there is nothing smart or discriminatory about sanctions; they are basically weapons of mass destruction. Hufbauer, for instance, notes how ineffective targeting is:

> In the recent North Korean case, UNSC sanctions were targeted at the country's top leader, Kim Jong-il. Rather than comprehensive sanctions, UNSC banned the sale of luxury goods to North Korea in response to North Korea's nuclear test in October 2006. This sanction was carefully tailored to annoy Kim Jong-il, known as a fan of Hennessy cognac, iPods, Harley Davidson motorcycles, and plasma televisions. Since the UNSC left the definition of luxury goods open to each country's interpretation, however, Kim Jong-il and his elite supporters probably found ample provisions.[18]

Whether or not Kim Jong Il really is a fan of Hennessy cognac, it is obvious that the UNSC sanctions would have been as ineffective in this regard as the Nazi blockade of wartime Britain was in limiting Winston Churchill's consumption of brandy. Indeed, there are so many contradictory and unsubstantiated stories about Kim Jong Il's supposed likes, and lifestyle, that they should all be treated with scepticism. For instance a *Time* magazine article about a purported former bodyguard of Kim Jong Il who has ended up in Seoul informed us that 'Kim refused to eat, drink or smoke anything from abroad, except for French wine. Even his hair oil had to be made in North Korea'.[19]

In Chapter 8 we discussed the personalisation of Kim Jong Il, and the way he is presented as embodying the North Korean state, so that his death is seen as cataclysmic and leading to the disintegration of that state. This also happens with the sanctions, whereby impounded goods are described as being for his personal use. Take, for instance, this story from the *Chosun Ilbo* about a hapless Austrian businessman who made the mistake of attempting to export to North Korea rather than, say, Saudi Arabia or the United States:

> An Austrian businessman has been slapped with a 3.3 million euro fine and a nine-month suspended sentence for selling luxury goods to North Korea in contravention of UN sanctions. The goods purchased from the Austrian are thought to be birthday gifts for North Korean leader Kim Jong-il ...
>
> Prosecutors initially indicted the entrepreneur for supplying two top-end Azimut Benetti yachts to North Korea. He also allegedly sold eight Mercedes S class cars and several Steinway grand pianos, dealing with a North Korean intermediary close to Kim Jong-il.[20]

Exactly how Kim Jong Il would manage to play with all those toys on his birthday was not explained. It is reported that when he was young he liked playing the piano, and was good at it – but the addition of several Steinway grand pianos to the collection would seem a bit of a tall story.[21] The reality, as anyone who has been to North Korea would know, is that such goods in general are not destined for Kim personally. They are passed on to institutions as gifts from the Dear Leader. The pianos would have ended up in concert halls, the music conservatory, or perhaps top schools. Music is a very important part of Korean life, and musical performances are an inevitable part of a visit to a school, or even a farm.[22]

Sanctions have an effect on the economy as a whole, and on ordinary people rather that elites. Again, Hufbauer observes that 'skeptics question whether sanctions are an effective instrument, especially when used unilaterally as a stand-alone weapon, since target regimes often can insulate themselves from the harsh impact even if the general population suffers'.[23] Hufbauer doesn't tackle this scepticism head-on, but it becomes clear that it all revolves around the question: 'Effective instrument for what goal?' If the goal is that of changing the policy of the target government, then the insulation of elites might be effective. However, if the goal is destabilisation and regime change, then the suffering of the 'general population' may well be an effective instrument.

One of the problems of discussing the effect of sanctions on North Korea is that, although the government rails against the

American policy of 'hostility' and sanctions, it does not publicly link those sanctions to economic problems, ascribing those to 'natural disasters'. This, in turn, is picked up by the media and international organisations.[24] The other causal explanation favoured by outside observers is 'economic mismanagement'.[25] Neither explanation accounts to any meaningful degree for the economic crisis that followed the collapse of the Soviet Union, which left the DPRK exposed and vulnerable to American policy. The reluctance of the US to admit to a link between its policy and famine in North Korea is understandable, but why does the DPRK government not make the charge more clearly and more often? Cuba, for instance, has calculated that the American embargo has cost it $82 billion, and the connection between that economic loss and the impact on living standards is easy to make.[26] However, the Cubans do not stress the linkage between sanctions and their economic problems.

The DPRK very seldom talks about the effect of sanctions, and never about the human cost. It does not release photographs of malnourished children with the caption: 'The dreadful effect of American sanctions.' This is partly a matter of pride, and partly of strategy.

Understandably, pride is an important factor. I have never come across a photograph of a malnourished child published by the DPRK government; all such photos are taken by foreigners. On various visits to the DPRK over the last decade and more, I have frequently been taken to places they were proud of, but never to anything which might demonstrate the effect of sanctions. As we know, there is often a tense relationship between the Koreans, who are reluctant to advertise their problems, and relief agencies, who want to publicise them in order to generate support and funding. There is, in fact, an important story to be told about the role of sanctions in producing deprivation, and the effectiveness of aid in reducing it.[27] The effectiveness of aid illustrates what would be possible if sanctions were lifted and North Korea had ordinary economic relations with the world, rather than just with China. However, while the North Koreans express gratitude for aid, they do not publicise it very much.[28]

So economic difficulties are usually ascribed to 'natural disasters', but occasionally the role of sanctions is mentioned. In 2000 vice-premier Jo Chang Dok answered questions about 'the recent serious shortage of electricity'. He was talking in the context of the failure of the US to implement the commitment under the

Agreed Framework to build two light water reactors for electricity generation:

> The serious shortage of electricity keeps us from meeting the growing needs in all sectors of the national economy, greatly hampering production and construction.
>
> There has never been such shortage of electricity as today in the DPRK.
>
> We are not to blame for this difficulty in the way of our economic growth. It is entirely attributable to the moves of the US-led imperialist allied forces to stifle the DPRK.[29]

In 2003 KCNA carried a fairly comprehensive overview of the US policy of hostility, which included military exercises and threats and the failure to implement the Agreed Framework, as well as the sanctions themselves:

> KCNA refutes US officials' lies about cause of economic difficulties
>
> Pyongyang, January 13 (KCNA) – Some elements of the Bush administration hostile to the DPRK are floating sheer lies that some economic difficulties in the DPRK are attributable to its wrong policy. This is nothing but a US hypocritical political propaganda to cover up the criminal nature of its blockade policy, a crime against humanity, committed against the DPRK for several decades.
>
> Temporary economic difficulties including the acute shortage of electricity and food in the DPRK were partly caused by consecutive years of natural disasters. But they are chiefly attributable to the US aggressive and hostile policy of blockade towards the DPRK.
>
> The US has pursued this policy for over half a century since its military occupation of South Korea in 1945 ...
>
> The US cooked up a 'COCOM' in 1949, taking advantage of its monopolistic position in the capitalist world after the [Second] World War and has controlled the export of technology and trade with the DPRK in different fields ...
>
> Since the 1970s the US has carried on extremely adventurous and provocative moves to ignite a nuclear war on the Korean Peninsula, annually staging 'Team Spirit' joint military exercises.
>
> The US policy of aggression and blockade became more vicious and desperate in the 1980s and the 1990s under the pretext of the non-existent 'nuclear issue' of the DPRK.

Taking advantage of the collapse of the former [S]oviet [U]nion and other socialist countries in East Europe and their return to capitalism, the US escalated its political and military offensive to destroy the DPRK's socialist system and tightened its economic blockade and sanctions against the DPRK to bring its economy to a total collapse ...

It refused to implement the DPRK–US Agreed Framework which calls for the provision of light water reactors to the DPRK in return for its freeze on nuclear facilities, thus causing a tremendous loss of electricity to the DPRK ...[30]

In 2010, on the occasion of the sixtieth anniversary of the outbreak of the Korean War, KCNA published a long (approximately 12-page) calculation of the 'Tremendous Damage Done to DPRK by US'. Much of the article was concerned with the Korean War itself, but it also listed actions in subsequent decades, and in some cases gave a dollar figure 'calculated by international practices'. Thus, for the war itself:

The US imperialists killed or wounded a total of at least 5,060,770 civilians of the DPRK: 1,247,870 killed, 911,790 abductees and more than 391,740 reported missing.

According to damages calculated by international practices, they total 26,168,823 million US dollars: 16,533,396 million for the dead, abductees and missing people and 9,635,427 million for the wounded and disabled when taking their possible working years and expected earnings, interest for the compensation unpaid and change in the US currency value into due consideration.[31]

One of the many charges against the United States relates to the bombing of Cubana Flight 455 in October 1976, in which five North Koreans were killed. This has been attributed to CIA operative Luis Posada Carriles, who over the years carried out a number of acts of terrorism. He has been in US custody for a few years, but in an interesting test of the real attitude of the US towards terrorism was only charged with immigration offences, of which he was acquitted in April 2011.[32] However, what concerns us here is the listing of damages inflicted on the DPRK by the hostility policy since the war, and the calculation of monetary value. The article is quite long, and the English translation is poor, but its main charges are clear: the damage caused to the economy and to people's living standards by the military threat, and the continual military exercises, which have forced the DPRK to 'put all the people under arms and turn the country into a fortress'; economic sanctions and 'blockade against all sectors including trade, finance, investment, real estate, insurance, transport, post and telecommunications and visits of people', and the impediment to foreign trade through physical and financial sanctions and harassment of North Korean traders; seizure of property of the DPRK government, and its individual citizens; failure to implement the commitments made under the Agreed Framework, particularly in relation to the light water reactors and the provision of heavy fuel oil. All in all, the statement claims that the economic damages inflicted by these measure alone on the DPRK by the United States 'in the six decades up to 2005' come to around '13,729,964 million US dollars'. The total damage during that period, including a monetary calculation for the loss of life during the war, was said to be US$64,959,854 million.[33]

Exactly how robust these calculations are is of course a matter of debate. However, a rough calculation of the disparity between the ROK and DPRK economies does suggest that the figure of US$13,729,964 million for economic damage is not unreasonable. According to the CIA World Factbook, the GDP of the ROK in 2010 was US$1,467,000 million, and that of the DPRK was US$40,000 million. The population of the ROK is twice that of the DPRK, so if we take half the ROK GDP and subtract that of the DPRK, we get a figure of US$693,500 million. Presuming that the figures in the DPRK statement are in contemporary dollars, we can multiply that difference for one year by 60 to get a very approximate figure for the six decades of US$41,610,000 million. Against that, the DPRK calculation of US$13,729,964 million seems within the bounds of probability. Whatever the actual amount, it is clear that the damage done has been, as the article put it, 'tremendous', and that it continues.

This lengthy charge sheet against the United States is very unusual. The normal practice has been to condemn sanctions but not admit the damage done. And even here the information is fairly generic, with no specific details. Crucially, there is no estimate of the number of people who died prematurely in the 1990s because of sanctions. Nor is there any calculation of child malnutrition. This information is available elsewhere, to some extent – mainly through the 2008 census and field assessment reports from the FAO and WFP.[34] There is, in fact, no thorough study of what is one of the greatest tragedies, or greatest crimes, of our times.

The reluctance of target nations to draw a connection between sanctions and their efficacy is surely due to a strategic need to deceive the enemy by not admitting vulnerability. Indeed, it will be recalled that, with what is arguably the greatest success in the recent history of sanctions – the collapse of the Soviet Union – the dire state of the regime was hidden from view. There is a story, perhaps apocryphal but illuminating nonetheless, that Defense Secretary Robert Gates, then at the CIA (he was director under Bush senior), told a meeting in the 1980s that the Soviet Union would not break up in his lifetime, or that of his children.[35]

The case of Iraq provides indications of what has happened in the DPRK. There are differences of course: Iraq had oil to provide revenue and bargaining power, but on the other hand it did not share a border with China. But Iraq was subject to sanctions, and went from one of the most economically and socially advanced countries in the Middle East to a state whose armed forces quickly collapsed under the American onslaught in 2003. In Iraq, as in North Korea and other sanctioned countries, it is the vulnerable who have suffered the most.[36] And among the vulnerable, it is children who naturally attract the most attention. There was an estimate by two FAO scientists in 1995 that UNSC sanctions had been responsible for the deaths of up to 576,000 Iraqi children.[37] It was this report that led to the famous exchange between an interviewer and Madeleine Albright, then US ambassador to the UN (and subsequently secretary of state):

CBS Reporter Lesley Stahl (speaking of post-war sanctions against Iraq): We have heard that a half million children have died. I mean, that's more children than died in Hiroshima. And – and you know, is the price worth it?

Madeleine Albright: I think this is a very hard choice, but the price – we think the price is worth it.[38]

Subsequently, in her autobiography, Albright bitterly regretted her admission, saying that she should have said it was all Saddam Hussein's doing: 'Saddam Hussein could have prevented any child from suffering by simply meeting his obligations'.[39] A bit disingenuous perhaps; it was written before the US invasion and the confirmation that Iraq had no weapons of mass destruction. But she had a point; had Saddam Hussein disbanded his army and marched off to the gallows, leaving the keys to the oil wells on his desk, then sanctions would not have been necessary – and they were, of course, lifted after conquest. But he did not surrender, and so sanctions, and the suffering of children and ordinary Iraqis, were considered necessary, and 'worth it'. Statistics on that suffering remain a matter of some dispute, as do calculations about the ravages of the invasion and resistance; one report in 2004 said that malnutrition among young children had doubled since the invasion.[40]

Although it is children who tend to suffer most from sanctions, they are not, of course, the real target. They are the objects, in that dreadful US military phrase, of 'collateral damage'. The real object is destabilisation – either the overthrow of the regime or the erosion of its military capability and the sapping of its resolve, so it is not strongly defended against invasion – and those are matters for adults.

The Americans, and their friends and allies, tend to have a disengaged attitude towards sanctions – disengaged both ethically and in terms of causality. Sanctions are, after all, but the modern version of the age-old military tactic of the siege. The aim of the siege is to reduce the enemy to such a state of starvation and deprivation that they open the gates, perhaps killing their leaders in the process, and throw themselves on the mercy of the besiegers. Leaders tend to be somewhat isolated from the effects of the siege, and have more to lose – the ordinary people might conceivably escape the sword or slavery, but they will not – and so are more reluctant to surrender. There are strong parallels between sanctions/sieges and terrorism: both inflict pain on ordinary, vulnerable, people in order to turn them against their leaders, who are less vulnerable. Whether the end justifies the means might be a matter of debate, but there is surely no doubt about the nature and effects of those means; unless, of course, like the good modern academic, journalist, or official, we are trained studiously to avoid noticing the obvious. Thus it is quite common to read descriptions of poverty, deprivation, malnutrition, and famine in North Korea with no mention being made of the role of sanctions. In the present context, moreover, we can obtain informed analysis of the possibility of the collapse of the DPRK without any acknowledgement of sanctions. We can find all sorts of fanciful explanations without the real and obvious causal factor being discussed. If the DPRK collapses, it is because the United States has brought it about. For instance, the study by Stares and Wit for the Council on Foreign Relations, euphemistically entitled 'Preparing for Sudden Change in North Korea', contains one occurrence of the word 'sanctions' in its nearly 50 pages – and that not in its capacity as a cause of 'sudden change'.[41] This might appear curious, considering that the ultimate objective of sanctions for many is to bring about the demise of the DPRK. One can understand the reluctance to admit, even (especially?) to themselves, that malnourished children and gaunt adults are the result of sanctions, but why does that extend to discussions of collapse? Perhaps because of the realisation that collapse, certainly in the short term, would have dreadful consequences.

One honourable exception to this blindness is former president Jimmy Carter. He frequently criticises sanctions, most recently when receiving an honorary doctorate at Korea University in Seoul in March 2010. He pointed out that 'common citizens, farmers and workers in the North suffer the most because of them':

> North Koreans have been suffering now for 50 years, not only because of the policy of their government in Pyongyang but because the international community increases their suffering by forbidding normal trade, commerce and the supply of the basic necessities of life.[42]

Of course, Carter cannot resist apportioning the blame away from the United States: sanctions are something emanating from 'the international community', and the suffering is also caused by 'the policy of their government in Pyongyang', even though before the international situation changed – especially with the collapse of the Soviet Union, making US sanctions effective – those same policies produced 'the good old days when they had no worries concerning what to eat under the late former leader Kim Il-sung'.[43]

Thus there is, in a sense, a double conspiracy about sanctions and North Korea. The Americans desire the consequences without admitting responsibility; no more Albright moments. The DPRK government, on the other hand, usually does not admit to the efficacy of sanctions, presumably because that would display vulnerability and invite their expansion. On the contrary, they often produce statements like this:

> Placing the production of fertilizers on a Juche [self-reliant] basis signifies an event which demonstrated once again the heroic spirit of Songun Korea rising to be a thriving nation, undeterred by the despicable moves on the part of the imperialist reactionaries to tighten the sanctions against the DPRK and stifle it and the

tremendous might of the foundation of the self-supporting national economy.[44]

In reality, a glance at the EarthTrends country profile on the DPRK shows the calamitous drop in fertiliser consumption per hectare of cropland in the 1990s, following the collapse of the Soviet Union and a concomitant drop in food production.[45] There is little doubt that sanctions, broadly defined, are the basic cause of the economic crisis, and that substantial economic rehabilitation and growth in North Korea is contingent on the removal of the hostility policy. Unfortunately, in the wake of the *Cheonan* incident, this is increasingly unlikely, as a belligerent Lee Myung-bak drags a disorientated Barack Obama along the road of tightened sanctions, heightened tension, and perhaps war.[46]

The broad contours of the effect of sanctions are obvious enough – the famous night-time satellite photo taken in 2000 showing South Korea, Japan, and China lit up, and North Korea mainly in darkness, is a graphic demonstration.[47] Electricity is not merely a major sinew of a the modern economy, but also its symbol. Sanctions, as defined here, affect virtually every portion of the economy, and hence the life of the population. Tough though circumstances are for most people, we should not over-dramatise them. There are all sorts of positive signs that the economy has adjusted to some extent to the unnatural external constraints. Information and communications technology products and services are an active area, with mobile phones, e-libraries and e-books much talked about, and 'informationalisation' seen, as elsewhere, to be a key economic driver.[48]

Paul Tjia, a Dutch ICT consultant who takes business delegations to the DPRK to explore outsourcing opportunities, notes that 'SEK Studio in Pyongyang is now one of the world's largest animation studios, producing films for French, Italian and Spanish film and television companies'.[49] Much attention, if perhaps not enough, has been paid to new agricultural methods – for instance, those that reduce the need for chemical fertiliser, and hence for imported inputs.[50] There has been a major effort over the last decade and more to promote potato cultivation and improve seeds.[51] Factories are praised for success in 'boost[ing] production by solving many scientific and technological problems by their own efforts and with their own technology through a full display of creative wisdom and effective cooperation'.

Karin Janz, the retiring country director for the German NGO Welthungerhilfe, was reported as saying that:

[i]n her five years travelling across nine provinces of North Korea, [she had] not come across a single case of starvation. The food situation is bad, but it is not as grave as the western media tended to show, she said. The government has also done a fairly good job of developing infrastructure and providing school education although the conditions are still a far cry from what prevails in the developed world, she said.[52]

In April 2010 Dr Margaret Chan, the director-general of the World Health Organization, visited the DPRK and was reported as saying that the 'health system would be the envy of many developing countries' because of the high number of medical personnel.[53] She said that she 'was impressed with some of the notable public health achievements', and commented: 'So what struck me was what they have managed to do under very difficult conditions'.[54]

The WHO is also the original source of data for the figures in Table 11.1. The data are fragmentary (there are no figures for Iraq, for instance), but we do have information for North Korea, and for various other countries, for 2002. While the rate of child malnutrition in North Korea is shocking, it is remarkably good in the circumstances and compared to other countries who are not burdened with sanctions. In particular, the comparison with Indonesia is telling. The archipelagic country has substantial problems – 17,508 islands does not make for easy governance – but it has considerable resources, and no constraints on trade or investment. Nor is it under military threat. My personal impressions of Java and Bali, at least, is of lush and fertile landscapes with no long North Korean-style winter. The high incidence of child malnutrition in Indonesia seems to be a product of social forces – inequality and a lack of economic drive – rather than of environmental or other economic ones.

Economies, like people, learn coping strategies in adversity. Whether it could have done better, or worse, remains disputed. Also disputed is the number of people who have died in the economic crisis. There have been all sorts of estimates over the years, with the journalist Jasper Becker apparently coming up with the highest figure, of 4 million.[55] A recent calculation based on the 2008 census, conducted in cooperation with the United Nations Population Fund, gives a figure of 340,000.[56] It seems that the DPRK has been more successful than Iraq was in coping with sanctions. A grisly – and inexact – comparison, but important nonetheless.

Table 11.1   Child Malnutrition, 2002

Malnutrition prevalence, weighted for age (% of children under five)

Country Name	%
Bangladesh	43.1
Timor-Leste	40.6
Eritrea	34.5
Djibouti	25.4
Zambia	23.3
Indonesia	23.0
DPRK	17.8
Guatemala	17.7
Algeria	11.1
Uzbekistan	7.1
China	6.8
Uruguay	5.4
Dominican Republic	4.2
Jordan	3.6
Romania	3.5
Jamaica	2.6
Czech Republic	2.1
United States	1.1

Source: 'World Development Indicators 2010', Washington: World Bank, 2010.
Original source: World Health Organization, 'Global Database on Child Growth and Malnutrition'.

Even if the DPRK has been relatively successful in withstanding the onslaught of sanctions (due in no small measure to China), it has still been grievously damaged. Whether that damage has succeeded in destabilisation is, as we have seen, a contested issue. If destabilisation has been successful, then the DPRK will be vulnerable to schism and infighting that will invite intervention, and would reduce the country's will to resist. If sanctions, instead of destabilising North Korea, have produced unity in the face of adversity and hardened resolve, then any invading force will face powerful resistance. That is the theme of the next chapter.

12
The Costs and Consequences of Invasion

If serious war – as opposed, say, to a skirmish at sea – does break out on the Korean peninsula, its primary objective will be the invasion and takeover of the North, the elimination of the DPRK, and the unification of Korea under the nominal sovereignty of the ROK. The ROK would remain subordinate to the United States and its military would continue to remain under American control, perhaps beyond the 2015 deadline. It became ever more evident during the discussion following the *Cheonan* incident that a limited military action was not feasible because the North would counterattack, and that message was reiterated in the Yeonpyeong incident. This, in effect, was a reprise of discussions going back to the 1990s, when a 'surgical strike' was contemplated. For Washington/Seoul, there could be no limited war against Pyongyang: it would have to be all or nothing.[1] That, at least, would be the anticipated scenario, but reality sometimes disappoints.

The costs of such action fall under two headings: financial and military.

THE FINANCIAL COSTS

Kim Dae-jung envisaged a gradual economic coming together of the two Korean economies. Their historic complementarity (agriculture in the south, industry and mining in the north) has been much diminished by 60 years of separate economic development, but complementarities remain – especially in relation to cheap, skilled, Korean-speaking labour in the North, as well as a sizeable potential market for products from the South. If peace did break out, if sanctions and other economic barriers were removed, and if aid, investment and reparations from Japan (disguised as aid) flowed in, it is likely that there would be rapid growth of the North Korean economy and that the South would benefit from this in many ways. The explosive expansion of the mobile phone market is just one example of what can happen when conditions are ripe.[2] As the late President Roh put it on the eve of his summit with Kim Jong Il in 2007,

> When the armistice regime is transformed into a peace regime and when the South and North join hands to bring in a new economic era, the (Korean) Peninsula will certainly become the hub of the Northeast Asian economy.
>
> The South will energetically expand into the Eurasian continent and place itself on the map as the hub of trade in logistics, financial services and business, he said. 'And the North will enjoy an opportunity to achieve epoch-making economic development.'[3]

Costs following an invasion or forced absorption are another matter. What was previously an investment to realise a future business opportunity becomes a burden. If Seoul takes over the North, it also takes over responsibility for feeding and sustaining the populace and for rehabilitating the infrastructure eroded by decades of sanctions. In that sense it would be hoisted by its own petard, being – at least for certain periods – a partner in the economic warfare.

Estimates of the cost of such unification vary, but one in March 2010 put it at $1.7 trillion – nearly twice the ROK's nominal GDP.[4] By September a figure of $3 trillion had been calculated.[5] It seems likely, in such a case, that the Korean peninsula would not become the economic hub of Northeast Asia but an economic waste ground. The German example of two decades of economic (and social) difficulties is frequently cited in comparison.[6]

MILITARY COSTS OF INVASION

The military costs fall under two categories: those of the probable DPRK counteroffensive, and those of the pacification of the North.

Counteroffensive

The DPRK has repeatedly threatened to counterattack (or strike pre-emptively) in the event of an invasion. In recent years it has explicitly mentioned nuclear weapons.

In terms of non-nuclear fighting, there are a number of scenarios that have some currency. Let us take just one. It is rather lurid, and certainly contains some errors, but it is a reasonably authoritative appraisal of what might happen – or at least what the Americans consider might happen. It comes from an article in the *Atlantic* magazine in 2005 describing a 'war game', which was in fact a discussion of the consequences of a US–DPRK war. The participants were senior members of the policy elite, including a lieutenant-general (Thomas McInerney), the president of the Carnegie Endowment for International Peace (Jessica Mathews) and Robert Gallucci, the man who negotiated the Agreed Framework for Bill Clinton.

> North Korea is widely believed to have as many as ten [nuclear weapons] already, and to be producing more every year. (It is also the first developing nation thought to be capable of striking the continental United States with a long-range ballistic missile.) And whereas Iraq did not, after all, have weapons of mass destruction, North Korea is believed to have large stockpiles of chemical weapons (mustard gas, sarin, VX nerve agent) and biological weapons (anthrax, botulism, cholera, hemorrhagic fever, plague, smallpox, typhoid, yellow fever). An actual war on the Korean peninsula would almost certainly be the bloodiest America has fought since Vietnam – possibly since World War II. In recent years Pentagon experts have estimated that the first ninety days of such a conflict might produce 300,000 to 500,000 South Korean and American military casualties, along with hundreds of thousands of civilian deaths. The damage to South Korea alone would rock the global economy.[7]

In reality, the US does not know what chemical and biological warfare capabilities the DPRK has (although we do know that the US has at least anthrax).[8] The failure of the satellite launch in 2009 indicated that – at least at the time – it did not have a rocket that could reach the continental United States, let alone the necessary weaponising and targeting capabilities.[9] In January Defense Secretary Robert Gates talked of the emergence of a North Korean missile threat to the continental US within five years, but this may well have represented politicking aimed at China, rather than a serious assessment.[10] The figure of 300,000 to 500,000 US and ROK military casualties in 90 days seems much too high, although it is frequently reported.

> The commander of American forces in Korea, Gary Luck, told Clinton at a White House briefing in May 1994 that a new Korean war would cost 52,000 American and 490,000 South Korean military casualties, dead and wounded, in the first ninety days as well as incalculable loss of civilian life and physical destruction.[11]

The DPRK has, it is claimed,

> highly trained Special Operations Forces – the North Korean equivalent of Saddam Hussein's elite Republican Guard. Consisting of some 125,000 troops, the SOF may be the largest such force in the world. In the event of a conflict on the peninsula, Gardiner said, we would find ourselves not only engaging these troops along the border but also combating their sneak attacks from the rear.[12]

The SOF are clearly not the equivalent of the Iraqi Republican Guard, but more akin to the British Special Air Service (SAS) and the American Special Operations Command (SOCOM).[13] Exactly how many of the troops would be able to penetrate the South in the event of war is unknown, but clearly the US is concerned enough to devote a special exercise – Foal Eagle – to the possibility. The right-wing *Chosun Ilbo* has been particularly active in running scare stories about North Korea's special forces, although what substance there is to the estimates is unknown.[14] It may be just a ploy to win increased spending for South Korea's Special Forces.

Major DPRK capabilities are artillery and multi-barrel rocket launchers, located along the Demilitarized Zone (DMZ), which can threaten Seoul.[15] One advantage that the DPRK does have is that the border is close to Seoul but quite distant from Pyongyang. There are all sorts of estimates about casualties in Seoul in the event of a Northern barrage, but General McInerney caused a stir during the *Atlantic* magazine war game when he claimed that they could be 'minimized':

> Director of National Intelligence Mathews disagreed that Seoul could be shielded: 'My understanding is that we cannot protect Seoul, at least for the first twenty-four hours of a war, and maybe for the first forty-eight.' McInerney disputed this, and Mathews asked him to explain.
> *McInerney*: 'There's a difference between "protecting" Seoul and [limiting] the amount of damage Seoul may take.'
> *Mathews*: 'There are a hundred thousand Americans in Seoul, not to mention ten million South Koreans.'
> *McInerney*: 'A lot of people are going to die, Jessica. But you still prevail.'
> *Mathews*: 'I just think we've got to be really careful. We've got to protect Seoul. If your daughter were living in Seoul, I don't

think you would feel the US military could protect her in those first twenty-four hours.'

McInerney: 'No, I do. I believe that we have the capability – whether from pre-emption or response – to minimize the casualties in Seoul.'

Mathews: '"Minimize" to roughly what level? A hundred thousand? Two hundred thousand?'

McInerney: 'I think a hundred thousand or less.'[16]

If McInerney has a daughter, she clearly does not live in Seoul. Interestingly, although McInerney at times comes across as a caricature of a blimpish 'cakewalk scenario' general, he is the one that comes out most strongly against invasion because of the difficulty of finding sufficient troops for the pacification of the North.

Pacification

How many troops would the US need? That largely depends on the degree of resistance an invasion would meet. As was shown in Iraq, among many other cases, popular resistance may survive and grow even after formal military opposition is overcome.

While the ostensible reason for the US military presence in South Korea, and for the joint military exercises, is to 'safeguard peace' and 'prevent an invasion from the North', no one in authority actually believes that. The preponderance of US/ROK force is overwhelming, and has been for decades. In fact, there is a tendency to revel in the weakness of the DPRK – US Director of National Intelligence Dennis Blair recently testified to Congress that the North has a 'crumbling military that cannot compete with South Korea [and an] army that struggles with aging weapons, poorly trained, out-of-shape soldiers, inflexible leaders, corruption, low morale and problems with command and control'.[17] The implications of such assessments is that an invasion of the North would be the cakewalk that Iraq and Afghanistan were anticipated to be.[18] However, Blair may well have been wrong in his assessment – and US intelligence does not have a good track record in respect of the DPRK. A recent study by two South Korean academics, Moon Chung-in and Lee Sangkeun had this to say:

The Korea Institute of Defense Analysis is known to have applied the Rand-developed Situation Force Scoring method to assess inter-Korean defense capabilities by taking into account variables such as fire power, mobility, sustainability, training, morale, combat readiness, combat scenarios, and overall terrain. Its findings show that ROK air power is superior to that of North Korea by 103 to 100, whereas naval power (90 vs. 100) and ground power (80 vs. 100) favor the North.[19]

While Moon and Lee express scepticism because of the disparity in equipment, which hugely favours the South, and this assessment unrealistically leaves out the Americans, it does provide some counterbalance to Blair's evaluation.

A common method of coming up with pacification requirement is to ignore niceties such as morale, patriotism and determination, and simply use a straightforward arithmetical calculation based on population size. Paul B. Stares and Joel S. Wit, in a report for the Council on Foreign Relations, came up with some estimates. Firstly, what might be called the 'cakewalk scenario':

> How large a force would be required to bring security and stability to North Korea would depend on the level of acquiescence to foreign intervention. Based on previous experiences elsewhere, the rule of thumb for the number of troops required for successful stability operations in a *permissive environment* is somewhere between five and ten per thousand people. Because North Korea has a population of approximately twenty-three million, a successful operation could require between 115,000 to 230,000 military personal [sic]. In addition, tens of thousands of police might also be needed to support these forces in more basic tasks.[20]

But, they add, permission might not be forthcoming:

> If former elements of the North Korean military, its security and intelligence forces, or its large special operations force were to resist the presence of foreign forces, the size of the needed stabilization force would escalate dramatically. Indeed, experience has shown that special operations forces are the most likely candidates to mount such resistance. Given the large number of such units in the North, the challenge could be considerable. In an insurgency, according to one Defense Science Board study, as many as twenty occupying troops are needed for every thousand persons, implying a force of 460,000 troops, more than three times the number of American troops in Iraq. Coping with such

a contingency would likely be impossible for the South Korean and American forces [alone].[21]

They do not suggest who might provide the additional troops. The Japanese? The British? There are no likely contenders.

The Stossel article came up with the 500,000 troops required, presumably using the same calculation.[22] A further study was reported at the beginning of 2010 by veteran Asia reporter, Donald Kirk. This was apparently conducted at the RAND Institute by analyst Bruce Bennett and Jennifer Lind, from Dartmouth College. The report does not seem to have been published by RAND, but we do have an illuminating description by Kirk of a presentation by Lind at the Center for Strategic and International Studies in Washington. Kirk's report does not offer much in the way of new information. The figures he quotes for the 'number of troops needed to subdue North Korea' is appreciably smaller than the nearly 500,000 given elsewhere, but presumably relies on the same sort of arithmetical calculation. What is interesting, and worrying, is the insouciance, carelessness and moral detachment it reveals, and which seems to take even Kirk aback:

'We don't envision large-scale organized resistance by the North Korean military,' she told a meeting at the Center for Strategic and International Studies in Washington. Nor, said Lind, in what presumably was an understatement, should anyone 'assume everyone in North Korea would welcome US forces' ...

Pressed to describe the legality of the deployment that she was suggesting, Lind acknowledged, 'There's no getting around it, this is an invasion of North Korea' in which 'we're sending military forces into a country that doesn't want you to come.'[23]

The idea of planning to invade a country that has been on a fairly constant war footing since the last time you were at war with them 60 years ago, on the assumption that there would be no 'large-scale organised resistance' seems somewhat over-confident. It is not without precedent. Both Napoleon and Hitler underestimated the difficulties of invading Russia, as did George W. Bush in respect of Iraq and Afghanistan.

Obviously the United States would expect the ROK to provide most of the troops, fill most of the body bags, and administer the conquered territory, under high-level US tutelage or control. The US would exercise direct control of the seizure of nuclear and

WMD capabilities, and presumably other assets it considers too valuable to fall into Korean hands. Lessons learned, it is claimed, in the pacification of Iraq and Afghanistan would be applied to Korea.[24] However, as the invasions of Iraq and Afghanistan demonstrated, plans to use others to do the fighting don't necessarily work. Opposition to the invasion of the North would surely grow in the South, perhaps to explosive levels, if casualties began to become substantial.

Lessons in wars are not confined to one side. One of the most significant weapons developed by the resistance in Iraq and Afghanistan have been improvised explosive devices – IEDs – and the US commander in Korea, General Walter Sharp, has warned that these will be employed by the Koreans.[25]

The preponderance of military power is clearly, and hugely, in the Americans' favour, but many wars – Vietnam, Iraq, Afghanistan – demonstrate that that alone does not guarantee success. As Bruce Cumings observes, 'For decades the South has towered over the North in military equipment; its current defense budget is greater than the North's annual GNP'; however, there is a 'fear among insiders that North Korean soldiers are much tougher than their southern counterparts'.[26] One of the games that tourists play at Panmunjom is comparing the relative sizes of the Southern and Northern soldiers; the Southerners, having been brought up on a hormone-enhanced diet are much larger than the Northerners, who have a traditional, and in recent years probably an inadequate diet, but look very tough and wiry. From personal observation in both Koreas, I think that Cumings' 'insiders' are correct, and agree that Northerners are tougher and more resilient. In addition, they would have the 'home player' advantage: defending your territory against an invader tends to strengthen motivation; and motivation would be a key factor in any drawn-out struggle. It is frequently reported that the younger generation of South Koreans is not interested in unification in the way their parents and grandparents were.[27] Yet these are the very people who would be expected to do the fighting in an invasion of the North. A survey conducted in 2006 by the *Korea Times* found that 48 per cent of youth 'would support N. Korea in case of US attack'.[28] Whether this level of support has changed, and how it would translate into action, are of course unknown, but the survey does suggest that young South Korean men might not be willing cannon fodder. This assumption was reinforced by a further survey carried out by the [South] Korea Institute for Defense Analyses in June 2010:

About four out of every 10 youngsters here said they would seek refuge further south from the border if a second Korean war broke out, a survey showed Wednesday. Only 15.5 percent said they would join the army to fight ...

They were also lukewarm toward unification through war. Nearly 60 percent of teens and 72.3 percent of those in their 20s said the South should absorb the North even if it involves a long war.

The portion rose to 76.3 percent among 30-somethings, 82.5 percent for those in their 40s and 85.8 percent among 50-somethings.[29]

The 15.5 percent who said they would join up were presumably thinking in terms of a defensive war on South Korean soil, as were the 40 percent who said they would move south, away from the border, or even abroad. How these attitudes can be reconciled with reported support for a 'unification war' is unclear, but it seems likely that if only 15.5 per cent were willing to join up for a defensive war, then an offensive one would attract less willing participation. Of course, in the event, they would have little choice, and would be conscripted; but their morale might well be low, and would likely sink further if the war in the north were protracted. On the other hand, a recent assessment of the North Korean football team does indicate the problems invaders might face:

Teamwork is the theme that runs through the North Korean side. The forwards sacrifice their attacking instincts and put the team first. This is a side with no egos and one that has been together for years with a collective spirit that is likely to be unmatched elsewhere.[30]

While it would be unwise to extrapolate from the elite football team to a mass army, some observers, at least, see the signs of social solidarity and cohesion in North Korea that could lead to firm and protracted resistance. Karin Janz of the German aid agency Welthungerhilfe commented after five years on the ground in the DPRK that 'patriotism runs high among the people and most have full faith in their leaders'.[31] To what degree one can give credence to a foreigner on such matters is uncertain, but she did have more experience in North Korea than virtually any other foreigner has had, so her opinion has some value.

But the North Koreans themselves are only part of the problem that the Americans, and the South Korean government, would encounter. Returning to Donald Kirk and his report on the Lind presentation:

> Yet another issue was the likely response of China, North Korea's ally ever since Chinese troops defended the North from advancing US and South Korean forces in the Korean War. The Chinese, as Bruce Klingner, a former Central Intelligence Agency analyst now with the conservative Heritage Foundation, noted: 'Do not want to talk about any contingency planning.'
>
> Lind seemed to think that somehow it would be possible to 'reassure China' that US and South Korean forces were not there to challenge China.
>
> It was as though the lessons of the Chinese role in the Korean War – and China's focus on insuring the stability of the North Korean regime against collapse – were no longer relevant.[32]

The Chinese reaction to an invasion of North Korea adds another hugely momentous dimension to the invasion scenario.

13
The China Factor: Into the Abyss?

THE CHINA FACTOR

The Chinese reaction is frequently mentioned in discussions of the intervention, as well it might be. Some, such as Jennifer Lind, blithely skirt around it and claim that the Chinese will be understanding about the US doing now what it was prevented by the Chinese from doing in the 1950s. Others, such as Bruce Klingner, refer to veiled Chinese warnings.[1]

Kenneth Quinones, a former State Department official familiar with Korean affairs, claims that the US and China have an informal agreement that neither will intervene in North Korea, and that, moreover, the US 'has assured China that the [it] will not supply [or] provide military or diplomatic support for any South Korean intervention in North Korea'.[2]

At first thought, it might be considered that the possibility of getting into another land war with China would sound the death-knell for any serious discussion in Washington, or Seoul, of invading North Korea. However the 'coming war with China' has a fairly substantial, and vociferous, constituency in America.[3] Every year since 2002 the Department of Defense has submitted a report to Congress on the 'Military Power of the People's Republic of China'.[4] It seems likely that there are those in the Pentagon and elsewhere who must consider that, if a war with China is inevitable, then the sooner it takes place the better. Similarly, if war is on its way, it would be sensible to have it in a place of one's choosing than to leave that to fate, or to the enemy.

War on the Korean peninsula would have the huge advantage for the US that it would automatically bring in the ROK military, one of the largest and best-equipped in the world. It might also bring in the Japanese. The Japanese armed forces have not been tested since 1945, but Japan's military expenditure ($46.3 billion in 2008) is twice that of South Korea ($24.2 billion). Both countries are of course well behind the United States in expenditure ($607 billion), as well as virtually all other measures of military might, but their combined expenditure is not far short of China's $84.9 billion.[5]

Moreover, whereas the United States has other wars it is fighting or needs to be prepared for around the world, South Korea and Japan could concentrate on China. So they would make a very valuable contribution to a US war with China.

In other words, for an American military strategist contemplating a war with China, this would be the place to have it start.

A CONFLUENCE LEADING TO WAR?

If war does break out in Korea, it will be not because of one particular factor, but a confluence of them. It is frequently said that no one wants war in Korea, and that – excepting the hypothetical military strategist above – is probably true. However, the same thing was said in 1914, and on countless other thresholds. What this book has sought to demonstrate is that there is a confluence of factors which might produce war.

The Challenges Facing Kim Jong Il

Kim Jong Il is faced with huge, existential challenges. Most books involving North Korea tend to put it in the centre, with talk of the 'North Korean nuclear problem' or the 'North Korean threat'. The reality is that the DPRK is a very small player, with little power and modest objectives – it wants to survive, it wants peace, and it wants prosperity. If there is a threat to peace in Northeast Asia it comes about not because of the DPRK (other than by its very existence), but because of the interplay of stronger forces. DPRK policy is essentially reactive, with little freedom of action.

If we are to understand what is going on, and what might happen, we need to look not to Pyongyang, but to where power resides – in Seoul, in Washington, and in Beijing.

Lee Myung-bak's Ambition

It is clear that Lee Myung-bak has a dream of uniting the Korean peninsula under his leadership. He has spoken of a 'Greater Republic of Korea' and proposed a 'unification tax' to cover the cost of absorbing the North: 'He said that reunification is a certainty, and that he thought that the time had come to prepare practical plans, such as a reunification tax in preparation for the day when it occurred.'[6] In public he has spoken of a 'three-stage unification plan – peace community, economic community and national community', but his actions give the lie to that camouflage.[7] Since he came to office, inter-Korean relations have plummeted, and there is no sign of a 'peace community' on the horizon. That might have been believable as an objective in the days of Kim Dae-jung and Roh Moo-hyun, but not in the days of Lee Myung-bak.

On the contrary, especially since the fabrication of the *Cheonan* sinking, the emphasis has been on confrontation and the build-up of tension, in the belief, as Jeong Seok-gu of the *Hankyoreh* put it, 'that if our government continues to apply pressure on North Korea, military tensions may flare in the short term, but before long the North Korean regime will collapse'.[8] What is anticipated with this 'collapse' has a number of versions. Here is one, not atypical, from Sung-Yoon Lee, a South Korean academic in the US, writing in the Washington journal *Foreign Policy*:

Although Kim's exit will certainly be cause to celebrate, it won't inevitably lead to a happy result; in fact, it could usher in a period of instability that triggers a regime collapse culminating in the unification of the two Koreas, a possibility that will require far more US involvement than President Barack Obama and his advisors may realize.

By its mere existence, Seoul poses an omnipresent existential threat to Pyongyang.

What's less commonly known is that the United States has done little to prepare for life after Kim Jong Il. It's true that US and South Korean officials have been quietly discussing a contingency plan for a drastic change in North Korea, dubbed OPLAN 5029 by the Pentagon. But beyond short-term emergency response measures such as securing the North's stockpiles of weapons of mass destruction, maintaining public safety, controlling borders, and providing humanitarian aid to displaced North Koreans, making plans for dealing with an alternative post-Kim Korea over the long term is critical to protecting US strategic interests in that vital region of the world. In view of America's political, economic, and human investment in South Korea and Northeast Asia over the past 65 years, it is also a moral imperative.

A power vacuum in Pyongyang will require the immediate dispatch of South Korean and US troops. Next will come other regional powers – Chinese peacekeeping forces securing the northern areas, followed by the Japanese Maritime Self-Defense Force transporting people and supplies along the Korean coastlines.[9]

There is clearly a mix of fantasising and foolishness in this scenario. One cannot imagine any foreign troops being readily accepted (and foreign here includes South Korean), but the Japanese would be the least welcome. And the thought of the Americans and Chinese happily cooperating on the dismemberment of North Korea is bizarre – and characteristic of those who want to invade North Korea but do not want to contemplate Chinese objections, or the possibility of war.

However, there is a dreadful logic to this train of thought. If you are not going to have peaceful reunification along the lines imagined by Kim Jae-jung and Roh Moo-hyun, if you are going to bank on collapse and are seeking to bring that about, then, if collapse occurs, it brings its own imperatives of necessity and opportunity. The collapse strategy is a slippery slope on which the actors, once embarked, have less and less control. Events may well take over.

Another driving factor is that time is running short for Lee Myung-bak, and perhaps for his confrontational policies. His term of office comes to an end in 2012. Many South Koreans oppose the policies of confrontation. Young South Koreans were not brought up under the indoctrination of the Cold War and the military dictatorships, and are turning away from the politics of those times.

US Decline and Strategic Paralysis

Although the United States is the imperial power and the Republic of Korea the client state, Lee Myung-bak does seem, at the moment at least, to be driving US Korea policy. This is in large measure because he knows what he wants; the United States, on the other hand, is in a state of strategic paralysis and is far from clear what it wants. This may change: there may be a shift of forces in Washington, perhaps propelled by a crisis in another part of the world, and it will be decided that Lee's course is too dangerous, or in conflict with wider objectives, and he will be restrained. Ultimately power lies with Washington. South Korea cannot invade the North on its own.

This strategic paralysis is a product of a number of factors I have talked about: the decline of the United States and the rise of China; the imbroglio in the Middle East, with no obvious way out; the Obama administration, exhilarated by its rhetoric but bereft of real power and drive to bring about change. All this is exacerbated by a long-standing and increasing infatuation with militarisation and its associated policies.

It is not surprising, then, that Lee Myung-bak seems attractive to Obama and his administration. Lee is driven and purposeful.

He is muscular. Supporting him means standing up to China and displaying strength. How much calculation there is in current US strategy is a puzzle. Is there an awareness of what is happening and where it may lead? Lee's gamble makes sense. If he pulls it off, he will go down in history as the man who succeed where Kim Il Sung failed – the man who reunified Korea. There are no such glittering prizes for Obama.

China's Dilemma

Finally, China's dilemma: how to cope with US resistance to its peaceful rise. This is now compounded by Lee's ambitions for Korea, which may bring things to a crisis. China and the United States compete, and cooperate, in many fields of endeavour and many parts of the world. Any of those contact points has the potential to become a scene of confrontation, and worse. In the past, it used to be thought that if there was to be a trigger for a US–China clash, it would be Taiwan. With the improvement of cross-straits relations between Beijing and Taipei in recent years, that prospect has faded, to be replaced by the situation in Korea. It might be argued that the confrontation between the United States and China is so deep-rooted that if there were not a crisis over Taiwan, or Korea, it would happen somewhere else. The crisis is often seen as a product of underlying tensions that must surface somewhere. There is truth in that, but the Korean situation has its own specific dynamics which may bring the two countries into conflict.

If a conflict over Korea can be avoided, then there is a good possibility that there will not be one elsewhere, and we may move to a world beyond American hegemony, in which Chinese ascendancy is accepted and is exercised relatively peacefully. Paradoxically, for that to happen and for the Korean situation to be defused before it gets out of hand, China will have to be more assertive and make it clear that it will not tolerate the invasion or destruction of North Korea.

STEPPING STONES TO AN UNCERTAIN FUTURE

The post-American world, and the role within it of China and other emerging powers, is a subject of huge importance and intense debate. The subject of the decline of the United States and the rise of China has been touched upon in this book, but there is much more to be said.[10] There are two issues here. If it does happen – and while the trends are clear there is no inevitability about it – will the transfer of primacy be peaceful? A theme of this book has been that the crisis in Korea may be a test of that. If the Korean situation is resolved peacefully then the chances of a Sino-American conflict elsewhere are reduced. If, on the other hand, there is a physical confrontation, or worse, between the two in Korea, then obviously it would exacerbate relations between the two countries on a global scale, with unpredictable consequences.

However, even if we get through this particular crisis, that does not mean that a bright future is assured. Far from it. A contested transfer of primacy from the United States to China will certainly make a world of Chinese ascendancy tense, bitter and belligerent. However, a peaceful transfer offers no guarantees about the allocation and exercise of power. A world of multi-polarity, where China is ascendant, but not overly dominant, and the United States plays a positive role consistent with the best of its history, would be the most desirable outcome. We know that the United States sought the unwise – and unobtainable – holy grail of full-spectrum dominance; it may be that China will be seduced along that path. The future is full of uncertainties, and all we can do is to press for solutions which offer the best possibilities for peace and prosperity.

In the meantime, perhaps we should observe Deng Xiaoping's adage about crossing the river one stone at a time. We do not know what the future holds, but we can still attempt to handle current events in a peaceful way because war breeds war, and bitterness engenders further bitterness. There are huge dangers and challenges in the contemporary world, and turmoil in the Middle East (for good and bad) and the war against the Gaddafi government in Libya tend to capture the headlines and overshadow events in Korea. However, the crisis in Korea is a very important stepping stone, and a slip here would have catastrophic ramifications, for this stone is where the waters of America and China, and other powerful countries, join and intermingle.

Notes

PART I

1. Associated Press, 'Wikileaks reveals plans for North Korean collapse', *Washington Post*, 30 November 2010.
2. Misinterpretation is a major issue in cross-cultural dialogue, whether in politics, business or love. We do not know in which languages these various conversations took place, or whether there were professional interpreters present. Discussions between people in a lingua franca – say, English – in which they are not completely fluent and fully aware of nuances, are especially liable to create misunderstanding.

1   IMPERIALISM, NATIONALISM, AND THE DIVISION AND REUNIFICATION OF KOREA

1. Michael Hastings, 'The Runaway General', *Rolling Stone*, 22 June 2010.
2. 'KOREA: The Walnut', *Time*, 9 March 1953.
3. 'Evidence of Park Chung-hee's Military Allegiance to Japan Surfaces', *Hankyoreh*, 6 November 2009.
4. Bruce Cumings, Francis M. Bator, Richard J. Bernstein and Richard Bernstein, 'The Korean War: An Exchange,' *New York Review of Books*, 22 November 2007.
5. I. F. Stone, *The Secret History of the Korean War*, New York: Monthly Review Press, 1952.
6. Richard J. Bernstein and Richard Bernstein, 'Good War Gone Bad (Review of *The Coldest Winter: America and the Korean War* by David Halberstam)', *New York Review of Books*, 25 October 2007.
7. Ibid.
8. 'N. Korea's War History Is Mirror Opposite World View', *Chosun Ilbo*, 24 June 2010; 'DPRK Committees Release Joint Statement on 60 Years after Korean War', *KCNA*, 24 June 2010.
9. Bruce Cumings, Francis M. Bator, Richard J. Bernstein and Richard Bernstein, 'The Korean War: An Exchange', *New York Review of Books*, 22 November 2007.
10. Jae-Jung Suh, 'Confronting War, Colonialism, and Intervention in the Asia Pacific', *Critical Asian Studies* 42: 4, 2011.
11. The very important role of the frequent joint US–ROK military exercises in laying the foundation for an invasion of the north is described in Chapter 10.
12. Sewell Chan and Jackie Calmes, 'US Keeps Command of Military in Seoul', *New York Times*, 26 June 2010; 'S. Korea, US Reschedule Wartime Operational Control Transfer', *Korea Herald*, 27 June 2010.
13. 'Experts Address Misconceptions about OPCON Transfer', *Hankyoreh*, 25 June 2010.

14. 'European Parliament Resolution of 17 June 2010 on the Situation in the Korean Peninsula', 17 June 2010; 'The DP Needs to Grow Up', *Chosun Ilbo*, 18 June 2010.

15. Georgy Toloraya, 'Peace or War? Do We Have to Choose?: A Russian Perspective', 38North.org, 27 May 2010.

16. 'FM Accuses US of Creating Atmosphere of International Pressure', *KCNA*, 28 May 2010.

17. Alexander Vorontsov and Oleg Revenko, 'The Conundrum of the South Korean Corvette (II)', *International Affairs*, 4 June 2010.

18. Min-seok Kim and Myo-ja Ser, 'US will command military exercise', *JoongAng Ilbo*, 17 June 2010; Peter Lee, 'Short Shelf Life for China–US Reset', *Asia Times Online*, 8 June 2010.

19. The role of sanctions, broadly defined to include the military threat, is discussed in Chapter 11.

20. Robert Carlin and John W. Lewis, 'What North Korea Really Wants', *Washington Post*, 27 January 2007.

21. François Lequiller and Derek Blades, *Understanding National Accounts*, Paris: OECD, 2006.

22. Eun-joo Lee, 'Six Decades Later, the North–South Gap Grows', *JoongAng Ilbo*, 26 June 2010.

23. 'KCNA on Tremendous Damage Done to DPRK by US', *KCNA*, 24 June 2010.

24. 'Uninterrupted Advance Toward Thriving Nation Called For', *KCNA*, 3 May 2010.

25. Peter James Spielmann, 'Carter: If No Palestine, Israel Sees "Catastrophe"', *Associated Press*, 26 January 2009.

2   KOREA AND THE POSTCOLONIAL WORLD

1. Nick Turse, 'Black Sites in the Empire of Bases', *Asia Times* online, 11 February 2010.

2. 'The United Nations and Decolonization', available at <www.un.org/Depts/dpi/decolonization/main.htm>.

3. Roy Richard Grinker, *Korea and its Futures: Unification and the Unfinished War*, New York: St Martin's Press, 1998.

4. Min-seok Kim and Myo-ja Ser, 'Just a Reminder: Seoul's Cruise Missiles', *JoongAng Ilbo*, 8 July 2006.

5. 'F-22 Fighter Jets Emblazoned with the Rising Sun', *Chosun Ilbo*, 27 April 2007.

6. 'Korea's Neighbors Catch Up with US Stealth Technology', *Chosun Ilbo*, 9 August 2010.

7. Richard F. Grimmett, 'Conventional Arms Transfers to Developing Nations, 2002–2009', *Congressional Research Service*, 10 September 2010.

8. Yoichi J. Dreazen and Amol Sharma, 'US Sells Arms to South Asian Rivals', *Wall Street Journal*, 25 February 2010.

9. Mark Thompson, 'There's No Business Like the Arms Business', *Time*, 14 September 2010.

10. Ibid.

11. Written and premiered in 1905.

12. Christopher Drew and Nicola Clark, 'BAE Settles Corruption Charges', *New York Times*, 5 February 2010.

13. 'Foreign Corrupt Practices Act', US Department of Justice, available at <www.justice.gov/criminal/fraud/fcpa>.

14. Thompson, 'There's No Business Like the Arms Business'.

15. John Feffer, 'Ploughshares into Swords: Economic Implications of South Korean Military Spending', *Korea Economic Institute Academic Paper Series* 3, 2009.

16. Sung-ki Jung, 'Uncertainty Clouds Prospects of Korean Fighter Plans', *Korea Times*, 24 March 2010.

17. 'Dassault Folds Tent, Swears Off Korea', *JoongAng Ilbo*, 6 June 2002.

18. 'Fighter's Crash: Though Time-Consuming, Thorough Probes Are Needed', *Korea Times*, 9 June 2006.

19. Jae-Jung Suh, 'Allied to Race? The US–Korea Alliance and Arms Race', *Asian Perspective* 33: 4, 2009 – emphasis added.

20. Sung-ki Jung, 'S. Korea May Join US Missile Shield', *Defense News*, 17 February 2010; Elaine M. Grossman, 'Cost to Test US Global-Strike Missile Could Reach $500 Million', *Global Security Newswire*, 15 March 2010.

21. Se-jeong Kim, 'Is NK the Biggest Threat to Americans?', *Korea Times*, 7 July 2009.

22. Tae-ho Kwon, 'S. Korea and US Chart New Path Following End of Iraq Combat Mission', *Hankyoreh*, 2 September 2010.

23. Martin Fackler and Mark Landler, 'Ties to US Played Role in Downfall of Japanese Leader', *New York Times*, 2 June 2010; Jitsuro Terashima, 'The US–Japan Alliance Must Evolve: The Futenma Flip-Flop, the Hatoyama Failure, and the Future,' *Asia-Pacific Journal* 32–4–10, 9 August 2010.

24. 'S. Korea Prepares for Face-to-Face Negotiations', *Hankyoreh*, 9 August 2007.

25. 'Lee Government Must Cancel Troop Redeployment to Afghanistan', *Hankyoreh*, 31 October 2009; 'Troop Dispatch to Afghanistan Is No Military Adventure', *Chosun Ilbo*, 2 November 2009.

26. Jae-hoon Lee, 'Clinton Announces New Sanctions against N. Korea', *Hankyoreh*, 22 July 2010; Doo-hyong Hwang, 'Korea's Troop Deployment in Afghanistan Serves Korea's National Interest: Scholar', *Yonhap*, 4 January 2010.

27. 'Gov't Must Tell Muslim World of Ashena Unit's Mission of Peace', *Chosun Ilbo*, 1 July 2010.

28. 'South Korean Companies Face Increasing Attacks in Afghanistan', *Hankyoreh*, 12 November 2009.

29. 'Lee Announces Expanded International Role for Military', *Hankyoreh*, 28 September 2009.

30. Rick Rozoff, 'Afghanistan: North Atlantic Military Bloc's Ten-Year War In South Asia', *Global Research*, 1 September 2010.

31. Troy Stangarone, 'Korea's Conundrum: Dealing with US Sanctions on Iran', *Korea Insight*, 3 September 2010.

32. Christian Oliver and Najmeh Bozorgmehr, 'S. Korea Ban Ends Tehran's Kia Imports', *Financial Times*, 13 September 2010.

33. 'N. Korea's GNI is One One-Hundreth of that of S. Korea', *Hankyoreh*, 12 March 2010. See also Eun-joo Lee, 'Six Decades Later, the North–South Gap Grows', *JoongAng Ilbo*, 26 June 2010.

34. Joseph Sang-Hoon Chung, *The North Korean Economy: Structure and Development*, Stanford, CA: Hoover Institution Press, 1974.

35. Christopher Hellman, 'Putting the Pentagon on a Diet,' *TomDispatch*, 20 May 2010.

36. Chung, *North Korean Economy*.

37. Robert Ash, 'Review of The North Korean Economy: Structure and Development. By Joseph Sang-Hoon Chung', *China Quarterly* 60, 1974.

38. Ibid.

39. Tim Beal, *North Korea: The Struggle Against American Power* (London and Ann Arbor: Pluto Press, 2005).

40. Chalmers Johnson, 'The Guns of August: Lowering the Flag on the American Century', *TomDispatch*, 17 August 2010. Chalmers Johnson has extended his original designation from Japan to South Korea and Dengist China, but would probably baulk at North Korea. However, essentially the term fits North Korea.

41. '"Iron Silkroad" to Connect Korean Peninsula and Europe Envisaged', *Yonhap*, 16 June 2000.

42. David I. Steinberg, 'Development Lessons from the Korean Experience – A Review Article', *Journal of Asian Studies* 42: 1, 1982.

43. 'South Korea: Country Study', Federal Research Divison, Library of Congress, 27 July 2010 – emphasis added.

44. Steinberg, 'Development Lessons from the Korean Experience'.

45. Mark E. Manyin, 'Japan–North Korea Relations: Selected Issues', Washington: Congressional Research Service, 2003.

46. Marshall I. Goldman, 'A Balance Sheet of Soviet Foreign Aid', *Foreign Affairs* 43: 2, 1965.

47. Joungwon Alexander Kim, 'Soviet Policy in North Korea', *World Politics* 22: 2, 1970.

48. Charles Armstrong, 'The Destruction and Reconstruction of North Korea, 1950–1960', *Asia-Pacific Journal* 8: 51, 2, 2010.

49. Kim, 'Soviet Policy in North Korea'.

50. Ibid.

51. Hazel Smith, *Hungry For Peace: International Security, Humanitarian Assistance, and Social Change in North Korea*, Washington, DC: United States Institute of Peace, 2005.

52. Michael A. Levi, *Deterring State Sponsorship of Nuclear Terrorism*, Washington, DC: Council on Foreign Relations Press, 2008; Michael A. Levi, *On Nuclear Terrorism,* Washington, DC: Harvard University Press for Council on Foreign Relations, 2007; Charles D. Ferguson, *Preventing Catastrophic Nuclear Terrorism*, Washington, DC: Council on Foreign Relations, 2006.

53. 'DPRK Stance towards Terrorist Attacks on US', *KCNA*, 12 September 2001; Young-jin Oh and Key-young Son, 'N.K. Sent US Private Cable on Anti-Terrorism', *Korea Times*, 23 September 2001; 'DPRK Signs Anti-Terror Conventions', *People's Korea*, 13 December 2001; 'DPRK Ready to Join 5 More Anti-Terror Pacts', *People's Korea*, 25 December 2001.

54. Jeff Stein, 'Wikileaks Documents: N. Korea Sold Missiles to al-Qaeda, Taliban', *Washington Post*, 26 July 2010.

55. Song-wu Park, 'KAL Bombing Constant Source of Dispute', *Korea Times*, 11 July 2004.

56. Tetsuo Kotani, 'Tip of the Spear: The 13 Missions for US Marines in Okinawa', *PacNet* 43, 2010.

3   THE COLLAPSE OF THE SOVIET UNION AND NORTH KOREA'S 'ARDUOUS MARCH'

1. Charles Whelan, 'North Korea: A Living, Breathing Stalinist State', *Sydney Morning Herald*, 5 March 2003.
2. Bruce Cumings, 'Fear and Loathing on the Pyongyang Trail: North Korea and the United States', *Japan Focus*, 12 December 2005.
3. Syng-il Hyun, 'Industrialization and Industrialism in a Developing Socialist Country: Convergence Theory and the Case of North Korea', PhD Thesis, Utah State University, 1982.
4. Ruediger Frank, 'Can Economic Theory Demystify North Korea?', *Korea Review of International Studies* 9: 1, 2006.
5. Hyun, 'Industrialization and Industrialism', p. 213.
6. 'FAO/WFP Crop and Food Supply Assessment Mission to the Democratic People's Republic of Korea', Rome: Food and Agriculture Organization/World Food Programme, 1998.
7. Kisan Gunjal, Swithun Goodbody, Joyce Kanyangwa Luma and Rita Bhatia, 'FAO/WFP Crop and Food Security Assessment Mission to the Democratic People's Republic of Korea', Rome: Food and Agriculture Organization of the United Nations, 16 November 2010.
8. Nathaniel Aden, 'North Korean Trade with China as Reported in Chinese Customs Statistics: Recent Energy Trends and Implications', in *DPRK Energy Experts Working Group Meeting*, San Francisco: Nautilus Institute, 2006.
9. Keith B. Richburg, 'In Chinese Border Town, Trade with North Korea Can Be Lucrative but Problematic', *Washington Post*, 26 November 2010; 'Over 600,000 N. Koreans starve from 1995–2005', *Hankyoreh*, 23 November 2010.
10. Hazel Smith, *Hungry for Peace: International Security, Humanitarian Assistance, and Social Change in North Korea*, Washington, DC: United States Institute of Peace, 2005.
11. *2008 Population Census National Report*, Pyongyang: Central Bureau of Statistics, 2009, available at <unstats.un.org/unsd/demographic/sources/census/2010_PHC/North_Korea/Final%20national%20census%20report.pdf>.
12. In addition to those cited above, see also 'N. Korea's Youth Population Dwindles Due to Food Shortage', *Chosun Ilbo*, 6 December 2010; Ji-sook Bae, 'Seoul Not Safe from Artillery Attacks', *Korea Times*, 26 November 2010; 'Extent of NK Damage Remains Uncertain', *Chosun Ilbo*, 26 November 2010.
13. Tim Lister, 'North Korea's Military Aging but Sizable', *CNN*, 25 November 2010; 'Korean People's Army Estimated to Number 700 Thousand Troops', *Hankyoreh*, 19 March 2010.
14. Chang Jae Lee, 'Trade and Investment in North Korea', in *Future Multilateral Economic Cooperation With the Democratic People's Republic of Korea*, The Stanley Foundation in cooperation with the German Council on Foreign Relations (DGAP), 2005.
15. 'Exchanges & Cooperation', ROK Ministry of Unification, at <eng.unikorea.go.kr/eng/default.jsp?pgname=AFFexchanges_overview>; '2005 White Paper on Korean Unification', ROK Ministry of Unification, 2005.
16. See Statistical Appendix, Table A1.
17. Amelia Gentleman, 'US Senate Vote on Nuclear Deal Draws Guarded Praise by India', *New York Times*, 17 November 2006; Dafna Linzer, 'Senate Backs White House Plan for India Nuclear Deal', *Washington Post*, 17 November

2006; Thom Shanker, 'Nuclear Deal with India Wins Senate Backing', *New York Times*, 17 November 2006.

18. Statistical Appendix, Table A3.

19. Tim Beal, 'Multilayered confrontation in East Asia: North Korea–Japan', *Asian Affairs* 36: 3, 2005.

20. Jonathan D. Pollack, 'The United States, North Korea, and the End of the Agreed Framework', *Naval War College Review* LVI: 3, 2003.

21. Leon V. Sigal, 'Looking for Leverage in All the Wrong Places', *38 North: US–Korea Institute at SAIS*, Johns Hopkins University, 1 May 2010.

22. Eun-joo Lee, 'Six Decades Later, the North-South Gap Grows', *JoongAng Ilbo*, 26 June 2010.

23. Kaesong is also spelled Gaesong. Jin-joo Eoh, 'Inter-Korean Trade Through Gaesong Industrial Park Increases in 2010', *Arirang*, 22 December 2010; Seung-hyun Jung, 'Inter-Korean Trade Rose Despite New Sanctions', *JoongAng Ilbo*, 30 September 2010. Note that the December report contains a misprint – 'million' for 'billion'.

24. 'Investors in DPRK Take Huge Hits; Interest in FDI Plummets', *Institute for Far Eastern Studies*, 18 October 2010.

25. Young Chul Chung, 'Political Economy of the US Economic Sanctions against North Korea: Past, Present and Future', *Development and Society* 34: 2, 2005.

26. Tim Beal, 'The United Nations and the North Korean Missile and Nuclear Tests', *NZ Journal of Asian Studies* 9: 2, 2007.

4   THE RISE OF CHINA AND THE DECLINE OF AMERICA

1. Thailand was also never formally a colony, but because of its relatively small size and its neo-colonial status, it does not have the significance of China.

2. 'Discussion at the 150th meeting of the National Security Council (Presidential memo)', *White House*, 19 June 1953.

3. James P. Warburg, 'United States Postwar Policy in Asia', *Annals of the American Academy of Political and Social Science* 318, 1958; Joseph S. Clark, 'An American Policy toward Communist China', *Annals of the American Academy of Political and Social Science* 330, 1960; Edgar Snow and Shao-Chang Hsu, 'Recognition of the People's Republic of China', *Annals of the American Academy of Political and Social Science* 324, 1959; Harold M. Vinacke, 'United States Policy towards China: An Appraisal', *Far Eastern Survey* 29: 5, 1960.

4. Hugh White, 'Power Shift: Australia's Future between Washington and Beijing', *Quarterly Essay* 39, 2010.

5. Ralph Cossa, 'Fears of New "Nixon shock"', *Japan Times*, 25 May 2007.

6. Yong-hyun Ahn, 'The Country Needs True Independence', *Chosun Ilbo*, 19 July 2010; 'Is There Really No Rift Between Seoul and Washington?', *Chosun Ilbo*, 9 October 2009.

7. Gerald Segal, 'China and the Great Power Triangle', *China Quarterly* 83 (1980); Stanley Karnow, 'East Asia in 1978: The Great Transformation', *Foreign Affairs* 57: 3, 1978.

8. Arvind Subramanian, 'Is China Already Number One? New GDP Estimates', *East Asia Forum*, 3 February 2011.

9. Craig VanGrasstek, 'The Benefits of US–China Trade in Services', *United States Council Foundation*, July 2006.

10. Daniel J. Ikenson, 'Thriving in a Global Economy: The Truth about US Manufacturing and Trade', *Cato Institute*, 28 August 2007; Paul Craig Roberts, 'Blinded by Ideology: Cato, Trade and Outsourcing', *Counterpunch*, 9 October 2007; David Chen, 'China Emerges as a Scapegoat in Campaign Ads', *New York Times*, 9 October 2010.

11. Shengxia Song, 'Moon Landing Gets Timetable', *Global Times*, 20 September 2010; Ian Sample, 'Lunar Eclipse: US Retreat Leaves China Leading Way in Race to Return to Moon', *Guardian*, 2 February 2010.

12. Kendra Marr, 'As Detroit Crumbles, China Emerges as Auto Epicenter', *Washington Post*, 18 May 2009; Keith Bradsher, 'Ford Agrees to Sell Volvo to a Fast-Rising Chinese Company', *New York Times*, 28 March 2010; 'The Rise of China's Auto Industry and Its Impact on the US Motor Vehicle Industry', *Congressional Research Service*, 16 November 2009.

13. Keith Bradsher, 'China Leading Global Race to Make Clean Energy', *New York Times*, 30 January 2010.

14. 'China's BYD Aims to Be World's Biggest Carmaker by 2025', *Chosun Ilbo*, 14 January 2010.

15. Michael T. Klare, 'Twenty-First Century Energy Superpower', *Tomdispatch.com*, 19 September 2010.

16. Patrick Jenkins, 'China Banks Eclipse US Rivals', *Financial Times*, 10 January 2010; Ariana Eunjung Cha, 'Chinese Banks Find Their Credit in High Demand', *Washington Post*, 2 January 2010; Melissa Murphy and Wen Jin Yuan, 'Internationalization of the Renminbi and Its Implications for the United States', *CSIS Freeman Chair in China Studies*, October 2009.

17. Robert Wright, 'China to Loosen West's Grip on Rail Sector', *Financial Times*, 13 September 2010; Keith Bradsher, 'China Is Eager to Bring High-Speed Rail Expertise to the US', *New York Times*, 7 April 2010; Jingyin Deng, 'China's Speedy Rails Going Overseas', *Global Times*, 15 March 2010; Bill Powell, 'China's Amazing New Bullet Train', *Fortune*, 6 August 2009.

18. Keith Bradsher, 'China Drawing High-Tech Research From US', *New York Times*, 17 March 2010; 'China Becoming Superpower in Scientific Research ', *Chosun Ilbo*, 27 January 2010; Clive Cookson, 'China Set for Global Lead in Scientific Research', *Financial Times*, 26 January 2010.

19. John Markoff, 'Chinese Supercomputer Is Ranked World's Second-Fastest, Challenging US Dominance', *New York Times*, 31 May 2010.

20. John Markoff and David Barboza, 'Chinese Telecom Giant in Push for US Market', *New York Times*, 25 October 2010.

21. 'China Transforms from Copycat to Patent Powerhouse', *Chosun Ilbo*, 5 October 2010.

22. Robert Fogel, '$123,000,000,000,000*. *China's estimated economy by the year 2040. Be warned', *Foreign Policy*, January/February 2010; Joel Kotkin, 'The China Syndrome', *Forbes*, 24 August 2010; Ross Garnaut, 'The Turning Period in Chinese Development', *East Asia Forum*, 2010; Subramanian, 'Is China Already Number One?'.

23. 'China to Become Top Favorite Nation of Koreans Studying Abroad', *Korea Times*, 21 June 2010.

24. John Pomfret, 'From China's Mouth to Texans' Ears: Outreach Includes Small Station in Galveston', *Washington Post*, 25 April 2010; Amako Satoshi, 'China as a 'Great Power' and East Asian Integration', *East Asia Forum*, 2010; Tae-hoon Lee, 'Book on China's Soft Power Released', *Korea Times*,

18 January 2010; Sunny Lee, 'China Embraces Soft Power for Image', *Korea Times*, 11 September 2009.

25. 'Joint Vision 2020', Washington, DC: US Department of Defense, 2000.

26. 'Military and Security Developments Involving the People's Republic of China 2010', Washington, DC: US Department of Defense 2010. 'International public goods' are peacekeeping operations in conformity with US foreign policy objectives.

27. Karen Jacobs, 'China Military Build-Up Seems US-focused: Mullen', *Reuters*, 4 May 2009.

28. Bill Gertz, 'China's "Aggressive" Buildup Called Worry', *Washington Times*, 14 January 2010.

29. 'Pentagon Sounds Alarm at China's Military Buildup', *Wall Street Journal*, 17 August 2010.

30. 'Chinese Military Buildup Far Exceeds its Defensive Needs: US', *IndianExpress.com*, 16 December 2010.

31. 'China "Has More Warships than US"', *Chosun Ilbo*, 1 September 2010.

32. 'China's Anti-Aircraft Carrier Missile "Closer to Completion"', *Chosun Ilbo*, 29 December 2010.

33. Robert Gates, 'Speech at Navy League Sea-Air-Space Exposition' *US Department of Defense*, 3 May 2010.

34. See Statistical Appendix, Table A14.

35. Bruce Russett, 'The Mysterious Case of Vanishing Hegemony; Or, Is Mark Twain Really Dead?', *International Organization* 39: 2, 1985.

36. Serge Halimi, 'The World Turned Upside Down: US Seen to Decline … Even Back in 1952', *Le Monde Diplomatique*, 1 November 2008.

37. Gideon Rachman, 'Think Again: American Decline: This Time It's for Real', *Foreign Policy*, 7 January 2011.

38. Michel Collon, 'What Will the US Foreign Policy be Tomorrow?', *MichelCollon. info*, 1 September 2008.

39. Niall Ferguson, 'America: An Empire in Denial', *Chronicle Review*, 28 March 2003, and 'Hegemony or Empire? (Review of *Two Hegemonies* by O'Brien and Clesse)', *Foreign Affairs*, 2003; Arno Mayer, 'The US Empire will Survive Bush', *Le Monde Diplomatique*, October 2008; Josef Joffe, 'The Default Power: The False Prophecy of America's Decline', *Foreign Affairs*, September/October 2009.

40. Stephen M. Walt, 'Taming American Power', *Foreign Affairs*, September/October 2005.

41. Russett, 'The Mysterious Case of Vanishing Hegemony'; Charles Krauthammer, 'Decline Is a Choice: The New Liberalism and the End of American Ascendancy', *Weekly Standard*, 19 October 2009.

42. Peter Liberman, 'What to Read on American Primacy', *Foreign Affairs*, 12 March 2009.

43. Nathan Gardels, 'Madeleine Albright Interviewed by Nathan Gardels', *New Perspectives Quarterly* 27: 4, 2004.

44. Mark Landler, 'Clinton Speech Offers Policy Overview', *New York Times*, 8 September 2010.

45. Fareed Zakaria and Condoleezza Rice, 'Interview With Fareed Zakaria of CNN', US State Department, 19 June 2008; Carlos Pascual, Madeleine Albright, Strobe Talbott, Thomas Pickering, Javier Solana and Bruce Jones, 'A Plan for

Action: Renewed American Leadership and International Cooperation for the 21st Century', Washington, DC: Brookings Institution, 20 November 2008.

46. Liz Sly, 'Amid Arab Protests, US Influence Has Waned', *Washington Post*, 4 February 2011.

47. Niall Ferguson, 'Complexity and Collapse: Empires on the Edge of Chaos', *Foreign Affairs*, March/April 2010, and 'America, the Fragile Empire', *Los Angeles Times*, 28 February 2010; 'Russian Analyst Predicts Decline and Breakup of US', *Novosti*, 24 November 2008.

48. Michael Cox, 'Is the United States in Decline – Again?', *International Affairs* 83: 4, 2007; John Gray, 'A Shattering Moment in America's Fall from Power', *Guardian*, 28 September 2008.

49. M. J. Williams, 'The Empire Writes Back (to Michael Cox)', *International Affairs* 83: 5, 2007; Chalmers Johnson, 'The Guns of August : Lowering the Flag on the American Century' *TomDispatch*, 17 August 2010; Julian Borger, 'David Miliband: China Ready to Join US as World Power', *Guardian*, 17 May 2009.

50. Mark Selden, 'As the Empire Falls: Lessons Learned and Unlearned in "America's Asia"', *Critical Asian Studies* 41: 3, 2009; Steve Yetiv, 'Reports of America's Decline are Greatly Exaggerated', *Christian Science Monitor*, 12 March 2009; Joel Achenbach, 'Bet on America: Forget the Doom and Gloom. In 50 Years, We'll Still Be No. 1', *Washington Post*, 2 September 2007.

51. Josef Joffe, 'The Default Power: The False Prophecy of America's Decline', *Foreign Affairs* September/October 2009; Daniel Deudney and G. John Ikenberry, 'The Myth of the Autocratic Revival: Why Liberal Democracy Will Prevail', *Foreign Affairs* 88: 1, 2009; Achenbach, 'Bet on America'.

52. Russett, 'The Mysterious Case of Vanishing Hegemony'.

53. *Global Trends 2025: A Transformed World* (Washington, DC: National Intelligence Council, 2008).

54. Joel Garreau, 'The Future Is So Yesterday', *Washington Post*, 20 July 2008; Nancy A. Youssef, 'As Iraq Winds Down, US Army Confronts a Broken Force', *McClatch Newspapers*, 17 September 2010; Anne Applebaum, '"It's Too Soon to Tell" How the Iraq War Went', *Washington Post*, 30 August 2010; Blaine Harden and John Pomfret, 'South Korea to Officially Blame North Korea for March Torpedo Attack on Warship', *Washington Post*, 19 May 2010; William D. Eggers and John O'Leary, 'Can the US Still Tackle Big Problems? Lessons from the Health-Care Battle', *Washington Post*, 21 March 2010; Janine Zacharia, 'Iraqis Still Reliant on Power Generators as US Prepares to Leave', *Washington Post*, 2 October 2010; Shaila Dewan, 'US Suspends Haitian Airlift in Cost Dispute', *New York Times*, 29 January 2010; Ezra Klein, 'California's Scary Sneak Preview', *Washington Post*, 3 January 2010.

55. Jonathan S. Landay, 'China's Thirst for Copper Could Hold Key to Afghanistan's Future', *McClatchy Newspapers*, 8 March 2009; Helena Cobban, 'Global Implications of China's Big Investment in Iraq and Afghanistan', *Asia-Pacific Journal: Japan Focus*, 2008.

56. Peter Marsh, 'China to Overtake US as Largest Manufacturer', *Financial Times*, 10 August 2008.

57. Associated Press, 'US Concerned over China's Rapid Development of New Weapons', *Guardian*, 9 January 2011.

58. Chris McGreal, 'Obama's State of the Union Address: US Must Seize "Sputnik Moment"', *Guardian*, 26 January 2011; 'Obama's Second State of the Union (Text)', *New York Times*, 25 January 2011.

59. Emanuel Pastreich, 'Is China the Nemesis in a New Cold War?', *Nautilus Policy Forum Online*, 6 March 2006. The *Guardian's* Gary Younge, writing on the invasion of Afghanistan, mentions America's 'militaristic reflexes and proclivities': Gary Younge, 'The US is Moving On from Afghanistan, but Its Troops Are Still Dying There', *Guardian*, 30 January 2011.

5   OBAMA'S STRATEGIC PARALYSIS

1. For a selection, see Paul Rogers, 'The Road to Endless War', *OpenDemocracy. net*, 25 November 2010; Thomas E. Woods, Jr, 'The Neglected Costs of the Warfare State: An Austrian Tribute to Seymour Melman', *Journal of Libertarian Studies* 22: 1, 2010; Robert Higgs, 'The Defense Budget Is Bigger Than You Think', *San Francisco Chronicle*, 18 January 2004; Seymour Melman, *Our Depleted Society*, New York: Holt, Rinehart & Winston, 1965, 'In the Grip of a Permanent War Economy', *Counterpunch*, 15 March 2003, and 'Economic Consequences of the Arms Race: The Second-Rate Economy', *American Economic Review* 78: 2, 1988; Jonathan Michael Feldman, 'From Warfare State to "Shadow State": Militarism, Economic Depletion, and Reconstruction', *Social Text* 91, 2007.

2. See Statistical Appendix, Tables A13, A14.

3. This was ostensibly an action of the Thai government but, as press reports made clear, it was basically following instructions from Washington. Thomas Fuller and David E. Sanger, 'Thais Seize Plane With Weapons From N. Korea', *New York Times*, 12 December 2009.

4. For a small selection, see 'DPRK Foreign Ministry's Spokesman on US Lifting of Major Economic Sanctions against DPRK', *KCNA*, 27 June 2008; Martin Fackler, 'Obama Speech Marks Shift on North Korea', *New York Times*, 11 November 2010; 'US Urged to Adopt Policy of Peaceful Co-Existence with DPRK', *KCNA*, 16 January 2005.

5. Again, just a small sample: Jimmy Carter, 'North Korea Wants to Make a Deal', *New York Times*, 15 September 2010; Mike Chinoy, 'No Hostile Intent: A Look Back at Kim Jong Il's Dramatic Overture to the Clinton Administration', *38 North* 11 November 2010; 'Pak: North Waiting for End to "Hostile" US Policy', *JoongAng Ilbo*, 3 August 2007; Bruce Cumings, 'Creating Korean Insecurity: The US Role', in Hazel Smith, ed., *Reconstituting Korean Security: A Policy Primer* (Tokyo, New York, Paris: United Nations University Press, 2008); 'N. Korea Proposed Secret Contacts with US in 1974: Document', *Kyodo News Service*, 21 December 2008; Sue-young Kim, 'North Korea Impatient for Dialogue With US', *Korea Times*, 4 September 2009.

6. The Agreed Framework collapsed during the Bush administration, which is discussed in my book, *North Korea: The Struggle Against American Power*. However, the failure of the treaty does not detract from its importance as an indicator of what both sides wanted.

7. 'Agreed Framework between the United States of America and the Democratic People's Republic of Korea', Korean Peninsula Energy Development Organization (KEDO), 21 October 1994, at <www.kedo.org/pdfs/AgreedFramework.pdf>.

8. Siegfried S. Hecker, 'Lessons Learned from the North Korean Nuclear Crises', *Nautilus Policy Forum Online* 10: 55, 2010, and 'A Return Trip to North Korea's Yongbyon Nuclear Complex', Center for International Security and Cooperation, Stanford University, 2010, at <iis-db.stanford.edu/pubs/23035/Yongbyonreport.pdf>.

9. Even on a less catastrophic level, trying to get the Americans to fulfil their commitments can be a problem, as the Libyans found out: Michael Slackman, '5 Years After It Halted Weapons Programs, Libya Sees the US as Ungrateful', *New York Times*, 10 March 2009.

10. Farnaz Fassihi, 'Iran Tightens Security as Subsidy Cuts Loom', *Wall Street Journal*, 4 November 2010.

11. 'DPRK Stand on Denuclearization of Korea Remains Unchanged', *KCNA*, 26 January 2011.

12. Richard C. Bush, 'The Challenge of a Nuclear North Korea: Dark Clouds, Only One Silver Lining', *PacNet* 44, 2010; Victor Cha, 'Five Myths About North Korea', *Washington Post*, 10 December 2010.

13. Associated Press, 'Son Says North Korean Leader Opposed Succession', *Washington Post*, 28 January 2011 – emphasis added.

14. KCNA carried 194 articles containing the phrase 'peace treaty' between 1 January 1996 and 24 January 2011. Two recent examples are 'Rodong Sinmun Calls for Confidence-Building Between DPRK and US', *KCNA*, 11 January 2011; 'FM Spokesman Accuses US of Sidestepping Proposals for Dialogue', *KCNA*, 16 December 2010.

15. Mike Chinoy, *Meltdown: The Inside Story of the North Korean Nuclear Crisis*, New York: St Martin's Press, 2008.

16. Mike Chinoy, 'North Korean Denuclearization Pact Is Collapsing', *San Francisco Chronicle*, 30 September 2008.

17. Peter M. Beck, 'The Bush Administration's Failed North Korea Policy', Friends Committee on National Legislation website, 14 April 2004; Victor Cha, 'Korea's Place in the Axis (update)', *Foreign Affairs*, November 2002.

18. Glenn Kessler, 'Analysis: North Korea Tests US policy of "strategic patience"', *Washington Post*, 27 May 2010.

19. Jong-seok Lee, 'Can the US Afford to "Muddle through" the N. Korea Nuclear Issue?', *Hankyoreh*, 22 March 2010.

20. James E. Goodby and Donald Gross, 'Strategic Patience Has Become Strategic Passivity', Nautilus Policy Forum Online, 2010.

21. For example, Paul Liem, 'A New Opportunity to Engage North Korea', Korea Policy Institute, 14 September 2009; 'Protests Across US to Demand: "No New Korean War!"', ANSWER Coalition, 27 November 2010; Christine Ahn, 'Sixty Years is Enough: One Woman's Dream for Peace in Korea', Korea Policy Institute, 25 June 2010.

22. Tim Shorrock, 'Obama's Only Choice on North Korea', *Daily Beast*, 24 November 2010; John Feffer, 'North Korea: Why Engagement Now?', *38 North*, 12 August 2010.

23. Tae-ho Kwon, 'Scope of Carter's Visit Remains in Question', *Hankyoreh*, 26 August 2010; 'Report on Jimmy Carter's Visit to DPRK', *KCNA*, 27 August 2010.

24. Peter James Spielmann, 'Carter: If No Palestine, Israel Sees "Catastrophe"', Associated Press, 26 January 2009.

25. Robert Carlin and John W. Lewis, 'Review US Policy Toward North Korea', *Washington Post*, 22 November 2010.
26. John Pomfret and Chico Harlen, 'North Korea Makes Some Gestures Toward Calm', *Washington Post*, 20 December 2010.
27. Donald P. Gregg, 'Why We Need Talks with North Korea', *Washington Post*, 22 December 2010.
28. Slackman, '5 Years After It Halted Weapons Programs, Libya Sees the US as Ungrateful'.
29. 'Pentagon Sees N. Korea as Rising Threat', *Chosun Ilbo*, 28 January 2011 – emphasis added.
30. Mike Chinoy, 'Is the South Korean Tail Wagging the American Dog?', *38 North*, 2010.
31. Stephen Gowans, 'The Sinking of the *Cheonan*: Another Gulf of Tonkin Incident', *What's Left*, 3 June 2010; 'Lee proposes unification tax', *Hankyoreh*, 16 August 2010.
32. Hugh White, 'Why War in Asia Remains Thinkable', *Survival* 50: 6 (2008).

PART II

1. James Hoare, 'Why the Sunshine Policy Made Sense', *38 North*, 29 March 2010.
2. 'Memorandum of DPRK Foreign Ministry', *KCNA*, 3 March 2005.
3. Jeong-ju Na, '"We Should Deal Resolutely with N. Korea"', *Korea Times*, 27 December 2010.

6   THE MYSTERIOUS SINKING OF THE CHEONAN, AND THE OFFICIAL INVESTIGATION

1. 'What Caused the *Cheonan* to Sink?', *Chosun Ilbo*, 29 March 2010; 'N. Korea "Runs Naval Suicide Squads"', *Chosun Ilbo*, 30 March 2010; Jean H. Lee, 'South Korea Says Mine from the North May Have Sunk Warship', *Washington Post*, 30 March 2010.
2. 'Broadcasters Baselessly Link Sunken Ship to N. Korean attack', *Hankyoreh*, 29 March 2010.
3. 'Information About Shipwreck Must Be Handled with Care', *Chosun Ilbo*, 7 April 2010.
4. Ministry of National Defense, 'Investigation Result on the Sinking of ROKS "Cheonan"', *Korea.net*, 20 May 2010.
5. Myung-bak Lee, 'Full Text of President Lee's National Address', *Korea Times*, 24 May 2010.
6. <www.cheonan46.go.kr/100>.
7. Lee, 'Full Text of President Lee's National Address.'
8. 'Defense Minister Told Off for Speculating About Shipwreck', *Chosun Ilbo*, 6 April 2010.
9. 'US Has No Evidence on N. Korea's Involvement: State Dept', *Yonhap*, 26 March 2010; Yonghak Jo, 'South Korea Rules Out Navy Ship Sunk by North Korea', *Washington Post*, 27 April 2010; Se-jeong Kim, '"Chances of

North Korea's Involvement Are Slim"', *Korea Times*, 28 March 2010; 'US Finds No North Link to Cheonan', *JoongAng Ilbo*, 7 April 2010.

10. Fred Hiatt, 'Fred Hiatt Interviews South Korean President Lee Myung-bak', *Newsweek*, 12 April 2010.

11. Editorial, 'Verification of the *Cheonan* Investigation at the National Assembly', *Hankyoreh*, 28 May 2010.

12. Hae-in Shin, 'N. K. Emerges as Key Election Issue', *Korea Herald*, 20 May 2010; Andray Abrahamian, 'North Korea: Ghost of Roh vs. Living Lee', *38North*, 27 May 2010.

13. 'Information About Shipwreck Must Be Handled with Care.'

14. 'Public's Faith in Military Authorities Shaken After *Cheonan* Sinking', *Hankyoreh*, 12 April 2010; Myo-ja Ser and Jung-ae Ko, 'Public Losing Faith in Authority After Sinking', *Chosun Ilbo*, 12 April 2010.

15. 'Defense Minister Told Off for Speculating About Shipwreck.'

16. Christian Oliver, 'Man in the News: Lee Myung-bak', *Financial Times*, 28 May 2010. Oliver's article attracted quite a few critical comments from South Korean readers, who saw it as a bit of PR for Lee.

17. Tae-Hwan Kwak, 'The Cheonan Incident and Its Impact on the Six-Party Process', *IFES Forum*, 4 June 2010.

18. Chan-ho Kang and Gwang-lip Moon, 'China Mulls No-Naming UN Censure', *JoongAng Ilbo*, 21 June 2010; 'Russian Military Experts Study *Cheonan* Sinking Probe Files', *Itar-Tass*, 9 June 2010.

19. '2 Koreas Brief UN Security Council on Cheonan Sinking', *Chosun Ilbo*, 16 June 2010 – emphasis added.

20. Kyung-min Jung and Ha-won Jung 'Two Versions of *Cheonan* Blast at UN', *JoongAng Ilbo*, 16 June 2010.

21. Tim Beal, 'The United Nations and the North Korean Missile and Nuclear Tests', *NZ Journal of Asian Studies* 9: 2, 2007.

22. '"UN Security Council Understands Probe into Ship Sinking"', *Korea Times*, 15 June 2010.

23. Ministry of National Defense, 'Investigation Result on the Sinking of ROKS "Cheonan"'.

24. Tae-hoon Lee, 'Gov't Seeks to Replace *Cheonan* Investigator', *Korea Times*, 13 May 2010.

25. Myo-ja Ser, 'Probe Member Summoned on False Rumor Allegations', *JoongAng Ilbo*, 29 May 2010.

26. S. C. Shin, 'Letter to Hillary Clinton, U.S. Secretary of State: There Was No Explosion. There Was No Torpedo', 26 May 2010.

27. Ser, 'Probe Member Summoned on False Rumor Allegations'.

28. Editorial, 'Punishment of *Cheonan* Opinions Contrary to Government Must Stop', *Hankyoreh*, 26 May 2010.

29. Hyun-jung Bae, 'Police Crack Down on *Cheonan* Rumors', *Korea Herald*, 24 May 2010; Si-soo Park, 'Police Hunt for *Cheonan* Rumors', *Korea Times*, 1 June 2010.

30. Ben Richardson and Saeromi Shin, 'South Korea Faces Domestic Skeptics Over Evidence Against North', *Bloomberg Businessweek*, 29 May 2010.

31. 'The DP Is Making a Fool of Itself Over the Cheonan Sinking', *Chosun Ilbo*, 18 May 2010.

32. Ibid.

33. Editorial, 'Verification of the Cheonan Investigation at the National Assembly'.

34. 'An Important Lesson for the Conspiracy Theorists', *Chosun Ilbo*, 1 June 2005.

35. Jee-ho Yoo, 'Scientist Co-Chairs *Cheonan* Probe Team', *JoongAng Ilbo*, 12 April 2010.

36. Ibid.

37. Ibid.

38. 'Military Commentator on Truth Behind "Story of Attack by North" (1)', *KCNA*, 28 May 2010; 'Military Commentator on Truth Behind "Story of Attack by North" (2)', *KCNA*, 29 May 2010.

39. Claudia Rodas, 'North Korea Declares Sweden an Enemy', *The Local*, 19 August 2008.

40. 'Seoul Rebuts N. Korean Denials in Cheonan Sinking', *Chosun Ilbo*, 31 May 2010.

41. Richardson and Shin, 'South Korea Faces Domestic Skeptics Over Evidence Against North'.

42. 'Diplomat Meets Detained Journalists in NK', *Korea Times*, 16 May 2009.

43. 'UD INFO – Fact Sheet: Sweden's Cooperation with NATO in EAPC/PfP', *Ministry for Foreign Affairs*, May 2005.

44. John McGlynn, 'Politics in Command: The "International" Investigation into the Sinking of the *Cheonan* and the Risk of a New Korean War', *Asia-Pacific Journal*, 14 June 2010.

45. Vyacheslav Solovyov, 'North Korea Flexes Muscles', Voice of Russia, 16 June 2010.

46. Editorial, 'Verification of the *Cheonan* Investigation at the National Assembly'.

47. 'Pyongyang Cites Forgotten Inter-Korean Agreement for Demands', *Chosun Ilbo*, 24 May 2010.

48. Editorial, 'A Joint North Korea–South Korea Investigation in Compliance with the Basic Agreement of 1991', *Hankyoreh*, 24 May 2010.

49. Alexander Vorontsov and Oleg Revenko, 'The Conundrum of the South Korean Corvette (I)', *International Affairs*, 25 May 2010.

50. 'Russia wants "100% proof" N. Korea Sunk Ship', *AFP*, 27 May 2010; 'Russian Experts Inspect Results of Cheonan Probe', *Korea Times*, 31 May 2010.

51. Young Jin Kim, '"Russia Unlikely to Back *Cheonan* Findings"', *Korea Times*, 7 June 2010.

52. 'Russia Urges Seoul, Pyongyang to Show Restraint over Ship Sinking', *RIA Novosti*, 20 May 2010.

53. 'Russian Experts "Unconvinced by *Cheonan* Evidence"', *Chosun Ilbo*, 10 June 2010; 'Russians Doubt About Ship Sinking by NK Attack', *Korea Times*, 9 June 2010.

54. Young-joon Ahn, 'China Premier: Korean Tensions Must Be Defused', *Washington Post*, 30 May 2010.

55. 'ChoJoongDong has greatly increased pro-administration coverage, study says', *Hankyoreh*, 27 May 2010; 'Conservative Newspapers and Lee Administration Strengthen Symbiotic Relationship', *Hankyoreh*, 27 May 2010; 'Defense Minister Told Off for Speculating About Shipwreck'; 'Torpedo Attack "Could Be Proved from State of Wreck Alone"', *Chosun Ilbo*, 30 April 2020.

56. Tae-hoon Lee, 'Explosives from Torpedo Found on Sunken Ship', *Korea Times*, 7 May 2010; 'Torpedo Explosive Detected in Sunken Ship: Official', *Yonhap*, 7 May 2010; 'Probe Concludes Torpedo Sank South Korea Ship: Report', Reuters, 6 May 2010; '*Cheonan* Probe Finds RDX, Alloy Used in Torpedoes', *JoongAng Ilbo*, 8 May 2010; Min-seok Kim and Myo-ja Ser, '*Cheonan* Probe

Detects TNT Type', *JoongAng Ilbo*, 14 May 2010; 'Torpedo Gunpowder Found in *Cheonan* Wreckage', *Chosun Ilbo*, 7 May 2010; 'Military Commentator on Truth behind "Story of Attack by North" (2)'.

57. 'Torpedo Gunpowder Found in *Cheonan* Wreckage'; Nari Kim, '*Cheonan* Investigators: N. Korean Torpedo Caused *Cheonan*'s Sinking', *Arirang*, 20 May 2010; McGlynn, 'Politics in Command'.

58. 'Serial Number of Torpedo Traced to N. Korea', *Chosun Ilbo*, 19 May 2010.

59. Ministry of National Defense, 'Investigation Result on the Sinking of ROKS "Cheonan"'.

60. Jae-hyon Cho, 'Evidence Scooped Up by Fishing Trawler', *Korea Times*, 20 May 2010.

61. John Sudworth, 'How South Korean Ship Was Sunk', BBC, 20 May 2010.

7 FROM 'SMOKING GUN' TO RUSTY TORPEDO

1. See, for instance, 'European Parliament Resolution of 17 June 2010 on the Situation in the Korean Peninsula', 17 June 2010.

2. Barbara Demick and John M. Glionna, 'Doubts Surface on North Korea's Role in Ship Sinking', *Los Angeles Times*, 23 July 2010. Demick is also the author of a recent book based on interviews with North Korean refugees: Barbara Demick, *Nothing to Envy: Ordinary Lives in North Korea*, New York: Spiegel & Grau, 2009.

3. Namgung Min, 'South Korea Splits along Political Lines', *Daily NK*, 20 May 2010.

4. 'Young People Less Inclined to Blame N. Korea for Shipwreck', *Chosun Ilbo*, 24 June 2010.

5. 'Most S. Koreans Skeptical About *Cheonan* Findings, Survey Shows', *Chosun Ilbo*, 8 September 2010.

6. Ben Richardson and Saeromi Shin, 'South Korea Faces Domestic Skeptics Over Evidence Against North', *Bloomberg Businessweek*, 29 May 2010.

7. Jeong-ju Na, 'Lee Regrets Speculations over Ship Sinking', *Korea Times*, 13 October 2010.

8. Ji-sook Bae, 'KBS Program Raises Questions about Cause of *Cheonan* Sinking', *Korea Times*, 18 November 2010.

9. Junghye Kwak , Huisun Kim and Taeho Lee, 'The PSPD's Stance on the Naval Vessel *Cheonan* Sinking', Peoples Solidarity for Participatory Democracy, Center for Peace and Disarmament, 1 June 2010; Gregory Elich, 'The Sinking of the *Cheonan* and Its Political Uses', *Counterpunch*, 28 July 2010; Mark E. Caprio, 'Plausible Denial? Reviewing the Evidence of DPRK Culpability for the *Cheonan* Warship Incident', *Asia-Pacific Journal* 26 July 2010.

10. 'Civic Group Takes Unresolved *Cheonan* Issues to UN', *Hankyoreh*, 15 June 2010; 'Activists Urge UNSC to Reinvestigate *Cheonan* Sinking', *Chosun Ilbo*, 15 June 2010; Ji-hyun Kim, 'UN Starts Discussions on *Cheonan* Sinking', *Korea Herald*, 15 June 2010.

11. Kyung-min Jung and Ha-won Jung, 'Two Versions of *Cheonan* Blast at UN', *JoongAng Ilbo*, 16 June 2010.

12. 'DPRK UN Representative on '*Cheonan*' Case', *KCNA*, 16 June 2010; 'Impartial Discussion on '*Cheonan*' Case Urged', *KCNA*, 18 June 2010; 'UNSC Urged to

Properly Know about Truth of '*Cheonan*' Case', *KCNA*, 21 June 2010; 'UN Discussions on Ship Sinking Stalled: Sources', *Yonhap*, 2 July 2010.

13. Hyun-kyung Kang and Young-jin Kim, 'Seoul Regrets NGO Sending *Cheonan* Report to UNSC', *Korea Times*, 14 June 2010; 'STOP Oppression & Prosecutors' Investigation on PSPD: Urgent Letter to Friends, Human Rights Defenders and Peace Activities', People's Solidarity for Participatory Democracy, 21 June 2010; 'Scholars Call for End to PSPD Witch-Hunt', *Hankyoreh*, 22 June 2010; 'Far-Right Groups Launch Violent Protests against PSPD', *Hankyoreh*, 18 June 2010.

14. Tomoko A. Hosaka, 'US, Japan to Keep US Military Base in Okinawa', *Washington Post*, 28 May 2010; Wooksik Cheong, 'The *Cheonan* Sinking and a New Cold War in Asia', *Nautilus Policy Forum Online* 29 June 2010; Gowans, 'The Sinking of the *Cheonan*: Another Gulf of Tonkin Incident', *What's Left*, 3 June 2010.

15. Joe Lauria, 'N. Korea: Ship's Sinking Helped US', *Wall Street Journal*, 15 June 2010.

16. F. William Engdahl, 'The Korean Crisis Breaking News, Cui Bono?', *Market Oracle*, 31 May 2010.

17. Martin Fackler, 'Ship Sinking Aids Ruling Party in S. Korean Vote', *New York Times*, 1 June 2010.

18. Chi-dong Lee, '(2nd LD) Main Opposition Heading for Stunning Victory in Local Elections', *Yonhap*, 3 June 2010.

19. Cheong-mo Yoo, 'Election Defeat Casts Gloom over Lee Administration, Ruling Party', *Yonhap*, 3 June 2010.

20. Some suggest 'friendly fire', but that would still be an accident rather than something deliberate: Myong Chol Kim, 'Pyongyang Sees US Role in *Cheonan* Sinking', *Asia Times Online*, 5 May 2010; 'An Important Lesson for the Conspiracy Theorists', *Chosun Ilbo*, 1 June 2005; 'South Korea in the Line of Friendly Fire', *Asia Times Online*, 26 May 2010; Sakai Tanaka, 'Who Sank the South Korean Warship *Cheonan*? A New Stage in the US-Korean War and US–China Relations', *Asia-Pacific Journal*, 24 May 2010.

21. Tetsuya Endo, 'What To Do about North Korea Now?', *East Asia Forum* (2011). Endo is a senior Japanese official and a former ambassador to New Zealand.

22. 'North Korea Seems To Have a Sort of Death Wish', *Der Spiegel*, 21 May 2010.

23. Christian Oliver, 'Theories Why Pyongyang Sank Warship', *Financial Times*, 24 May 2010.

24. John Feffer, 'Kim Jong-Il: Right-Wing Mole?', *World Beat 5*: 20, 2010; Bruce Klingner, 'US Must Respond Firmly to North Korean Naval Attack', *Heritage Foundation*, 20 May 2010; Sunny Lee, '*Cheonan* Tragedy: Is There an Exit Strategy?', *Korea Times*, 8 June 2010.

25. Tania Branigan, 'North Korea Threatens South Over Report on Sinking of Warship', *Guardian*, 20 May 2010.

26. 'NIS says N. Korean Attack on *Cheonan* Impossible Sans Kim Jong-il Approval', *Hankyoreh*, 7 April 2010.

27. 'European Parliament Resolution of 17 June 2010 on the Situation in the Korean Peninsula'.

28. Pauline Jelinek, 'AP Enterprise: Sub Attack Came Near Drill', *Washington Post*, 5 June 2010; 'S. Korea–US Anti-Submarine Drill Conducted Night of *Cheonan* Sinking', *Hankyoreh*, 8 June 2010.

29. Jeff Stein, 'Analysts Question Korea Torpedo Incident', *Washington Post*, 27 May 2010.

30. 'US Has No Evidence on N. Korea's Involvement: State Dept', *Yonhap*, 26 March 2010; Yonghak Jo, 'South Korea Rules Out Navy Ship Sunk by North Korea', *Washington Post*, 27 April 2010; Se-jeong Kim, 'Chances of North Korea's Involvement Are Slim', *Korea Times*, 28 March 2010.

31. Ministry of National Defense, 'Investigation Result on the Sinking of ROKS '*Cheonan*'', *Korea.net*, 20 May 2010.

32. Hyuk-chul Kwon, 'Military Believed N. Korean Submarine Was at Shipyard During *Cheonan* Incident', *Hankyoreh*, 23 October 2010.

33. 'Questions Raised Following *Cheonan* Announcement', *Hankyoreh*, 21 May 2010; Brewerstroupe, 'The Miraculous Torpedo', *Slate*, 27 May 2010.

34. 'Questions Raised Following *Cheonan* Announcement'.

35. Richardson and Shin, 'South Korea Faces Domestic Skeptics Over Evidence Against North.'; John McGlynn, 'Politics in Command: The "International" Investigation into the Sinking of the *Cheonan* and the Risk of a New Korean War', *Asia-Pacific Journal*, 24 January 2010; Elich, 'Sinking of the *Cheonan* and Its Political Uses'.

36. S. C. Shin, 'Letter to Hillary Clinton, US Secretary of State: There Was No Explosion. There Was No Torpedo', 26 May 2010.

37. 'Scientists question *Cheonan* investigation findings', *Hankyoreh*, 28 June 2010; 'Questions Linger 100 days after the *Cheonan* Sinking', *Hankyoreh*, 3 July 2010; Seunghun Lee and J.J. Suh, 'Rush to Judgment: Inconsistencies in South Korea's *Cheonan* Report', *Asia-Pacific Journal* 28 January 2010; David Cyranoski, 'Controversy Over South Korea's Sunken Ship', *Nature*, 14 July 2010, 'More Questions Raised Over South Korea's Sunken Ship', *Nature*, 2010, and 'Questions Raised Over Korean Torpedo Claims', *Nature*, 2010.

38. Hyun-Ik Hong, 'Strategic Cooperation between South Korea and Russia', *Korea Focus*, 17 May 2002; 'Accord is Reached on Russian Debt', *JoongAng Ilbo*, 20 June 2003.

39. 'Korea, Russia at Odds Over Rocket Launch Failure', *Chosun Ilbo*, 1 February 2011.

40. Alexander Vorontsov and Oleg Revenko, 'The Conundrum of the South Korean Corvette (I)', *International Affairs*, 25 May 2010).

41. 'Russian Experts to Report *Cheonan* Sinking Conclusions to Defense Ministry Soon', *RIA Novosti*, 8 June 2010.

42. Leonid Petrov, 'Interview', Radio Free Asia, 28 May 2010.

43. Min-seok Kim, 'Russian team wraps up probe', *JoonAng Ilbo*, 8 June 2010.

44. Ibid. – emphasis added.

45. 'Government protests Russia's Conflicting *Cheonan* findings', *Hankyoreh*, 12 July 2010.

46. Ibid.

47. Elich, 'Sinking of the *Cheonan* and Its Political Uses'; Gwang-lip Moon, 'Russia Says Sea Mine Sunk *Cheonan*: Report', *JoongAng Ilbo*, 28 July 2010; Cyranoski, 'More Questions Raised Over South Korea's Sunken Ship'.

48. 'Russia's *Cheonan* Investigation Suspects that the Sinking *Cheonan* Ship Was Caused by a Mine in Water', *Hankyoreh*, 28 July 2010.

49. 'Russian Navy Expert Team's Analysis on the *Cheonan* Incident', *Hankyoreh*, 29 July 2010.

50. 'Lee Administration Responds to Russian Investigation Report', *Hankyoreh*, 28 July 2010.
51. 'A Thorough Reinvestigation into the Sinking of the *Cheonan*', *Hankyoreh*, 28 July 2010.
52. Ibid.
53. You Ju-hyun Lee, 'Opposition Calls for *Cheonan* Reinvestigation', *Hankyoreh*, 15 September 2010; Tae-ho Kwon, 'Academics Call for *Cheonan* Reinvestigation', *Hankyoreh*, 12 October 2010.
54. 'China Proposes UN Military Armistice Commission Convene for Reinvestigation into *Cheonan*', *Hankyoreh*, 29 May 2010; 'N. Korea's Reinvestigation Proposal Alters *Cheonan* Situation', *Hankyoreh*, 21 May 2010.
55. 'A thorough reinvestigation into the sinking of the *Cheonan*'.
56. 'Russian Specialists Have Questions on S. Korean Corvette's Sinking – Navy Commander', InterFax.com, 24 July 2010; 'Russian Experts Unable to Give Answers on *Cheonan* Sinking – Navy Commander', *RIA-Novosti*, 24 July 2010; Tae-ho Kwon, 'South Korean Government Impeded Russian Team's *Cheonan* Investigation: Donald Gregg', *Hankyoreh*, 4 September 2010.
57. Kwon, 'South Korean Government Impeded Russian Team's *Cheonan* Investigation: Donald Gregg'.
58. 'Government Protests Russia's Conflicting *Cheonan* Findings'.
59. Donald P. Gregg, 'Testing North Korean Waters', *International Herald Tribune*, 31 August 2010.
60. See text in Reports on the Cheonan sinking in the online appendix at <www.timbeal.net.nz/Crisis_in_Korea>.
61. 'Russian Navy Expert Team's Analysis on the *Cheonan* Incident'.
62. 'Russia's *Cheonan* Investigation Suspects that the Sinking *Cheonan* Ship Was Caused by a Mine in Water'.
63. 'Russian Navy Expert Team's Analysis on the *Cheonan* Incident'.
64. 'Questions Raised Following *Cheonan* Announcement'; '*Cheonan* Findings Raise More Questions', *Chosun Ilbo*, 24 May 2010; '*Cheonan* Investigators Presented Wrong Torpedo Diagram', *Chosun Ilbo*, 30 June 2010; Won-je Son, 'N. Korea Reiterates Innocence, Offers Evidence', *Hankyoreh*, 3 November 2010.
65. 'Russian Navy Expert Team's Analysis on the *Cheonan* Incident' – emphasis added.
66. Ibid. – emphasis added.
67. 'Military Commentator on Truth behind "Story of Attack by North" (1)', *KCNA*, 28 May 2010; 'Questions Linger 100 Days after the *Cheonan* Sinking'; Cyranoski, 'Controversy over South Korea's Sunken Ship'; Demick and Glionna, 'Doubts Surface on North Korea's Role in Ship Sinking'; Ronda Hauben, 'Netizens Question Cause of *Cheonan* Tragedy', *OhmyNews*, 8 June 2010; Bo-keun Kim, 'No. 1 Torpedo Remains Source of Controversy', *Hankyoreh*, 11 September 2010.
68. Sung-ki Jung, 'Questions Raised about "Smoking Gun"', *Korea Times*, 20 May 2010.
69. *Joint Investigation Report: On the Attack Against ROK Ship Cheonan*, Seoul: Ministry of National Defense, 2010.
70. Kim, 'No. 1 Torpedo Remains Source of Controversy'.
71. International Crisis Group, 'North Korea: The Risks of War in the Yellow Sea', *Asia Report* 198, 2010 – emphasis added.

72. Technically, the torpedo remnant was not 'rusty', because that only applies to corrosion of iron and its alloys, whereas this metal was said to be an aluminium alloy. That brings in another twist to the story. According to the North Koreans this remnant was not of one of their torpedoes, because they are made out of 'steel alloy'. Ironically, if that is true, then any corrosion on a fired, sunken North Korean torpedo would, in fact, have been rust. This torpedo was not, strictly speaking, rusty; but it seems that the story was. 'Letter dated 2 November 2010 from the Permanent Representative of the Democratic People's Republic of Korea to the United Nations addressed to the President of the Security Council', United Nations Security Council, 3 November 2010.

73. '"Cheonan" Case Termed Most Hideous Conspiratorial Farce in History', KCNA, 2 November 2010.

74. Rob Green is a member of the New Zealand Peace Foundation's Disarmament and Security Centre: <www.disarmsecure.org/people.php>.

75. Personal communication, 26 January 2011.

76. 'Questions Raised Following Cheonan Announcement'.

77. Demick and Glionna, 'Doubts Surface on North Korea's Role in Ship Sinking'.

78. 'Are we prepared?', Korea Herald, 30 March 2010; 'NIS Says N. Korean Attack on Cheonan Impossible Sans Kim Jong-il Approval'; 'US Won't Stand for Leaks of Classified Data, NIS Chief Warns', Chosun Ilbo, 7 April 2010; Branigan, 'North Korea Threatens South over Report on Sinking of Warship'; Jelinek, 'AP Enterprise: Sub Attack Came Near Drill'.

79. McGlynn, 'Politics in Command: The "International" Investigation into the Sinking of the Cheonan and the Risk of a New Korean War'.

80. 'Q and A With Rear Admiral Thomas J. Eccles', CorrDefense 5: 3, 2009.

81. I cover this incident in some detail in Tim Beal, 'Korean Brinkmanship, American Provocation, and the Road to War: The Manufacturing of a Crisis', Asia-Pacific Journal 8: 51 (1), 2010.

82. Hyo-sik Lee, 'Families of Yeonpyeong Civilian Victims Want National Merits', Korea Times, 1 December 2010.

83. Editorial, 'Time for Pyongyang to Take Responsibility for Attack', Hankyoreh, 25 November 2010; 'North Korea's Provocation Must Never Be Tolerated', Kyunghyang Daily News, 24 November 2010.

84. 'KPA Supreme Command: World Should Know Who Is Provoker', KCNA, 20 December 2010.

85. 'Gift from Governor of New Mexico State of US', KCNA, 20 December 2010.

86. 'US governor visits North Korea', Al Jezeera, 17 December 2010; 'UN Security Council in Emergency Talks on Korean Tensions', Voice of America, 19 December 2010.

87. Martin Fackler and Mark McDonald, 'North Korea Again Opts for the Unexpected: Restraint', New York Times, 21 December 2010; John Pomfret and Chico Harlen, 'North Korea Makes Some Gestures Toward Calm', Washington Post, 20 December 2010.

88. 'Signs Suggest that N. Korean Regime Is Cracking', Chosun Ilbo, 13 December 2010.

PART III

1. Aidan Foster-Carter, 'The Gradualist Pipe-Dream: Prospects and Pathways for Korean Reunification', in Andrew Mack, ed., Asian Flashpoint: Security and

the Korean Peninsula, Canberra: Allen & Unwin, 1993. Timisoara was the seat of the Romanian revolution of 1989. It will be recalled that Ceausescu made himself extremely unpopular with a draconian austerity programme in order to pay back a $10 billion debt to the IMF. He paid back the debt, but was overthrown and executed shortly afterwards.

2. Bryan Kay, 'Is Collapse of NK Regime Imminent?', *Korea Times*, 15 November 2009.

3. 'Signs Suggest that N. Korean Regime Is Cracking', *Chosun Ilbo*, 13 December 2010.

4. 'US Military Exercises', Federation of American Scientists, available at <www. fas.org/programs/ssp/man/usmillogistics/military_exercises.html>.

5. Robert Stirrup, 'Ships Depart Pearl Harbor for RIMPAC 2010 Exercises', *US Navy*, 8 July 2010.

6. Kathrin Hille, 'China Blasts Clinton's Maritime Venture', *Financial Times*, 30 July 2010.

7. Jennifer Rubin, 'Stuart Levey Departs', *Washington Post*, 25 January 2011.

8. Peter Lee, 'Good-bye, Mr Insubordination', *Asia Times Online*, 4 February 2011.

9. George A. Lopez and David Cortright, 'Containing Iraq: Sanctions Worked', *Foreign Affairs* 83: 4, 2004.

10. Abbas Alnasrawi, 'Iraq: Economic Sanctions and Consequences, 1990–2000', *Third World Quarterly* 22: 2, 2001. Lopez and Cortright admit to 'hundreds of thousands' of children killed; Lopez and Cortright, 'Containing Iraq: Sanctions Worked'.

11. John Pomfret, 'Military Strength Eludes China, Which Looks Overseas for Arms', *Washington Post*, 25 December 2010.

12. White, 'Why War in Asia Remains Thinkable', *Survival* 50: 6, December 2008.

13. China Hand, 'It's Official: America Has a China-Containment Policy', *China Matters*, 9 July 2010. 'China Hand' also frequently publishes in *Asian Times Online* as Peter Lee.

8   SCENARIO BUILDING: FAILED SUCCESSION AND COLLAPSE

1. Oliver Arlow, 'Kim Jong-il Keeps $4bn 'Emergency Fund' in European Banks', *Daily Telegraph*, 14 March 2010; 'The Last Emperor', *New York Times*, 19 October 2003.

2. Michael Howard, 'US Troops Kill 300 in Najaf Raid', *Guardian*, 7 August 2004.

3. 'US at Work on Strangling Kim Jong-il's Cash Flow', *Chosun Ilbo*, 12 November 2009.

4. Arlow, 'Kim Jong-il Keeps $4bn 'Emergency Fund' in European Banks'.

5. Gerhard L. Weinberg, 'Hitler's Image of the United States', *American Historical Review* 69: 4 (1964).

6. Michael Ha, '"North Korean Leader Had Another Stroke"', *Korea Times*, 26 November 2008; Mark Mazzetti and Sang-hun Choe, 'North Korea's Leader Is Seriously Ill, US Intelligence Officials Say', *New York Times*, 9 September 2008.

7. Se-jeong Kim, 'Kim Jong-il Looking Leaner Than Before', *Korea Times*, 22 March 2009.

8. Patrick Goodenough, 'North Korea Steps Up Reports of Alleged Kim Jong-il Outings', *CNS*, 30 December 2008.

9. 'Amid Authenticity Dispute, Kim Jong-il Makes Brisk Inspections', *Korea Times*, 7 November 2009.

10. '09BEIJING1247, BEIJING-BASED G-5 CHIEFS OF MISSION ON DPRK, GTMO', *WikiLeaks*, 8 May 2009.

11. 'Protests across US to Demand: "No New Korean War!"'.

12. 'US Official: Kim Jong-il in Full Control in N. Korea', *Chosun Ilbo*, 10 August 2009.

13. Perhaps the most consistent and articulate exponent of the negotiator's position is Leon Sigal. See, for instance, Leon V. Sigal, 'What Obama should offer North Korea', *Bulletin of the Atomic Scientists* (2009), 'Why Punishing North Korea Won't Work … and What Will', *Asia-Pacific Journal: Japan Focus* 23 January 2009, 'The Only Way Out: Negotiate with North Korea – An Interview with Leon Sigal on Recent Events and US–DPRK Relations', *Korea Policy Institute*, 16 June 2009, and 'North Korea Policy on the Rocks: What Can Be Done to Restore Constructive Engagement?', *GlobalAsia* 4: 2 (2009).

14. James Traub, 'The Accidental Domestic President', *Foreign Policy*, 2010.

15. 'US Expert Casts Doubt on "Grand Bargain" for N. Korea', *Chosun Ilbo*, 9 October 2009.

16. Victor Cha, 'Obama's Korea Inheritance', *Comparative Connections* 10: 4, 2009.

17. Martin Fackler and Mark McDonald, 'South Korea Reassesses Its Defenses after Attack', *New York Times*, 26 November 2010.

18. For example, Andrei Lankov, 'Kim Jong-un Unlikely Candidate for NK Leader', *Korea Times* 2009; '31st MEU reflects on 2009', *US Marine Corps News*, 11 December 2009; '"N. Korea Stops Promoting Leader's Son"', *Korea Times*, 10 October 2009; Ji-hyun Kim, 'Nation Divided over Possible N. K. Collapse ' *Korea Herald*, 23 March 2010.

19. Sang-hoon Yang, 'Seoul Must Prepare for the Worst-Case Scenario', *Chosun Ilbo*, 17 June 2009.

20. John Feffer, 'Kim Jong-Il: Right-Wing Mole?', *World Beat* 5: 20, 2010.

21. Christian Oliver, 'Theories Why Pyongyang Sank Warship', *Financial Times*, 24 May 2010 – emphasis added.

22. Martin Fackler, 'From the North, a Pattern of Aggression', *New York Times*, 23 November 2010.

23. 'What Will Be the Impact of S.Korean Sanctions on N.Korea?', *Chosun Ilbo*, 25 May 2010.

24. Associated Press, 'Son Says North Korean Leader Opposed Succession', *Washington Post*, 28 January 2011.

25. Ibid.

26. Emma John, 'William, Kate and the Strange Law of Promogeniture', *Observer*, 23 January 2011.

27. Scott Snyder, 'Symposium on OpCon Transfer and Its Implications for the US–ROK Alliance', *Asia Foundation*, 25 March 2010.

28. Ruediger Frank, 'The Stability of North Korea and a Long-Term Strategy for Transformation', *Institute for Far Eastern Studies Forum*, 26 February 2010.

29. '"N. Korea Not in Danger of Imminent Collapse"', *Dong-A Ilbo*, 8 April 2010. Hwang died in October 2010.

30. Associated Press, 'Wikileaks Reveals Plans for North Korean Collapse', *Washington Post*, 30 November 2010; David E. Sanger, 'North Korea Keeps the World Guessing', *New York Times*, 29 November 2010; Simon Tisdall, 'Wikileaks Cables Reveal China "Ready to Abandon North Korea"', *Guardian*, 29 November 2010, and 'WikiLeaks Cables: How China Lost Patience with North Korea', *Guardian*, 29 November 2010; Chico Harlan, 'Seoul Undertakes Effort to Measure North Korea's Longevity', *Washington Post*, 19 December 2010; Philippe Pons, 'North Korea, Fortress State', *Le Monde diplomatique*, January 2011.

31. Drew Thompson, 'China's Perspective of Post-*Cheonan* Regional Security', in *Post-Cheonan Regional Security* (Seoul: Asia Foundation's Center for US–Korea Policy and the Asan Institute for Policy Studies, 2010).

32. Yong-in Yi, 'Cold War Alliances Reborn with Regional Tension', *Hankyoreh*, 30 November 2010.

33. Saibal Dasgupta, 'Economic Sanctions Strengthen North Korea's Dictatorship, Says German NGO', *Times of India*, 20 April 2010.

34. Hyung-jin Kim, 'S. Korea: Nuclear Push Could Bring North's Collapse', *Washington Post*, 17 January 2011.

35. 'USFK Chief Warns of Instability in N. Korea', *Chosun Ilbo*, 26 March 2010.

36. Jonathan Lynn, 'North Korea Has Plenty of Doctors: WHO', *Washington Post*, 30 April 2010; Dr Margaret Chan, 'Dr Margaret Chan, WHO Director-General: Visit to DPR Korea; Virtual Press Conference', *MaximsNewsNetwork*, 1 May 2010.

37. Bradley Graham, 'Rumsfeld Remains Largely Unapologetic in Memoir', *Washington Post*, 3 February 2011.

38. Bonnie Glaser and Scott Snyder, 'Preparations Needed for North Korean Collapse', *PacNet* 27, 20 May 2010. See also Scott Snyder and See-Won Byun, 'The Obama Administration and Preparations for North Korean Instability', *International Journal of Korean Unification Studies* 18: 2, 2009.

39. Michael J. Finnegan, 'Preparing for the Inevitable in North Korea', *PacNet* 28B, 28 April 2009.

40. Fareed Zakaria, 'When North Korea Falls …' *Washington Post*, 18 October 2010.

41. John Bolton, 'North Korea: Not the Time For Talks', *Wall Street Journal*, 4 January 2011.

42. Ibid.

43. Gang Ding, 'Coordination Will Stave Off Another Korean War', *Global Times*, 30 December 2010.

44. Yuan Luo, 'All-Out War Unlikely on the Korean Peninsula', *Global Times*, 23 December 2010.

45. Jianyu Jin, Ziyu Wang and Hae-hoon Choung, 'Pragmatism Propels South Korean Attitudes', *Global Times*, 28 January 2011.

46. 'US Embassy Cables: China "Would Accept" Korean Reunification', *Guardian*, 1 December 2010.

47. 'Lee proposes unification tax', *Hankyoreh*, 16 August 2010; Gwang-lip Moon, 'Little Enthusiasm for Lee's Unification Tax Proposal', *JoongAng Ilbo*, 17 August 2010; Chico Harlan, 'South Korean Leader Has Reunification Plan', *Washington Post*, 16 August 2010; Tae-hoon Lee, 'Would You Pay $1 a Month for Unification Tax?', *Korea Times*, 28 October 2010.

48. 'N. Korea Policy to Shift from Engagement to Reunification', *Chosun Ilbo*, 27 December 2010.

49. 'Lee Pushes Constitutional Amendment in Televised Dialogue', *Hankyoreh*, 2 February 2011. Lee is pushing for a move to a two-term presidency, and at the moment that would come in too late for him. A crisis, and a war in the North, might well change things.

50. Jingxian Lu and Young-ghil Kwon, 'Multilateral Alliances Critical for Korean Future', *Global Times*, 1 February 2011.

9 THE NORTHERN LIMIT LINE: KEEPING THE WAR ALIVE

1. 'Text of the Korean War Armistice Agreement', 1953, available at <news. findlaw.com/wp/docs/korea/kwarmagr072753.html>. Regrettably, the website does not include the maps.

2. Ben S. Malcom, '"White Tigers" Prowled North Korea', *VFW Magazine*, May 2002.

3. For a good analysis of the NLL in the context of the Yeonpyeong clash, see Stephen Gowans, 'US Ultimately to Blame for Korean Skirmishes in Yellow Sea', *What's Left*, 5 December 2010.

4. Jon M. Van Dykea, Mark J. Valencia and Jenny Miller Garmendia, 'The North/ South Korea Boundary Dispute in the Yellow (West) Sea', *Marine Policy* 27: 2, 2003.

5. 'DPRK Takes Merciless Action to Defend MDL ', *KCNA*, 13 November 2009; Sang-hun Choe, 'Korean Navies Skirmish in Disputed Waters', *New York Times*, 10 November 2009.

6. 'South Korea Deviated from Previous Rules of Engagement in West Sea Clash', *Hankyoreh*, 11 November 2009.

7. Nicole Finnemann, 'The Sinking of the *Cheonan*', *Korea Insight*, 1 April 2010.

8. Van Dykea et al., 'The North/South Korea Boundary Dispute in the Yellow (West) Sea'.

9. John Barry Kotch and Michael Abbey, 'Ending Naval Clashes on the Northern Limit Line and the Quest for a West Sea Peace Regime', *Asian Perspectives* 27: 2, 2003.

10. 'KPA Navy Command's Important Communiqué', *KCNA*, 23 March 2000; 'Northern Limit Line Rejected', *KCNA*, 2 August 2002. See map in Tim Beal, 'Korean Brinkmanship, American Provocation, and the Road to War: The Manufacturing of a Crisis', *Asia-Pacific Journal* 8: 51 (1), 2010.

11. 'DPRK Foreign Ministry's Spokesman Blasts US Delaying Tactics in Solution · of Nuclear Issue', *KCNA*, 28 March 2008.

12. 'KPA Panmunjom Mission Clarifies Revolutionary Armed Forces' Principled Stand', *KCNA*, 27 May 2009.

13. Mark Thompson, 'There's No Business Like the Arms Business', *Time*, 14 September 2010; Grimmett, 'Conventional Arms Transfers to Developing Nations, 2002–2009', *Congressional Research Service*, 10 September 2010; Roula Khalaf and James Drummond, 'Gulf States in $123bn US Arms Spree', *Financial Times*, 20 September 2010.

14. Hazel Smith, 'North Korea Shipping: A Potential for WMD Proliferation?', *East–West Center: AsiaPacific Issues* 87, 2009.

15. 'Northern Limit Line Rejected'; 'Truth About West Sea Naval Clash; "NLL" Questioned', *People's Korea*, 13 July 2002; 'Truth behind "Northern Limit Line" Disclosed', *KCNA*, 25 June 2007.
16. 'Press Conference on Issue of MDL at West Sea of Korea', *KCNA*, 26 August 1999.
17. 'KPA Navy Command's Important Communiqué'. See also 'KNPC warns US and S. Korea against Acting Recklessly', *KCNA*, 9 April 2000; 'S. Korea's Challenge to Measure of Navy Command of KPA Blasted', *KCNA*, 31 March 2000; 'S. Korean Authorities' Intensified Military Provocations', *KCNA*, 28 February 2000.
18. Jon Van Dyke, 'The Maritime Boundary between North & South Korea in the Yellow (West) Sea', *38 North*, 29 July 2010.
19. Ibid.
20. Ibid.
21. Daniel Ten Kate and Peter S. Green, 'Defending Korea Line Seen Contrary to Law by Kissinger Remains US Policy', *Bloomberg*, 17 December 2010.
22. Paul Liem, 'Honor the *Cheonan* Dead with Peace', *Korea Policy Institute*, 3 June 2010.
23. Kate and Green, 'Defending Korea Line Seen Contrary to Law by Kissinger Remains US Policy'.
24. Ibid.
25. Joint State/Defense message, 'ROKG LEGAL MEMORANDUM ON NORTHWEST COASTAL INCIDENTS (Cable to US embassy, Seoul)', *State Department*, 22 December 1973.
26. Francis Underhill, 'DEFUSING WESTERN COASTAL ISLAND SITUATION', *State Department*, December 1973.
27. Kate and Green, 'Defending Korea Line Seen Contrary to Law by Kissinger Remains US Policy.'
28. Selig S. Harrison, 'Drawing a Line in the Water', *New York Times*, 12 December 2010.
29. International Crisis Group, 'North Korea: The Risks of War in the Yellow Sea', *Asia Report* 198, 2010.

10 MILITARY EXERCISES: PRECIPITATING COLLAPSE, PREPARING FOR INVASION

1. Jee-ho Yoo, 'Korea, US Could Delay Wartime Control Transfer', *JoongAng Ilbo*, 24 March 2010. The wrangling over this issue is intriguing and warrants exploration.
2. Tae-hoon Lee, 'Army, Air Force to Stage Largest-Ever Joint Drill', *Korea Times*, 22 December 2010.
3. 'KOREA CRISIS: Basic Facts and Historical Context', *National Campaign to End the Korean War*, 27 November 2010.
4. Tetsuo Kotani, 'Tip of the Spear: The 13 Missions for US Marines in Okinawa', *PacNet* 43, 2010; '31st Marine Expeditionary Unit', Wikipedia, at <en.wikipedia.org/wiki/31st_Marine_Expeditionary_Unit>; 31st Marine Expeditionary Unit home page, at <www.marines.mil/unit/31stmeu/Pages/default.aspx>; '31st MEU Reflects on 2009', *US Marine Corps News*, 11 December 2009; Rebekka

S. Heite, '31st MEU's Long-Range Raid Capabilities Tested', US Air Force (Andersen Air Force Base), 15 April 2010.

5. Min-seok Kim and Myo-ja Ser. 'US Will Command Military Exercise', *JoongAng Ilbo*, 17 June 2010; Sung-ki Jung, 'USFK to Retake Control over Drill with ROK', *Korea Times*, 17 June 2010.

6. 'Experts Address Misconceptions about OPCON Transfer', *Hankyoreh*, 25 June 2010; 'No Reason to Postpone OPCON Transfer', *Hankyoreh*, 24 June 2010, Ha-won Jung, 'Minister: Transfer of Wartime Control May Be Delayed', *JoongAng Ilbo*, 25 June 2010; Sewell Chan and Jackie Calmes, 'US Keeps Command of Military in Seoul', *New York Times*, 26 June 2010; 'Ratify OPCON Transfer Delay at the National Assembly', *Hankyoreh*, 29 June 2010.

7. 'OPCON Transfer Delay Signals Abrupt Strategic Change', *Hankyoreh*, 24 June 2010.

8. *Reception, Staging, Onward Movement, And Integration field Manual* (Washington, DC: Headquarters, Department of the Army, 1999). For a trenchant and informed look at the logistical challenges faced by the US military, see Tom Engelhardt, 'Believe It or Not (2010 Imperial Edition) US War-Fighting Numbers to Knock Your Socks Off', TomDispatch.com, 6 April 2010.

9. Nick Turse, 'Black Sites in the Empire of Bases', *Asia Times Online*, 11 February 2010).

10. Sung-ki Jung, 'USFK Seeks to Expand Role Outside Peninsula', *Korea Times*, 24 February 2010.

11. Sung-ki Jung, 'USFK Chief Pledges Naval, Air-Centric Reinforcement', *Korea Times*, 1 February 2009.

12. Doo-hyong Hwang, 'US to Mobilize More Troops in Case of N. Korean Contingency: Official', *Yonhap*, 4 February 2010, and 'Extra US Troops Not Likely to Arrive in Time in Case of N. K. Crisis: Gates', *Yonhap*, 3 February 2010.

13. John Pike, 'Foal Eagle', Global Security.org, at <www.globalsecurity.org/military/ops/foal-eagle.htm>.

14. Sang-Hun Choe, 'Last Communist Rebel Dies in South Korea', *Associated Press*, 2 April 2004.

15. Sung-ki Jung, 'S. Korea, US to Tone Down War Games Next Week', *Korea Times*, 10 August 2009.

16. Korean Committee for Solidarity with the World People, 'Joint Military Exercises', by email from Pyongyang, 5 August 2009.

17. Daniel Pinkston, 'US–ROK Military Exercises', *International Crisis Group*, 7 March 2011.

18. Sue-young Kim, '2 Koreas Open Modern Military Hot Lines', *Korea Times*, 30 March 2009.

19. Max Boot, 'The New American Way of War', *Foreign Affairs* (2003).

20. Sung-ki Jung, 'Minister Vows Preemptive Strike Against NK Nuclear Attack', *Korea Times*, 20 January 2010; Ji-hyun Kim, '"Preemptive Strikes Would Be Needed to Stop N. K. attack"', *Korea Herald*, 21 January 2010.

21. Carlton Meyer, 'The Mythical North Korean Threat', 2003, at <www.g2mil.com/korea.htm>; Chung-in Moon and Sangkeun Lee, 'Military Spending and the Arms Race on the Korean Peninsula', *Asian Perspectives* 33: 4, 2009. This latter paper appeared with revisions in the *Asia Pacific Journal*, 28 March 2010.

22. Byeong-tae Kang, '"North Korea Does Not Pose a Threat"', *Korea Focus*, 28 July 2009.

23. Ironically, North Korea has picked up the spun meaning of 'pre-emptive', and so criticises 'bellicose forces' for contemplating 'mounting preemptive attacks on the DPRK'; 'US and S. Korean "OPLAN 5029" Blamed', *KCNA*, 9 November 2009. Jimmy Carter also uses 'pre-emptive' incorrectly; Duk-kun Byun, 'Jimmy Carter Calls on US, S. Korea to Talk Directly with N. Korea', *Yonhap*, 23 March 2010.

24. 'US Commander Reveals True Purpose of Troops in Okinawa is to Remove N. Korea's Nukes', *Mainichi*, 1 April 2010; John Feffer, 'Can Japan Say No to Washington?', *Foreign Policy in Focus*, 4 March 2010.

25. Jackson Diehl, 'Obama's Foreign Policy Needs an Update', *Washington Post*, 22 November 2010.

26. 'Kim Jong Il Inspects Command of KPA Unit 630', *KCNA*, 31 January 2010.

27. 'Analysts Say N. Korea Highlights Peace Negotiations through Artillery Fire Near NLL', *Hankyoreh*, 28 January 2010.

28. Se-jeong Kim, 'Is N. K. the Biggest Threat to Americans?', *Korea Times*, 7 July 2009.

29. 'Are we prepared?', *Korea Herald*, 30 March 2010.

30. 'NIS says N. Korean Attack on *Cheonan* Impossible Sans Kim Jong-il Approval' *Hankyoreh*, 7 April 2010; 'US Won't Stand for Leaks of Classified Data, NIS Chief Warns', *Hankyoreh*, 7 April 2010.

31. Bruce Cumings, 'Korea: Forgotten Nuclear Threats', *Le Monde Diplomatique*, December 2004.

32. John Pike, 'Operation Plans [OPLAN]', GlobalSecurity.org, at <www.globalsecurity.org/military/ops/oplan.htm>.

33. John Pike, 'Garden Plot/CONPLAN 2502 (Civil Disturbance Operations)', *GlobalSecurity.org*, 31 July 2008.

34. William Arkin, 'Not Just A Last Resort? A Global Strike Plan, With a Nuclear Option', *Washington Post*, 15 May 2005.

35. 'US Plot for Preemptive Nuclear Attack Blasted', *KCNA*, 24 May 2005.

36. John Pike, 'OPLAN 5026 – Air Strikes', *GlobalSecurity.org*, at <www.globalsecurity.org/military/ops/oplan-5026.htm>.

37. 'Seoul Simulated Bombing of N. Korean Nuclear Plant', *Chosun Ilbo*, 6 June 2005.

38. Ibid.

39. 'Seoul Simulated Bombing of N. Korean Nuclear Plant', *Chosun Ilbo*, 6 June 2005.

40. 'Korean People Will Deal Merciless Annihilating Strike to Aggressors.' *KCNA*, 21 August 2009.

41. 'OPLAN 5027 Major Theater War – West', *GlobalSecurity.org*, at <www.globalsecurity.org/military/ops/oplan-5027.htm>.

42. Charles 'Jack' Pritchard, 'What I Saw in North Korea', *New York Times*, 21 January 2004.

43. Dong-shin Seo, 'Asians Cooperate to Counter Japan's Rising Militarism', *Korea Times*, 25 March 2005; Richard Tanter, 'Japanese Militarization and the Bush Doctrine', *Japan Focus* 17 February 2005; Mari Yamaguchi, 'Japan Capable of Making Nuclear Weapon', *Guardian*, 30 November 2006.

44. Min-seok Kim and Jee-ho Yoo, 'North Adopts New War Invasion Strategy: Source', *JoongAng Ilbo*, 27 April 2010; Brian Lee, 'Behind the Front Line, a Shrouded Military', *JoongAng Ilbo*, 29 April 2010; Chung-in Moon and

Sangkeun Lee, 'Military Spending and the Arms Race on the Korean Peninsula', *Asia-Pacific Journal*, 13 February 2010.

45.   Pike, 'OPLAN 5027 Major Theater War – West'.

46.   'Is Our Military Up to the Job of Protecting the Country?', *Chosun Ilbo*, 18 December 2009. See also 'N. Korea "Hacks into S. Korea–US Defense Plans"', *Chosun Ilbo*, 18 December 2009; Justin McCurry, 'North Korean Hackers May Have Stolen US War Plans', *Guardian*, 18 December 2009.

47.   Pike, 'OPLAN 5027 Major Theater War – West.'

48.   Selig S. Harrison, 'Was the North Korean Launch a "Provocation"?', *Hankyoreh*, 14 April 2009.

49.   Bruce B. Auster, Kevin Whitelaw and Thomas Omestad, 'Upping the Ante for Kim Jong Il; Pentagon Plan 5030, A New Blueprint for Facing Down North Korea', *US News and World Report, Nation & World*, 21 July 2003.

50.   Ibid.

51.   'US War Scenario against DPRK Assailed', *KCNA*, 5 August 2003.

52.   'Chinese in Series of Diplomatic Gaffes in Seoul', *Chosun Ilbo*, 30 November 2010.

53.   'Korea, US Agree to Compromise N. Korea "Concept Plan"', *Chosun Ilbo*, 5 June 2005; Victor Cha, 'We Have No Plan', *Nautilus Policy Forum Online*, 15 June 2008.

54.   Sung-ki Jung, 'S. Korean Army to Deploy 2,000 Wheeled Armored Vehicles from 2013', *Korea Times*, 5 October 2008.

55.   'Korea, US Agree to Compromise N. Korea "Concept Plan".'

56.   'OPLAN 5029 – Collapse of North Korea', *GlobalSecurity.org*, at <www.globalsecurity.org/military/ops/oplan-5029.htm>; 'OPLAN 5029 Risks Ceding South Korean Sovereignty to the US', *Hankyoreh*, 2 November 2009; 'Time for Dialogue Not OPLAN 5029', *Hankyoreh*, 2 November 2009; 'US and S. Korean "OPLAN 5029" Blamed'.

57.   'US and S. Korean "OPLAN 5029" Blamed.'

58.   Simon Tisdall, 'Wikileaks Cables Reveal China "Ready to Abandon North Korea"', *Guardian*, 29 November 2010.

59.   R. Jeffrey Smith and Joby Warrick, 'Nuclear Aims by Pakistan, India Prompt US Concern', *Washington Post*, 28 May 2009; Jane Perlez, 'A Visit to a US Ally, but an Increasingly Wary One' *New York Times*, 8 February 2009; Matthew Bunn, *Securing the Bomb 2010: Securing All Nuclear Materials in Four Years*, Washington, DC: Washington Nuclear Threat Initiative, 2010; Seymour M. Hersh, 'Watching the Warheads: The Risks to Pakistan's Nuclear Arsenal.', *New Yorker*, 5 November 2001; Christina Lamb, 'Elite US Troops Ready to Combat Pakistani Nuclear Hijacks', *Sunday Times*, 17 January 2010.

60.   George P. Shultz, William J. Perry, Henry A. Kissinger and Sam Nunn, 'Toward a Nuclear-Free World', *Wall Street Journal*, 15 January 2009.

61.   Scott Ritter, 'The End of Obama's Vision of a Nuke-Free World', *TruthDig. org*, 16 February 2010.

62.   Bunn, *Securing the Bomb 2010*.

63.   Hyuk-chul Kwon, 'Joint Drills Will Be Far from NLL, Military Reports', *Hankyoreh*, 27 November 2010; Min-seok Kim and Min-yong Lee, 'Drill Under Way to Remove WMDs', *JoongAng Ilbo*, 12 March 2010.

64.   'S. Korea, US "Complete N. Korea Contingency Plan"', *Chosun Ilbo*, 2 November 2009.

65. Sung-ki Jung, 'S. Korea, Japan Can Build Nuclear Weapons Quickly', *Korea Times*, 18 March 2010.
66. Emma Chanlett-Avery and Mary Beth Nikitin, *Japan's Nuclear Policy Future: Policy Debate, Prospects, and US Interests*, Washington, DC: Congressional Research Service, 2009.
67. Ibid.

11 THE SIEGE: SANCTIONS, THEIR ROLE AND EFFECT

1. 'United Nations Sanctions (Democratic People's Republic of Korea) Regulations 2006', NZ Government, 10 September 2009, available at <www.legislation. govt.nz/regulation/public/2006/0382/latest/DLM421679.html>.
2. 'US at Work on Strangling Kim Jong-il's Cash Flow', *Chosun Ilbo*, 12 November 2009.
3. Donald Greenlees and David Lague, 'How a US Inquiry Held Up the N. Korea Peace Talks', *International Herald Tribune*, 11 April 2007; China Hand, 'David Asher's Dead End', at <chinamatters.blogspot.com/2007/04/david-ashers-dead-end.html>; John McGlynn, 'Banco Delta Asia, North Korea's Frozen Funds and US Undermining of the Six-Party Talks: Obstacles to a Solution', *Japan Focus*, 9 June 2007; Jenifer Rubin, 'Stuart Levey Departs', *Washington Post*, 25 January 2011.
4. Leon V. Sigal, 'North Korea's Tactics', *Nautilus Policy Forum Online*, 15 February 2005.
5. 'Memorandum of DPRK Foreign Ministry', *KCNA*, 3 March 2005.
6. For an excellent analysis of the last two decades, see Samuel S. Kim, 'North Korea's Nuclear Strategy and the Interface between International and Domestic Politics', *Asian Perspective* 34: 1, 2010.
7. Joel S. Wit, 'Don't Sink Diplomacy', *New York Times*, 18 May 2010.
8. Myoung-Ky Park and Philo Kim, 'Inter-Korean Relations in Nuclear Politics', *Asian Perspective* 34: 1, 2010; Mike Chinoy, 'He's Not the Crazy One', *Daily Beast*, 13 July 2009; 'White Paper Declares Sunshine Policy Dead and Buried', *Chosun Ilbo*, 18 November 2010.
9. 'USFK Chief Warns of Instability in N. Korea', *Chosun Ilbo*, 26 March 2010.
10. Suk Kim, 'Will UN Economic Sanctions Against a Nuclear North Korea Work?', IFES Forum, Kungnam University, 20 November 2006.
11. Steve Herman, 'Sanctions Expected to Harm North Korean Economy', Voice of America, 23 July 2010.
12. House Committee on Foreign Affairs Subcommittee on Asia, the Pacific and the Global Environment, 'Smart Power: Remaking US Foreign Policy in North Korea', Testimony by Scott Snyder, Director, Center for US–Korea Policy, The Asia Foundation, 12 February 2009.
13. Emma Chanlett-Avery and Mary Beth Nikitin, *Japan's Nuclear Policy Future: Policy Debate, Prospects, and US Interests* (Washington, DC: Congressional Research Service, 2009).
14. Marcus Noland, 'The (Non) Impact of UN Sanctions on North Korea', Peterson Institute for International Economics Working Paper WP08–12, December 2008; Stephan Haggard and Marcus Noland, 'Sanctioning North Korea: The Political Economy of Denuclearization and Proliferation', Peterson Institute for International Economics Working Paper WP09–4 (2009).

15. Gary Clyde Hufbauer, Jeffrey J. Schott, Kimberley Ann Elliott and Barbara Oegg, *Economic Sanctions Reconsidered*, 3rd edn, Washington, DC: Institute for International Economics, 2007.
16. Ibid., Table 1A.1.
17. Ibid., p. 70.
18. Ibid., pp. 138–9.
19. Donald Macintyre, 'The Supremo in His Labyrinth', *Time*, 18 February 2002.
20. 'Austrian Guilty Over Lavish Birthday Presents for Kim Jong-il', *Chosun Ilbo*, 8 December 2010.
21. Jae-Cheon Lim, *Kim Jong Il's Leadership of North Korea*, Abingdon: Routledge, 2009. He was also fond of playing cards and soccer, shooting, watching movies and driving cars.
22. 'Kim Jong Il Enjoys Performance Given by State Symphony Orchestra', *KCNA*, 28 November 2010; 'Joint Concert Held on Chopin's 200th Birthday', *KCNA*, 11 November 2010.
23. Hufbauer et al., *Economic Sanctions Reconsidered*, p. 1.
24. 'UN to Send Review Mission to North Korea', AFP, 18 May 2010.
25. Ben Blanchard, 'North Korea Farmers Shun New Won – Former Aid Worker', XE.com, 20 April 2010.
26. Ciaran Giles, 'Foreign Ministers Urge End to Cuba Embargo', *Washington Post*, 13 October 2005.
27. Hazel Smith, 'Overcoming Humanitarian Dilemmas in the DPRK (North Korea)', United States Institute of Peace, July 2002; Hazel Smith, 'Brownback Bill Will Not Solve North Korea's Problems', *Jane's Intelligence Review*, February 2004, pp. 42–5.
28. 'Message to German Chancellor', *KCNA*, 14 November 2001; 'Gratitude Expressed for Appeal for International Assistance to DPRK', *KCNA*, 4 December 2000; 'DPRK–Japan Red Cross Talks Held in Beijing', *KCNA*, 13 March 2000; 'Timely Humanitarian Appeal – KCNA Commentary', *KCNA*, 11 July 1998.
29. 'Jo Chang Dok interviewed on Serious Shortage of Electricity', *KCNA*, 3 February 2000.
30. 'KCNA Refutes US Officials' Lies About Cause of Economic Difficulties', *KCNA*, 13 January 2003.
31. 'KCNA on Tremendous Damage Done to DPRK by US', *KCNA*, 24 June 2010.
32. 'Venezuela Demands US Extradition of Terrorist', *KCNA*, 14 April 2011; Associated Press, 'Cuba's Parliament Chief Denounces Acquittal of Ex-CIA Agent in US as a "Shameful Farce",' *Washington Post*, 9 April 2011; 'Cuban Ex-CIA Agent Acquitted of Charges Alleging He Lied During US Immigration Hearing', *Wasington Post*, 8 April 2011.
33. 'KCNA on Tremendous Damage Done to DPRK by US'.
34. Kisan Gunjal, Swithun Goodbody, Joyce Kanyangwa Luma and Rita Bhatia, 'FAO/WFP Crop and Food Security Assessment Mission to the Democratic People's Republic of Korea', Food and Agriculture Organization of the United Nations, 16 November 2010.
35. Aditya Chakrabortty, 'Prepare to be Pummelled by the Political Predictions', *Guardian*, 13 April 2010.
36. Gary Clyde Hufbauer, 'Sanctions-Happy USA', *Washington Post*, 12 July 1998.
37. Barbara Crossette, 'Iraq Sanctions Kill Children, UN Reports', *New York Times*, 1 December 1995.

38. Lesley Stahl, 'Albright: "Worth It"', at <home.comcast.net/~dhamre/docAlb. htm>. This site also has movie and sound clips of the exchange, along with an extract from Albright's autobiography.

39. Ibid.

40. Karl Vick, 'Children Pay Cost of Iraq's Chaos', *Washington Post*, 21 November 2004; George A. Lopez and David Cortright, 'Containing Iraq: Sanctions Worked', *Foreign Affairs* 83: 4, 2004.

41. Paul B. Stares and Joel S. Wit, *Preparing for Sudden Change in North Korea*, Washington, DC: Brookings Institution Press for Council on Foreign Relations, 2009.

42. Tae-hoon Lee, 'Jimmy Carter Opposes Sanctions Against North Korea', *Korea Times*, 24 March 2010.

43. Hyun-kyung Kang, 'Nostalgia for Kim Il-sung Rising in N. Korea', *Korea Times*, 21 March 2010.

44. 'Uninterrupted Advance Toward Thriving Nation Called For', *KCNA*, 3 May 2010.

45. 'Agriculture and Food – North Korea', World Resources Institute, at <earthtrends.wri.org/pdf_library/country_profiles/agr_cou_408.pdf>.

46. Olivia Hampton, 'North Korea: Obama's "Dumb War"?', *Guardian*, 25 May 2010.

47. Available from <en.wikipedia.org/wiki/File:Eastasia_lights.jpg>.

48. 'Kim Il Sung University Boasts Its E-Library', *KCNA*, 28 April 2010; 'DPRK stresses economic "Informationalization"', *NK Brief*, Institute for Far Eastern Studies, 4 November 2009; 'Mobile Phones Spread Fast in N. Korea', *Chosun Ilbo*, 10 December 2009; 'N. Korea says it has Developed Web Site for Mobile Phones', *Yonhap*, 22 May 2010.

49. Paul Tjia, 'The Next India', *The Broker*, 28 May 2009.

50. Gregory Elich and Christine Ahn, 'Inside North Korea: An Interview with Christine Ahn', *Counterpunch*, 17 September 2008; *Analysis of the Situation of Children and Women in the Democratic People's Republic of Korea*, Pyongyang: UNICEF, 2006.

51. 'Kim Jong Il Inspects Potato Farm', *KCNA*, 17 May 2010.

52. Saibal Dasgupta, 'Economic Sanctions Strengthen North Korea's Dictatorship, Says German NGO', *Times of India*, 20 April 2010.

53. Jonathan Lynn, 'North Korea Has Plenty of Doctors: WHO', *Washington Post*, 30 April 2010.

54. Margaret Chan, 'Dr Margaret Chan, WHO Director-General: Visit to DPR Korea; Virtual Press Conference', MaximsNewsNetwork, 1 May 2010.

55. Bruce Cumings, 'Fear and Loathing on the Pyongyang Trail: North Korea and the United States', *Japan Focus*, 12 December 2005.

56. Keith B. Richburg, 'In Chinese Border Town, Trade with North Korea Can Be Lucrative but Problematic', *Washington Post*, 26 November 2010. The report itself, some 273 pages long, is available from the UN at <unstats.un.org/unsd/ demographic/sources/census/2010_PHC/North_Korea/Final%20national%20 census%20report.pdf>.

12   THE COSTS AND CONSEQUENCES OF INVASION

1. Anne Flaherty and Matthew Lee, 'Pentagon Won't Say Ship Sinking Is an Act of War', *Washington Post*, 20 May 2010.

2. 'Govt to Produce Own Handsets as Demand for Mobile Phones Rises', *TeleGeography*, 20 April 2010.

3. Yon-se Kim, 'Roh Sees NK's Economic Boom', *Korea Times*, 15 August 2007.

4. Alexis Dudden, John Duncan, Henry Em, John Feffer, Martin Hart-Landsberg, Monica Kim, Suzy Kim, Namhee Lee, Jae-Jung Suh, Seung Hye Suh and Theodore Jun Yoo, 'ASCK Steering Committee Statement on the Current Crisis in Korea', 27 November 2010. For an earlier, substantial, study by the quoted authority, see Charles Wolf, Jr, and Kamil Akramov, 'North Korean Paradoxes: Circumstances, Costs, and Consequences of Korean Unification', RAND National Defense Research Institute, 2005.

5. 'Korean Reunification to Cost Over $3 Trillion', *Korea Times*, 14 September 2010.

6. 'How Reunification Cost Is Calculated', *Chosun Ilbo*, 17 August 2010; 'N. Korea "Will Take 30 Years to Catch Up with South"', *Chosun Ilbo*, 15 September 2010; James Hoare, 'Why the Sunshine Policy Made Sense', *38 North*, 29 March 2010.

7. Scott Stossel, 'North Korea: The War Game', *Atlantic*, July/August 2005.

8. 'N. Korea's Bio-Chem Warfare Threat', CNN, 3 March 2003; Matthew L. Wald, 'CIA Denies Being Source of Anthrax', *Los Angeles Times*, 17 December 2001.

9. Craig Covault, 'North Korean Rocket Flew Further than Earlier Thought', *Spaceflight Now*, 10 April 2009; 'S. Korean Govt Admits DPRK Rocket Followed Satellite Trajectory', *China Daily*, 14 April 2009.

10. Elisabeth Bumiller and David E. Sanger, 'Gates Warns of North Korea Missile Threat to US', *New York Times*, 11 January 2011; 'Pentagon Sees N. Korea as Rising Threat', *Chosun Ilbo*, 28 January 2011.

11. Richard J. Bernstein and Richard Bernstein, 'How Not to Deal with North Korea', *New York Review of Books*, 1 March 2007.

12. Stossel, 'North Korea: The War Game.'

13. Thom Shanker, Helene Cooper and Richard A. Oppel, Jr, 'Elite US Units Step Up Effort in Afghan City Before Attack', *New York Times*, 25 April 2010; 'United States Special Operations Command', *New York Times*, available at <www.nytimes.com/2010/04/26/world/asia/26kandahar.html?hp>.

14. 'N. Korea "Has 180,000 Special Forces Ready to Cross into South"', *Chosun Ilbo*, 16 June 2010; 'S. Korea Must Strengthen Its Special Forces', *Chousin Ilbo*, 7 January 2011; 'S. Korea's Special Forces "Vastly Outnumbered" by N. Korea's', *Chosun Ilbo*, 6 January 2011.

15. 'Kim Jong-il Watches Massive Military Drill', *Chosun Ilbo*, 26 April 2010.

16. Stossel, 'North Korea: The War Game'. Mathews, of course, is just role-playing the position of Director of National Intelligence.

17. Foster Klug, 'US Intelligence Chief: North Korean Military Crumbling', Gazette.com, 2 February 2010.

18. David Von Drehle, 'Wrestling With History: Sometimes You Have To Fight the War You Have, Not the War You Wish You Had', *Washington Post*, 13 November 2005.

19. This paper has appeared. The original version is Chung-in Moon and Sangkeun Lee, 'Military Spending and the Arms Race on the Korean Peninsula', *Asian Perspectives* 33: 4, 2009.

20. Paul B. Stares and Joel S. Wit, *Preparing for Sudden Change in North Korea*, Washington, DC: Brookings Institution Press for Council on Foreign Relations, 2009, p. 21 – emphasis added.

21. Ibid., p. 22.

22. Addressing David Kay, McInerney remarked that he couldn't afford to put 500,000 troops in North Korea if the Kim regime collapsed. 'I would like to do it', he said, 'but the resources aren't there.' Stossel, 'North Korea: The War Game'.

23. Donald Kirk, 'Rand: 400,000 Troops Needed to Secure N. Korea and its "Loose Nukes"', *WorldTribune*, 25 January 2010.

24. Michael J. Finnegan, 'US–ROK Cooperation in Post-Conflict Stabilization and Reconstruction', paper presented at the Expanding the Agenda for Cooperation between the United States and Republic of Korea, Washington, DC, 5 January 2010.

25. Lara Jakes, 'Gen: IEDs Are N. Korea's Latest Weapon', ABC News, 29 September 2009.

26. Bruce Cumings, 'Fear and Loathing on the Pyongyang Trail: North Korea and the United States', *Japan Focus*, 12 December 2005.

27. Emma Campbell, 'South Korea's G-Generation: A Nation Within a Nation, Detached from Unification', *East Asia Form*, 13 April 2010.

28. Song-wu Park, '48% of Youth Would Support N. Korea in Case of US Attack', *Korea Times*, 21 February 2006.

29. Ji-sook Bae, '"40% of Youngsters Would Flee from War"', *Korea Times*, 23 June 2010.

30. John Duerden, 'World Cup 2010 Special: Ten Things To Expect From North Korea In South Africa', Goal.com, 19 May 2010.

31. Saibal Dasgupta, 'Economic Sanctions Strengthen North Korea's Dictatorship, Says German NGO', *Times of India*, 20 April 2010.

32. Kirk, 'Rand: 400,000 Troops Needed to Secure N. Korea and Its "Loose Nukes"'.

13   THE CHINA FACTOR: INTO THE ABYSS?

1. Bonnie S. Glasser, Scott Snyder, See-Won Byun and David J. Szerlip, *Responding to Change on the Korean Peninsula: Impediments to US–South Korea–China Coordination,* Washington, DC: Center for Strategic and International Studies, 2010; 'China Declines to Discuss US Scenario for N. Korea', *Chosun Ilbo*, 3 August 2009.

2. '"US, China Agreed Not to Send Troops to NK"', *Korea Times*, 15 August 2009.

3. Some examples, just confined to books: Joseph Farah, 'A US–China War?', *Los Angeles Times*, 10 Ocbober 2007; Ted Galen Carpenter, *America's Coming War with China*, New York: Palgrave Macmillan, 2006; Jed Babbin and Edward Timperlake, *Showdown: Why China Wants War with the United States*, Washington: Regnery, 2006; Richard Bernstein and Ross H. Munro, *The Coming Conflict with China*, New York: Vintage, 1998; Steven W. Mosher, *Hegemon: China's Plan to Dominate Asia and the World,* New York: Encounter Books, 2001; Bill Gertz, *The China Threat: How the People's Republic Targets America*, Washington, DC: Regnery Publishing, Inc, 2002; Peter Navarro, *The Coming China Wars: Where They Will Be Fought and How They Can Be Won*, 2nd edn, Upper Saddle River, NJ: FT Press, 2008.

4. 'Annual Report to Congress: Military Power of the People's Republic of China', Department of Defense, available at <www.defense.gov/pubs/china.html>. This text is dated 2008, but it is unclear when it was submitted, and why there has not been one since then.
5. *Military Expenditure: SIPRI Yearbook 2008: Armaments, Disarmament and International Security*, Oxford: Oxford University Press, 2008.
6. 'Lee Proposes Unification Tax', *Hankyoreh*, 16 August 2010.
7. 'Lee's Reunification Plan Excludes Korean Commonwealth', *Hankyoreh*, 17 August 2010.
8. Seok-gu Jeong, 'President Lee's *Cheonan* Gamble', *Hankyoreh*, 25 May 2010.
9. Sung-yoon Lee, 'Planning For A Life After Kim', *Foreign Policy*, 16 February 2010.
10. I plan to return to this area in a book tentatively titled *Friends and Enemies: Declining America and Rising China*.

Bibliography

'09BEIJING1247, BEIJING-BASED G-5 CHIEFS OF MISSION ON DPRK, GTMO', *WikiLeaks*, 8 May 2009.

'2 Koreas Brief UN Security Council on *Cheonan* Sinking', *Chosun Ilbo*, 16 June 2010.

'31st Marine Expeditionary Unit', Wikipedia, <en.wikipedia.org/wiki/31st_Marine_Expeditionary_Unit>.

'31st Marine Expeditionary Unit home page', <www.marines.mil/unit/31stmeu/Pages/default.aspx>.

'31st MEU Reflects on 2009', *US Marine Corps News*, 11 December 2009.

'2005 White Paper on Korean Unification', Ministry of Unification, 2005.

'Accord is Reached on Russian debt', *JoongAng Ilbo*, 20 June 2003.

'Activists Urge UNSC to Reinvestigate *Cheonan* Sinking', *Chosun Ilbo*, 15 June 2010.

'Agreed Framework between the United States of America and the Democratic People's Republic of Korea', *Korean Peninsula Energy Development Organization (KEDO)*, 21 October 1994.

'Agriculture and Food – North Korea', World Resources Institute, <earthtrends.wri.org/pdf_library/country_profiles/agr_cou_408.pdf>.

'Amid Authenticity Dispute, Kim Jong-il Makes Brisk Inspections', *Korea Times*, 7 November 2009.

'Analysts Say N. Korea Highlights Peace Negotiations through Artillery Fire Near NLL', *Hankyoreh*, 28 January 2010.

'Annual Report to Congress: Military Power of the People's Republic of China', Department of Defense, <www.defense.gov/pubs/china.html>.

'Are We Prepared?' *Korea Herald*, 30 March 2010.

'Austrian Guilty Over Lavish Birthday Presents for Kim Jong-il', *Chosun Ilbo*, 8 December 2010.

'Broadcasters Baselessly Link Sunken Ship to N. Korean Attack', *Hankyoreh*, 29 March 2010.

'*Cheonan* Findings Raise More Questions', *Chosun Ilbo*, 24 May 2010.

'*Cheonan* Investigators Presented Wrong Torpedo Diagram', *Chosun Ilbo*, 30 June 2010.

'*Cheonan* Probe Finds RDX, Alloy Used in Torpedoes', *JoongAng Ilbo*, 8 May 2010.

'"*Cheonan*" Case Termed Most Hideous Conspiratorial Farce in History', *KCNA*, 2 November 2010.

'China's Anti-Aircraft Carrier Missile "Closer to Completion"', *Chosun Ilbo*, 29 December 2010.

'China's BYD Aims to Be World's Biggest Carmaker by 2025', *Chosun Ilbo*, 14 January 2010.

'China "Has More Warships than US"', *Chosun Ilbo*, 1 September 2010.

'China Becoming Superpower in Scientific Research', *Chosun Ilbo*, 27 January 2010.

'China Declines to Discuss US Scenario for N. Korea', *Chosun Ilbo*, 3 August 2009.

'China Proposes UN Military Armistice Commission Convene for Reinvestigation into *Cheonan*', *Hankyoreh*, 29 May 2010.

'China to Become Top Favorite Nation of Koreans Studying Abroad', *Korea Times*, 21 June 2010.

'China Transforms from Copycat to Patent Powerhouse', *Chosun Ilbo*, 5 October 2010.

'Chinese in Series of Diplomatic Gaffes in Seoul', *Chosun Ilbo*, 30 November 2010.

'Chinese Military Buildup Far Exceeds Its Defensive Needs: US', IndianExpress. com, 16 December 2010.

'ChoJoongDong Has Greatly Increased Pro-Administration Coverage, Study Says', *Hankyoreh*, 27 May 2010.

'Civic Group Takes Unresolved *Cheonan* Issues to UN', *Hankyoreh*, 15 June 2010.

'Conservative Newspapers and Lee Administration Strengthen Symbiotic Relationship', *Hankyoreh*, 27 May 2010.

'Dassault Folds Tent, Swears Off Korea', *JoongAng Ilbo*, 7 June 2002.

'Defense Minister Told Off for Speculating About Shipwreck', *Chosun Ilbo*, 6 April 2010.

'Diplomat Meets Detained Journalists in NK', *Korea Times*, 16 May 2009.

'Discussion at the 150th Meeting of the National Security Council (Presidential Memo)', White House, 19 June 1953.

'The DP Is Making a Fool of Itself Over the *Cheonan* Sinking', *Chosun Ilbo*, 18 May 2010.

'The DP Needs to Grow Up', *Chosun Ilbo*, 18 June 2010.

'DPRK–Japan Red Cross Talks Held in Beijing', *KCNA*, 13 March 2000.

'DPRK Committees Release Joint Statement on 60 Years after Korean War', *KCNA*, 24 June 2010.

'DPRK Foreign Ministry's Spokesman Blasts US Delaying Tactics in Solution of Nuclear Issue', *KCNA*, 28 March 2008.

'DPRK Foreign Ministry's Spokesman on US Lifting of Major Economic Sanctions against DPRK', *KCNA*, 27 June 2008.

'DPRK Ready to Join 5 More Anti-Terror Pacts', *People's Korea*, 25 December 2001.

'DPRK Signs Anti-Terror Conventions', *People's Korea*, 13 December 2001.

'DPRK Stance towards Terrorist Attacks on US', *KCNA*, 12 September 2001.

'DPRK Stand on Denuclearization of Korea Remains Unchanged', *KCNA*, 26 January 2011.

'DPRK Stresses Economic "Informationalization"', NK Brief, Institute for Far Eastern Studies, 4 November 2009.

'DPRK Takes Merciless Action to Defend MDL', *KCNA*, 13 November 2009.

'DPRK UN Representative on "*Cheonan*" Case', *KCNA*, 16 June 2010.

'European Parliament Resolution of 17 June 2010 on the Situation in the Korean Peninsula', 17 June 2010.

'Evidence of Park Chung-hee's Military Allegiance to Japan Surfaces', *Hankyoreh*, 6 November 2009.

'Exchanges & Cooperation', ROK Ministry of Unification, <eng.unikorea.go.kr/ eng/default.jsp?pgname=AFFexchanges_overview>.

'Experts Address Misconceptions about OPCON Transfer', *Hankyoreh*, 25 June 2010.

'Extent of NK Damage Remains Uncertain', *Chosun Ilbo*, 26 November 2010.

'F-22 Fighter Jets Emblazoned with the Rising Sun', *Chosun Ilbo*, 27 April 2007.

'FAO/WFP Crop and Food Supply Assessment Mission to the Democratic People's Republic of Korea', Rome: Food and Agriculture Organization/World Food Programme, 1998.

'Far-right Groups Launch Violent Protests against PSPD', *Hankyoreh*, 18 June 2010.

'Fighter's Crash: Though Time-Consuming, Thorough Probes Are Needed', *Korea Times*, 9 June 2006.

'FM Accuses US of Creating Atmosphere of International Pressure', *KCNA*, 28 May 2010.

'FM Spokesman Accuses US of Sidestepping Proposals for Dialogue', *KCNA*, 16 December 2010.

'Foreign Corrupt Practices Act', US Department of Justice, www.justice.gov/criminal/fraud/fcpa.

'Gift from Governor of New Mexico State of US', *KCNA*, 20 December 2010.

'Gov't Must Tell Muslim World of Ashena Unit's Mission of Peace', *Chosun Ilbo*, 1 July 2010.

'Government Protests Russia's Conflicting *Cheonan* Findings', *Hankyoreh*, 12 July 2010.

'Govt to Produce Own Handsets as Demand for Mobile Phones Rises', *TeleGeography*, 20 April 2010.

'Gratitude Expressed for Appeal for International Assistance to DPRK', *KCNA*, 4 December 2000.

'Health InterNetwork Access to Research Initiative (HINARI)', World Health Organization, <www.who.int/hinari/en>.

'How Reunification Cost Is Calculated', *Chosun Ilbo*, 17 August 2010.

'Impartial Discussion on "*Cheonan*" Case Urged', *KCNA*, 18 June 2010.

'An Important Lesson for the Conspiracy Theorists', *Chosun Ilbo*, 1 June 2005.

'Information About Shipwreck Must Be Handled with Care', *Chosun Ilbo*, 7 April 2010.

'Investors in DPRK Take Huge Hits; Interest in FDI Plummets', Institute for Far Eastern Studies, 18 October 2010.

'"Iron Silkroad" to Connect Korean Peninsula and Europe Envisaged', *Yonhap*, 16 June 2000.

'Is Our Military Up to the Job of Protecting the Country?', *Chosun Ilbo*, 18 December 2009.

'Is There Really No Rift Between Seoul and Washington?', *Chosun Ilbo*, 9 October 2009.

'Jo Chang Dok Interviewed on Serious Shortage of Electricity', *KCNA*, 3 February 2000.

'Joint Concert Held on Chopin's 200th Birthday', *KCNA*, 11 November 2010.

'KCNA on Tremendous Damage Done to DPRK by US', *KCNA*, 24 June 2010.

'KCNA Refutes US Officials' Lies About Cause of Economic Difficulties', *KCNA*, 13 January 2003.

'Kim Il Sung University Boasts Its E-Library', *KCNA*, 28 April 2010.

'Kim Jong-il Watches Massive Military Drill', *Chosun Ilbo*, 26 April 2010.

'Kim Jong Il Enjoys Performance Given by State Symphony Orchestra', *KCNA*, 28 November 2010.

'Kim Jong Il Inspects Command of KPA Unit 630', *KCNA*, 31 January 2010.

'Kim Jong Il Inspects Potato Farm', *KCNA*, 17 May 2010.

'KNPC Warns US and S. Korea Against Acting Recklessly', *KCNA*, 9 April 2000.

'Korea's Neighbors Catch Up with US Stealth Technology', *Chosun Ilbo*, 9 August 2010.

'KOREA CRISIS: Basic Facts and Historical Context', National Campaign to end the Korean War, 27 November 2010.

'Korea, Russia at Odds Over Rocket Launch Failure', *Chosun Ilbo*, 1 February 2011.

'Korea, US Agree to Compromise N. Korea "Concept Plan"', *Chosun Ilbo*, 5 June 2005.

'KOREA: The Walnut', *Time*, 9 March 1953.

'Korean People's Army Estimated to Number 700 Thousand Troops', *Hankyoreh*, 19 March 2010.

'Korean Reunification to Cost over $3 trillion', *Korea Times*, 14 September 2010.

'KPA Navy Command's Important Communiqué', *KCNA*, 23 March 2000.

'KPA Panmunjom Mission Clarifies Revolutionary Armed Forces' Principled Stand', *KCNA*, 27 May 2009.

'KPA Supreme Command: World Should Know Who Is Provoker', *KCNA*, 20 December 2010.

'The Last Emperor', *New York Times*, 19 October 2003.

'Lee Administration Responds to Russian Investigation Report', *Hankyoreh*, 28 July 2010.

'Lee Announces Expanded International Role for Military', *Hankyoreh*, 28 September.

'Lee Government Must Cancel Troop Redeployment to Afghanistan', *Hankyoreh*, 31 October 2009.

'Lee Proposes Unification Tax', *Hankyoreh*, 16 August 2010.

'Lee Pushes Constitutional Amendment in Televised Dialogue', *Hankyoreh*, 2 February 2011.

'Lee's Reunification Plan Excludes Korean Commonwealth', *Hankyoreh*, 17 August 2010.

'Memorandum of DPRK Foreign Ministry', *KCNA*, 3 March 2005.

'Message to German Chancellor', *KCNA*, 14 November 2001.

'Military and Security Developments Involving the People's Republic of China 2010', US Department of Defense, 2010.

'Military Commentator on Truth behind "Story of Attack by North" (1)', *KCNA*, 28 May 2010.

'Military Commentator on Truth behind "Story of Attack by North" (2)', *KCNA*, 29 May 2010.

'Mobile Phones Spread Fast in N. Korea', *Chosun Ilbo*, 10 December 2009.

'Most S. Koreans Skeptical About *Cheonan* Findings, Survey Shows', *Chosun Ilbo*, 8 September 2010.

'N. Korea's Bio-Chem Warfare Threat', CNN, 3 March 2003.

'N. Korea Not in Danger of Imminent Collapse', *Dong-A Ilbo*, 8 April 2010.

'N. Korea Proposed Secret Contacts with US in 1974: Document', Kyodo News Service, 21 December 2008.

'N. Korea Says It Has Developed Web Site for Mobile Phones', *Yonhap*, 22 May 2010.

'N. Korea Stops Promoting Leader's Son', *Korea Times*, 10 October 2009.

'N. Korea's War History Is Mirror Opposite World View', *Chosun Ilbo*, 24 June 2010.

'N. Korea's Youth Population Dwindles Due to Food Shortage', *Chosun Ilbo*, 6 December 2010.

'N. Korea "Hacks into S. Korea–US Defense Plans"', *Chosun Ilbo*, 18 December 2009.

'N. Korea "Has 180,000 Special Forces Ready to Cross into South"', *Chosun Ilbo*, 16 June 2010.

'N. Korea "Runs Naval Suicide Squads"', *Chosun Ilbo*, 30 March 2010.

'N. Korea "Will Take 30 Years to Catch Up with South"', *Chosun Ilbo*, 15 September 2010.

'N. Korea Policy to Shift from Engagement to Reunification', *Chosun Ilbo*, 27 December 2010.

'N. Korea's Reinvestigation Proposal Alters *Cheonan* Situation', *Hankyoreh*, 21 May 2010.

'NIS Says N. Korean Attack on *Cheonan* Impossible Sans Kim Jong-il Approval', *Hankyoreh*, 7 April 2010.

'North Korea's Provocation Must Never Be Tolerated', *Kyunghyang Daily News*, 24 November 2010.

'Northern Limit Line Rejected', *KCNA*, 2 August 2002.

'Obama's Second State of the Union (Text)', *New York Times*, 25 January 2011.

'OPCON Transfer Delay Signals Abrupt Strategic Change', *Hankyoreh*, 24 June 2010.

'OPLAN 5029 – Collapse of North Korea', GlobalSecurity.org, <www.globalsecurity. org/military/ops/oplan-5029.htm>.

'OPLAN 5029 Risks Ceding South Korean Sovereignty to the US', *Hankyoreh*, 2 November 2009.

'Over 600,000 N. Koreans Starve from 1995–2005', *Hankyoreh*, 23 November 2010.

'Pak: North Waiting for End to "Hostile" US Policy', *JoongAng Ilbo*, 3 August 2007.

'Pentagon Sees N. Korea as Rising Threat', *Chosun Ilbo*, 28 January 2011.

'Pentagon Sounds Alarm at China's Military Buildup', *Wall Street Journal*, 17 August 2010.

'Poll: Do You Think America's "Can-Do" Spirit Is Faltering?', LJWorld.com, June 2010.

'Posada Carriles Trial Hinges on Yacht', Fox News, 2 February 2011.

'Probe Concludes Torpedo Sank South Korea Ship: Report', *Reuters*, 6 May 2010.

'Protests across US to Demand: "No New Korean War!"', ANSWER Coalition, 27 November 2010.

'Public's Faith in Military Authorities Shaken after *Cheonan* Sinking', *Hankyoreh*, 12 April 2010.

'Pyongyang Cites Forgotten Inter-Korean Agreement for Demands', *Chosun Ilbo*, 24 May 2010.

'Q and A With Rear Admiral Thomas J. Eccles', *CorrDefense* 5: 3, 2009.

'Questions Linger 100 Days after the *Cheonan* Sinking', *Hankyoreh*, 3 July 2010.

'Questions Raised Following *Cheonan* Announcement', *Hankyoreh*, 21 May 2010.

'Report on Jimmy Carter's Visit to DPRK', *KCNA*, 27 August 2010.

'The Rise of China's Auto Industry and Its Impact on the US Motor Vehicle Industry', Congressional Research Service, 16 November 2009.

'Rodong Sinmun Calls for Confidence-Building between DPRK and US', *KCNA*, 11 January 2011.

'Russia Urges Seoul, Pyongyang to Show Restraint over Ship Sinking', *RIA Novosti*, 20 May 2010.

'Russia wants "100% proof" N. Korea Sunk Ship', AFP, 27 May 2010.

'Russia's *Cheonan* Investigation Suspects that the Sinking *Cheonan* Ship was Caused by a Mine in Water', *Hankyoreh*, 28 July 2010.

'Russian Analyst Predicts Decline and Breakup of US', *Novosti*, 24 November 2008.

'Russian Experts "Unconvinced by *Cheonan* Evidence"', *Chosun Ilbo*, 10 June 2010.

'Russian Experts Inspect Results of *Cheonan* Probe', *Korea Times*, 31 May 2010.

'Russian Experts to Report *Cheonan* Sinking Conclusions to Defense Ministry Soon', *RIA Novosti*, 8 June 2010.

'Russian Experts Unable to Give Answers on *Cheonan* Sinking – Navy Commander', *RIA-Novosti*, 24 July 2010.

'Russian Military Experts Study *Cheonan* Sinking Probe Files', *Itar-Tass*, 9 June 2010.

'Russian Navy Expert Team's Analysis on the *Cheonan* Incident', *Hankyoreh*, 29 July 2010.

'Russian Specialists Have Questions on S. Korean Corvette's Sinking – Navy Commander', InterFax.com, 24 July 2010.

'Russians Doubt about Ship Sinking by NK Attack', *Korea Times*, 9 June 2010.

'S. Korean Govt Admits DPRK Rocket Followed Satellite Trajectory', *China Daily*, 14 April 2009.

'S. Korea's Challenge to Measure of Navy Command of KPA Blasted', *KCNA*, 31 March 2000.

'S. Korea Prepares for Face-to-Face Negotiations', *Hankyoreh*, 9 August 2007.

'S. Korea, US Reschedule Wartime Operational Control Transfer', *Korea Herald*, 27 June 2010.

'S. Korean Authorities' Intensified Military Provocations', *KCNA*, 28 February 2000.

'S. Korea's Special Forces "Vastly Outnumbered" by N. Korea's', *Chosun Ilbo*, 6 January 2011.

'S. Korea–US Anti-Submarine Drill Conducted Night of *Cheonan* Sinking', *Hankyoreh*, 8 June 2010.

'S. Korea Must Strengthen Its Special Forces', *Chosun Ilbo*, 7 January 2011.

'S. Korea, US, "Complete N. Korea Contingency Plan"', *Chosun Ilbo*, 2 November 2009.

'Scholars Call for End to PSPD Witch-Hunt', *Hankyoreh*, 22 June 2010.

'Scientists Question *Cheonan* Investigation Findings', *Hankyoreh*, 28 June 2010.

'Seoul Simulated Bombing of N. Korean Nuclear Plant', *Chosun Ilbo*, 6 June 2005.

'Serial Number of Torpedo Traced to N. Korea', *Chosun Ilbo*, 19 May 2010.

'Signs Suggest that N. Korean Regime Is Cracking', *Chosun Ilbo*, 13 December 2010.

'South Korea Deviated from Previous Rules of Engagement in West Sea Clash', *Hankyoreh*, 11 November 2009.

'South Korea: Country Study', *Federal Research Divison, Library of Congress*, 27 July 2010.

'South Korean Companies Face Increasing Attacks in Afghanistan', *Hankyoreh*, 12 November 2009.

'STOP Oppression & Prosecutors: Investigation on PSPD: Urgent Letter to Friends, Human Rights Defenders and Peace Activities', People's Solidarity for Participatory Democracy, 21 June 2010.

'Text of the Korean War Armistice Agreement', 27 July 1953, <news.findlaw.com/wp/docs/korea/kwarmagr072753.html>.

'Timely Humanitarian Appeal – KCNA commentary', *KCNA*, 11 July 1998.

'Torpedo Attack "Could Be Proved from State of Wreck Alone"', *Chosun Ilbo*, 30 April 2020.

'Torpedo Explosive Detected in Sunken Ship: Official', *Yonhap*, 7 May 2010.

'Torpedo Gunpowder Found in *Cheonan* Wreckage', *Chosun Ilbo*, 7 May 2010.

'Troop Dispatch to Afghanistan Is No Military Adventure', *Chosun Ilbo*, 2 November 2009.

'Truth About West Sea Naval Clash; "NLL" Questioned', *People's Korea*, 13 July 2002.

'Truth Behind "Northern Limit Line" Disclosed', *KCNA*, 25 June 2007.

'UN discussions on Ship Sinking Stalled: Sources', *Yonhap*, 2 July 2010.

'US and S. Korean "OPLAN 5029" Blamed', *KCNA*, 9 November 2009.

'US at Work on Strangling Kim Jong-il's Cash Flow', *Chosun Ilbo*, 12 November 2009.

'US Commander Reveals True Purpose of Troops in Okinawa is to Remove N. Korea's Nukes', *Mainichi*, 1 April 2010.

'US Expert Casts Doubt on "Grand Bargain" for N. Korea', *Chosun Ilbo*, 9 October 2009.

'US Finds No North Link to *Cheonan*', *JoongAng Ilbo*, 7 April 2010.

'US Has No Evidence on N. Korea's Involvement: State Dept', *Yonhap*, 26 March 2010.

'US Military Exercises', Federation of American Scientists, <www.fas.org/programs/ssp/man/usmillogistics/military_exercises.html>.

'US Official: Kim Jong-il in Full Control in N.Korea', *Chosun Ilbo*, 10 August 2009.

'US Plot for Preemptive Nuclear Attack Blasted', *KCNA*, 24 May 2005.

'US Urged to Adopt Policy of Peaceful Co-Existence with DPRK', *KCNA*, 16 January 2005.

'US War Scenario against DPRK Assailed', *KCNA*, 5 August 2003.

'US Won't Stand for Leaks of Classified Data, NIS Chief Warns', *Chosun Ilbo*, 7 April 2010.

'UD INFO – Fact Sheet: Sweden's Cooperation with NATO in EAPC/PfP', Ministry for Foreign Affairs, May 2005.

'UN Security Council in Emergency Talks on Korean Tensions', Voice of America, 19 December 2010.

'"UN Security Council Understands Probe into Ship Sinking"', *Korea Times*, 15 June 2010.

'UN to Send Review Mission to North Korea', *AFP*, 18 May 2010.

'Uninterrupted Advance toward Thriving Nation Called For', *KCNA*, 3 May 2010.

'The United Nations and Decolonization', <www.un.org/Depts/dpi/decolonization/main.htm>.

'United Nations Sanctions (Democratic People's Republic of Korea) Regulations 2006', *NZ Government*, 10 September 2009.

'United States Special Operations Command', *New York Times*, <www.nytimes.com/2010/04/26/world/asia/26kandahar.html?hp>.

'UNSC Urged to Properly Know about Truth of "*Cheonan*" Case', *KCNA*, 21 June 2010.

'US Embassy Cables: China "Would Accept" Korean Reunification', *Guardian*, 1 December 2010.

'US, China Agreed Not to Send Troops to NK', *Korea Times*, 15 August 2009.

'US Governor Visits North Korea', *Al Jazeera*, 17 December 2010.

'USFK Chief Warns of Instability in N. Korea', *Chosun Ilbo*, 26 March 2010.

'What Caused the *Cheonan* to Sink?', *Chosun Ilbo*, 29 March 2010.

'What Will Be the Impact of S. Korean Sanctions on N. Korea?', *Chosun Ilbo*, 25 May 2010.

'White Paper Declares Sunshine Policy Dead and Buried', *Chosun Ilbo*, 18 November 2010.

'Young People Less Inclined to Blame N. Korea for Shipwreck', *Chosun Ilbo*, 24 June 2010.

2008 Population Census National Report, Pyongyang: Central Bureau of Statistics, 2009.

Abrahamian, Andray, 'North Korea: Ghost of Roh vs. Living Lee', *38North*, 27 May 2010.

Achenbach, Joel, 'Bet on America: Forget the Doom and Gloom. In 50 Years, We'll Still Be No. 1', *Washington Post*, 2 September 2007.

Aden, Nathaniel, 'North Korean Trade with China as Reported in Chinese Customs Statistics: Recent Energy Trends and Implications', in *DPRK Energy Experts Working Group Meeting*, San Francisco: Nautilus Institute, 2006.

Ahn, Christine, 'Sixty Years is Enough: One Woman's Dream for Peace in Korea', *Korea Policy Institute*, 25 June 2010.

Ahn, Yong-hyun, 'The Country Needs True Independence', *Chosun Ilbo*, 19 July 2010.

Ahn, Young-joon, 'China Premier: Korean Tensions Must Be Defused', *Washington Post*, 30 May 2010.

Alnasrawi, Abbas, 'Iraq: Economic Sanctions and Consequences, 1990–2000', *Third World Quarterly* 22: 2, 2001.

Analysis of the Situation of Children and Women in the Democratic People's Republic of Korea, Pyongyang: UNICEF, 2006.

Applebaum, Anne, '"It's Too Soon to Tell" How the Iraq War Went', *Washington Post*, 30 August 2010.

Arkin, William 'Not Just A Last Resort? A Global Strike Plan, With a Nuclear Option', *Washington Post*, 15 May 2005.

Arlow, Oliver, 'Kim Jong-il Keeps $4bn "Emergency Fund" in European Banks', *Daily Telegraph*, 14 March 2010.

Armstrong, Charles, 'The Destruction and Reconstruction of North Korea, 1950–1960', *Asia-Pacific Journal* 8: 51 (2), 2010.

Ash, Robert, 'Review of The North Korean Economy: Structure and Development. By Joseph Sang-Hoon Chung', *China Quarterly* 60, 1974.

Associated Press, 'Wikileaks Reveals Plans for North Korean Collapse', *Washington Post*, 30 November 2010.

——'US Concerned over China's Rapid Development of New Weapons', *Guardian*, 9 January 2011.

——'Son Says North Korean Leader Opposed Succession', *Washington Post*, 28 January 2011.

Auster, Bruce B. , Kevin Whitelaw and Thomas Omestad, 'Upping the Ante for Kim Jong Il; Pentagon Plan 5030, A New Blueprint for Facing Down North Korea', *US News and World Report, Nation & World*, 21 July 2003.

Babbin, Jed , and Edward Timperlake, *Showdown: Why China Wants War with the United States*, Washington: Regnery, 2006.

Bae, Hyun-jung 'Police Crack Down on *Cheonan* Rumors', *Korea Herald*, 24 May 2010.

Bae, Ji-sook, '40% of Youngsters Would Flee from War', *Korea Times*, 23 June 2010.

——'KBS Program Raises Questions about Cause of *Cheonan* Sinking', *Korea Times*, 18 November 2010.

——'Seoul Not Safe from Artillery Attacks', *Korea Times*, 26 November 2010.

Beal, Tim, 'Multilayered Confrontation in East Asia: North Korea–Japan', *Asian Affairs* 36: 3, 2005.

——*North Korea: The Struggle against American Power*, London and Ann Arbor: Pluto Press, 2005.

——'The United Nations and the North Korean Missile and Nuclear Tests', *NZ Journal of Asian Studies* 9: 2, 2007.

——'Korean Brinkmanship, American Provocation, and the Road to War: The Manufacturing of a Crisis', *Asia-Pacific Journal* 8: 51 (1), 2010.

Beck, Peter M., 'The Bush Administration's Failed North Korea Policy', Friends Committee on National Legislation website, 14 April 2004.

Bernstein, Richard J., and Richard Bernstein, 'How Not to Deal with North Korea', *New York Review of Books*, 1 March 2007.

——'Good War Gone Bad (Review of *The Coldest Winter: America and the Korean War* by David Halberstam)', *New York Review of Books*, 25 October 2007.

Bernstein, Richard, and Ross H. Munro, *The Coming Conflict with China*, New York: Vintage, 1998.

Blanchard, Ben, 'North Korea Farmers Shun New Won – Former Aid Worker', XE.com, 20 April 2010.

Bolton, John, 'North Korea: Not the Time For Talks', *Wall Street Journal*, 4 January 2011.

Boot, Max 'The New American Way of War', *Foreign Affairs*, July/August 2003.

Borger, Julian, 'David Miliband: China Ready to Join US as World Power', *Guardian*, 17 May 2009.

Bradsher, Keith, 'China Leading Global Race to Make Clean Energy', *New York Times*, 30 January 2010.

——'China Drawing High-Tech Research From US', *New York Times*, 17 March 2010.

——'Ford Agrees to Sell Volvo to a Fast-Rising Chinese Company', *New York Times*, 28 March 2010.

——'China Is Eager to Bring High-Speed Rail Expertise to the US', *New York Times*, 7 April 2010.

Branigan, Tania, 'North Korea Threatens South over Report on Sinking of Warship', *Guardian*, 20 May 2010.

'Brewerstroupe', 'The Miraculous Torpedo', *Slate*, 27 May 2010.

Bumiller, Elisabeth, and David E. Sanger, 'Gates Warns of North Korea Missile Threat to US', *New York Times*, 11 January 2011.

Bunn, Matthew, *Securing the Bomb 2010: Securing All Nuclear Materials in Four Years*, Washington Nuclear Threat Initiative, 2010.

Bush, Richard C., 'The Challenge of a Nuclear North Korea: Dark Clouds, Only One Silver Lining', *PacNet*, 30 September 2010.

Byun, Duk-kun, 'Jimmy Carter calls on US, S. Korea to Talk Directly with N. Korea', *Yonhap*, 23 March 2010.

Campbell, Emma, 'South Korea's G-Generation: A Nation Within a Nation, Detached from Unification', *East Asia Form*, 13 April 2010.

Caprio, Mark E., 'Plausible Denial? Reviewing the Evidence of DPRK Culpability for the *Cheonan* Warship Incident', *Asia-Pacific Journal*, 26 July 2010.

Carlin, Robert, and John W. Lewis, 'What North Korea Really Wants', *Washington Post*, 27 January 2007.

——'Review US Policy toward North Korea', *Washington Post*, 22 November 2010.

Carpenter, Ted Galen, *America's Coming War with China*, New York: Palgrave Macmillan, 2006.

Carter, Jimmy, 'North Korea Wants to Make a Deal', *New York Times*, 15 September 2010.

Cha, Ariana Eunjung, 'Chinese Banks Find Their Credit in High Demand', *Washington Post*, 2 January 2010.

Cha, Victor, 'Korea's Place in the Axis (update)', *Foreign Affairs*, November 2002.

——'We Have No Plan', *Nautilus Policy Forum Online*, 15 June 2008.

——'Obama's Korea Inheritance', *Comparative Connections* 10: 4, 2009.

——'Five Myths about North Korea', *Washington Post*, 10 December 2010.

Chakrabortty, Aditya, 'Prepare to be Pummelled by the Political Predictions', *Guardian*, 13 April 2010.

Chan, Margaret Dr., 'Dr Margaret Chan, WHO Director-General: Visit to DPR Korea; Virtual Press Conference', *MaximsNewsNetwork*, 1 May 2010.

Chan, Sewell, and Jackie Calmes, 'US Keeps Command of Military in Seoul', *New York Times*, 26 June 2010.

Chanlett-Avery, Emma, and Mary Beth Nikitin, *Japan's Nuclear Policy Future: Policy Debate, Prospects, and US Interests*, Washington DC: Congressional Research Service, 2009.

Chen, David, 'China Emerges as a Scapegoat in Campaign Ads', *New York Times*, 9 October 2010.

Cheong, Wooksik, 'The *Cheonan* Sinking and a New Cold War in Asia', Nautilus Policy Forum Online 10–034, 2010.

China Hand, 'David Asher's Dead End', *China Matters*, 28 April 2007, <chinamatters. blogspot.com/2007/04/david-ashers-dead-end.html>.

——'It's Official: America Has a China-Containment Policy', *China Matters*, 9 July 2010, <chinamatters.blogspot.com/2010/07/its-official-america-has-china.html>.

Chinoy, Mike, 'North Korean Denuclearization Pact is Collapsing', *San Francisco Chronicle*, 30 September 2008.

——*Meltdown: The Inside Story of the North Korean Nuclear Crisis*, New York: St Martin's Press, 2008.

——'He's Not the Crazy One', *Daily Beast*, 13 July 2009.

——'No Hostile Intent: A Look Back at Kim Jong Il's Dramatic Overture to the Clinton Administration', *38 North*, 11 November 2009.

——'Is the South Korean Tail Wagging the American Dog?' *38 North*, 22 July 2010.

Cho, Jae-hyon, 'Evidence Scooped Up by Fishing Trawler', *Korea Times*, 20 May 2010.

Choe, Sang-hun, 'Korean Navies Skirmish in Disputed Waters', *New York Times*, 10 November 2009.

Choe, Sang-Hun, 'Last Communist Rebel Dies in South Korea', *Associated Press*, 2 April 2004.

Chung, Joseph Sang-Hoon, *The North Korean Economy: Structure and Development*, Stanford, California: Hoover Institution Press, 1974.

Chung, Young Chul, 'Political Economy of the US Economic Sanctions against North Korea: Past, Present and Future', *Development and Society* 34: 2, 2005.

Clark, Joseph S., 'An American Policy toward Communist China', *Annals of the American Academy of Political and Social Science* 330, July 1960.

Cobban, Helena, 'Global Implications of China's Big Investment in Iraq and Afghanistan', *Asia-Pacific Journal: Japan Focus*, 1 September 2008.

Collon, Michel, 'What Will the US Foreign Policy be Tomorrow?' MichelCollen. info, 1 September 2008.

Cookson, Clive, 'China Set for Global Lead in Scientific Research', *Financial Times*, 26 January 2010.

Cossa, Ralph, 'Fears of New "Nixon Shock"', *Japan Times*, 25 May 2007.

Covault, Craig, 'North Korean Rocket Flew Further than Earlier Thought', *Spaceflight Now*, 10 April 2009.

Cox, Michael, 'Is the United States in Decline—Again?' *International Affairs* 83: 4, 2007.

Crossette, Barbara, 'Iraq Sanctions Kill Children, UN Reports', *New York Times*, 1 December 1995.

Cumings, Bruce, 'Korea: Forgotten Nuclear Threats', *Le Monde Diplomatique*, December 2004.

——'Fear and Loathing on the Pyongyang Trail: North Korea and the United States', *Japan Focus*, 12 December 2005.

——'Creating Korean Insecurity: The US Role', in Hazel Smith, ed., *Reconstituting Korean Security: A Policy Primer*, Tokyo–New York–Paris: United Nations University Press, 2008, pp. 21–42.

Cumings, Bruce, Francis M. Bator, Richard J. Bernstein and Richard Bernstein, 'The Korean War: An Exchange', *New York Review of Books*, 22 November 2007.

Cyranoski, David, 'Questions Raised over Korean Torpedo Claims', *Nature*, 14 July 2010.

——'Controversy over South Korea's Sunken Ship', *Nature*, 14 July 2010.

——'More Questions Raised over South Korea's Sunken Ship', *Nature*, 27 July 2010.

Dasgupta, Saibal, 'Economic Sanctions Strengthen North Korea's Dictatorship, Says German NGO', *Times of India*, 20 April 2010.

Demick, Barbara, *Nothing to Envy: Ordinary Lives in North Korea*, 1st edn, New York: Spiegel & Grau, 2009.

Demick, Barbara, and John M. Glionna, 'Doubts Surface on North Korea's Role in Ship Sinking', *Los Angeles Times*, 23 July 2010.

Deng, Jingyin 'China's Speedy Rails Going Overseas', *Global Times*, 15 March 2010.

Deudney, Daniel, and G. John Ikenberry, 'The Myth of the Autocratic Revival: Why Liberal Democracy Will Prevail', *Foreign Affairs* 88: 1, 2009.

Dewan, Shaila, 'US Suspends Haitian Airlift in Cost Dispute', *New York Times*, 29 January 2010.

Diehl, Jackson, 'Obama's Foreign Policy Needs an Update', *Washington Post*, 22 November 2010.

Ding, Gang, 'Coordination Will Stave Off Another Korean War', *Global Times*, 30 December 2010.

Dreazen, Yoichi J., and Amol Sharma, 'US Sells Arms to South Asian Rivals', *Wall Street Journal*, 25 February 2010.

Drew, Christopher, and Nicola Clark, 'BAE Settles Corruption Charges', *New York Times*, 5 February 2010.

Dudden, Alexis, John Duncan, Henry Em, John Feffer, Martin Hart-Landsberg, Monica Kim, Suzy Kim, Namhee Lee, Jae-Jung Suh, Seung Hye Suh and Theodore Jun Yoo, 'ASCK Steering Committee Statement on the Current Crisis in Korea', 27 November 2010.

Duerden, John, 'World Cup 2010 Special: Ten Things To Expect From North Korea In South Africa', Goal.com, 19 May 2010.

Eggers, William D., and John O'Leary, 'Can the US Still Tackle Big Problems? Lessons from the Health-Care Battle', *Washington Post*, 21 March 2010.

Elich, Gregory, 'The Sinking of the *Cheonan* and Its Political Uses', *Counterpunch*, 28 July 2010.

Elich, Gregory, and Christine Ahn, 'Inside North Korea: An Interview with Christine Ahn', *Counterpunch*, 17 September 2008.

Endo, Tetsuya, 'What to Do about North Korea Now?' *East Asia Forum*, 27 January 2011.

Engdahl, F. William, 'The Korean Crisis Breaking News, Cui Bono?', MarketOracle, 31 May 2010.

Engelhardt, Tom, 'Believe It or Not (2010 Imperial Edition) US War-Fighting Numbers to Knock Your Socks Off', TomDispatch.com, 6 April 2010.

Eoh, Jin-joo, 'Inter-Korean Trade Through Gaesong Industrial Park Increases in 2010', *Arirang*, 22 December 2010.

Fackler, Martin, 'Ship Sinking Aids Ruling Party in S. Korean Vote', *New York Times*, 1 June 2010.

——'Obama Speech Marks Shift on North Korea', *New York Times*, 11 November 2010.

——'From the North, a Pattern of Aggression', *New York Times*, 23 November 2010.

Fackler, Martin, and Mark Landler, 'Ties to US Played Role in Downfall of Japanese Leader', *New York Times*, 2 June 2010.

——'South Korea Reassesses Its Defenses After Attack', *New York Times*, 26 November 2010.

Fackler, Martin, and Mark McDonald, 'North Korea Again Opts for the Unexpected: Restraint', *New York Times*, 21 December 2010.

Farah, Joseph 'A US–China War?' *Los Angeles Times*, 10 October 2007.

Fassihi, Farnaz, 'Iran Tightens Security as Subsidy Cuts Loom', *Wall Street Journal*, 4 November 2010.

Feffer, John, 'Ploughshares into Swords: Economic Implications of South Korean Military Spending', Korea Economic Institute Academic Paper Series 3, 2009.

——'Can Japan Say No to Washington?' *Foreign Policy in Focus*, 4 March 2010.

——'North Korea: Why Engagement Now?' *38 North*, 12 August 2010.

——'Kim Jong-Il: Right-Wing Mole?' *World Beat* 5: 20, 2010.

Feldman, Jonathan Michael, 'From Warfare State to "Shadow State": Militarism, Economic Depletion, and Reconstruction', *Social Text*: 91, 2007.

Ferguson, Charles D., *Preventing Catastrophic Nuclear Terrorism*, Washington, DC: Council on Foreign Relations, 2006.

Ferguson, Niall, 'America: An Empire in Denial', *Chronicle Review*, 28 March 2003.

——'Hegemony or Empire? (Review of *Two Hegemonies* by O'Brien and Clesse)', *Foreign Affairs*, September/October 2003.

——'America, the Fragile Empire', *Los Angeles Times*, 28 February 2010.

——'Complexity and Collapse: Empires on the Edge of Chaos', *Foreign Affairs*, March/April 2010.

Finnegan, Michael J., 'Preparing for the Inevitable in North Korea', *PacNet* 28B, 28 April 2009.

Finnegan, Michael J., 'US–ROK Cooperation in Post-Conflict Stabilization and Reconstruction', paper presented at Expanding the Agenda for Cooperation between the United States and Republic of Korea, Washington DC, 5 January 2010.

Finnemann, Nicole, 'The Sinking of the *Cheonan*', *Korea Insight*, 1 April 2010.

Flaherty, Anne, and Matthew Lee, 'Pentagon Won't Say Ship Sinking Is an Act of war', *Washington Post*, 20 May 2010.

Fogel, Robert, '$123,000,000,000,000* *China's Estimated Economy by the Year 2040. Be Warned', *Foreign Policy*, January/February 2010.

Foster-Carter, Aidan, 'The Gradualist Pipe-Dream: Prospects and Pathways for Korean Reunification', in Andrew Mack, ed., *Asian Flashpoint: Security and the Korean Peninsula*, Canberra: Allen & Unwin, 1993.

Frank, Rudiger, 'Can Economic Theory Demystify North Korea?' *Korea Review of International Studies* 9: 1, 2006.

——'The Stability of North Korea and a Long-Term Strategy for Transformation', IFES Forum 10–2–26–1, 2010.

Fuller, Thomas, and David E. Sanger, 'Thais Seize Plane With Weapons From N. Korea', *New York Times*, 12 December 2009.

Gardels, Nathan, 'Madeleine Albright Interviewed by Nathan Gardels', *New Perspectives Quarterly* 27: 4, 2004.

Garnaut, Ross, 'The Turning Period in Chinese Development', *East Asia Forum*, 1 August 2010.

Garreau, Joel, 'The Future Is So Yesterday', *Washington Post*, 20 July 2008.

Gates, Robert, 'Speech at Navy League Sea–Air–Space Exposition', US Department of Defense, 3 May 2010.

Gentleman, Amelia, 'US Senate Vote on Nuclear Deal Draws Guarded Praise by India', *New York Times*, 17 November 2006.

Gertz, Bill, *The China Threat: How the People's Republic Targets America*, Regnery Publishing, Inc, 2002.

——'China's "Aggressive" Buildup Called Worry', *Washington Times*, 14 January 2010.

Giles, Ciaran, 'Foreign Ministers Urge End to Cuba Embargo', *Washington Post*, 13 October 2005.

Glaser, Bonnie, and Scott Snyder, 'Preparations Needed for North Korean Collapse', *PacNet* 27, 2010.

Glasser, Bonnie S., Scott Snyder, See-Won Byun and David J. Szerlip, *Responding to Change on the Korean Peninsula: Impediments to US–South Korea–China Coordination*, A Report of the CSIS Freeman Chair in China Studies, 6 May 2010.

Global Trends 2025: A Transformed World, Washington DC: National Intelligence Council, 2008.

Goldman, Marshall I., 'A Balance Sheet of Soviet Foreign Aid', *Foreign Affairs* 43: 2, 1965.

Goodby, James E., and Donald Gross, 'Strategic Patience Has Become Strategic Passivity', *Nautilus Policy Forum Online*, 22 December 2010.

Goodenough, Patrick, 'North Korea Steps Up Reports of Alleged Kim Jong-il Outings', *CNS*, 30 December 2008.

Gowans, Stephen, 'The Sinking of the *Cheonan*: Another Gulf of Tonkin incident', *What's Left*, 3 June 2010.

——'US Ultimately to Blame for Korean Skirmishes in Yellow Sea', *What's Left*, 5 December 2010.

Graham, Bradley, 'Rumsfeld Remains Largely Unapologetic in Memoir', *Washington Post*, 3 February 2011.

Gray, John, 'A Shattering Moment in America's Fall From Power', *Guardian*, 28 September 2008.

Greenlees, Donald, and David Lague, 'How a US Inquiry Held up the N. Korea Peace Talks', *International Herald Tribune*, 11 April 2007.

Gregg, Donald P, 'Testing North Korean Waters', *International Herald Tribune*, 31 August 2010.

——'Why We Need Talks with North Korea', *Washington Post*, 22 December 2010.

Grimmett, Richard F., 'Conventional Arms Transfers to Developing Nations, 2002–2009', *Congressional Research Service*, 10 September 2010.

Grinker, Roy Richard, *Korea and its Futures: Unification and the Unfinished War*, New York: St Martin's Press, 1998.

Grossman, Elaine M., 'Cost to Test US Global-Strike Missile Could Reach $500 Million', *Global Security Newswire*, 15 March 2010.

Gunjal, Kisan, Swithun Goodbody, Joyce Kanyangwa Luma and Rita Bhatia, 'FAO/WFP Crop and Food Security Assessment Mission to the Democratic People's Republic of Korea', Food and Agriculture Organization of the United Nations, 16 November 2010.

Ha, Michael, 'North Korean Leader Had Another Stroke', *Korea Times*, 26 November 2008.

Haggard, Stephan, and Marcus Noland, 'Sanctioning North Korea: The Political Economy of Denuclearization and Proliferation', *Peterson Institute for International Economics Working Paper* WP09–4, 2009.

Halimi, Serge, 'The World Turned Upside Down; US Seen to Decline … Even Back in 1952', *Le Monde Diplomatique*, 1 November 2008.

Hampton, Olivia, 'North Korea: Obama's "Dumb War"?' *Guardian*, 25 May 2010.

Hankyoreh (editorial), 'Time for Dialogue not OPLAN 5029', *Hankyoreh*, 2 November 2009.

——'A Joint North Korea–South Korea Investigation in Compliance with the Basic Agreement of 1991', *Hankyoreh*, 24 May 2010.

——'Punishment of *Cheonan* Opinions Contrary to Government Must Stop', *Hankyoreh*, 26 May 2010.

——'Verification of the *Cheonan* Investigation at the National Assembly', *Hankyoreh*, 28 May 2010.

——'No Reason to Postpone OPCON Transfer', *Hankyoreh*, 24 June 2010.

——'Ratify OPCON Transfer Delay at the National Assembly', *Hankyoreh*, 29 June 2010.

——'A Thorough Reinvestigation into the Sinking of the *Cheonan*', *Hankyoreh*, 28 July 2010.

——'Time for Pyongyang to Take Responsibility for Attack', *Hankyoreh*, 25 November 2010.

Harden, Blaine, and John Pomfret, 'South Korea to Officially Blame North Korea for March Torpedo Attack on Warship', *Washington Post*, 19 May 2010.

Harlan, Chico, 'South Korean Leader Has Reunification Plan', *Washington Post*, 16 August 2010.

——'Seoul Undertakes Effort to Measure North Korea's Longevity', *Washington Post*, 19 December 2010.

Harrison, Selig S., 'Was the North Korean Launch a "Provocation"?' *Hankyoreh*, 14 April 2009.

——'Drawing a Line in the Water', *New York Times*, 12 December 2010.

Hastings, Michael, 'The Runaway General', *Rolling Stone*, 22 June 2010.

Hauben, Ronda, 'Netizens Question Cause of *Cheonan* Tragedy', *OhmyNews*, 8 June 2010.

Hecker, Siegfried S., 'Lessons Learned from the North Korean Nuclear Crises', *Nautilus Policy Forum Online* 10–055, 2010.

——'A Return Trip to North Korea's Yongbyon Nuclear Complex', Center for International Security and Cooperation, Stanford University, 20 November 2010.

Heite, Cpl. Rebekka S., '31st MEU's Long-Range Raid Capabilities Tested', US Air Force (Andersen Air Force Base), 15 April 2010.

Hellman, Christopher, 'Putting the Pentagon on a Diet', *TomDispatch*, 20 May 2010.

Herman, Steve, 'Sanctions Expected to Harm North Korean Economy', *Voice of America*, 23 July 2010.

Hersh, Seymour M., 'Watching the Warheads: The Risks to Pakistan's Nuclear Arsenal', *New Yorker*, 5 November 2001.

Hiatt, Fred, 'Fred Hiatt Interviews South Korean President Lee Myung-bak', *Newsweek*, 12 April 2010.

Higgs, Robert, 'The Defense Budget Is Bigger Than You Think', *San Francisco Chronicle*, 18 January 2004.

Hille, Kathrin, 'China Blasts Clinton's Maritime Venture', *Financial Times*, 30 July 2010.

Hoare, James, 'Why the Sunshine Policy Made Sense', *38 North*, 29 March 2010.

Hong, Hyun-Ik 'Strategic Cooperation between South Korea and Russia', *Korea Focus*, 17 May 2002.

Hosaka, Tomoko A., 'US, Japan to Keep US Military Base in Okinawa', *Washington Post*, 28 May 2010.

Howard, Michael, 'US Troops Kill 300 in Najaf Raid', *Guardian*, 7 August 2004.

Hufbauer, Gary Clyde, 'Sanctions-Happy USA', *Washington Post*, 12 July 1998.

Hufbauer, Gary Clyde, Jeffrey J. Schott, Kimberley Ann Elliott and Barbara Oegg, *Economic Sanctions Reconsidered*, 3rd edn, Washington, DC: Institute for International Economics, 2007.

Hwang, Doo-hyong, 'Korea's Troop Deployment in Afghanistan Serves Korea's National Interest: Scholar', *Yonhap*, 4 January 2010.

——'US to Mobilize More Troops in Case of N. Korean Contingency: Official', *Yonhap*, 4 February 2010.

Hwang, Doo-hyong 'Extra US Troops Not Likely to Arrive in Time in Case of NK Crisis: Gates', *Yonhap*, 3 February 2010.

Hyun, Syng-il, 'Industrialization and Industrialism in a Developing Socialist Country: Convergence Theory and the Case of North Korea', PhD, Utah State University, 1982.

Ikenson, Daniel J., 'Thriving in a Global Economy: The Truth about US Manufacturing and Trade', Cato Institute, 28 August 2007.

International Crisis Group, 'North Korea: The Risks of War in the Yellow Sea', *Asia Report* 198, 2010.

Jacobs, Karen, 'China Military Build-Up Seems US-Focused: Mullen', *Reuters*, 4 May 2009.

Jakes, Lara, 'Gen: IEDs Are N. Korea's Latest Weapon', *ABC News*, 29 September 2009.

Jelinek, Pauline, 'AP Enterprise: Sub Attack Came Near Drill', *Washington Post*, 5 June 2010.

Jenkins, Patrick, 'China Banks Eclipse US Rivals', *Financial Times*, 10 January 2010.

Jeong, Seok-gu, 'President Lee's *Cheonan* gamble', *Hankyoreh*, 25 May 2010.

Jin, Jianyu, Ziyu Wang and Hae-hoon Choung, 'Pragmatism Propels South Korean Attitudes', *Global Times*, 28 January 2011.

Jo, Yonghak, 'South Korea Rules Out Navy Ship Sunk by North Korea', *Washington Post*, 27 April 2010.

Joffe, Josef, 'The Default Power: The False Prophecy of America's Decline', *Foreign Affairs*, September/October 2009.

John, Emma, 'William, Kate and the Strange Law of Promogeniture', *Observer*, 23 January 2011.

Johnson, Chalmers, 'The Guns of August: Lowering the Flag on the American Century', *TomDispatch*, 17 August 2010.

Joint Investigation Report: On the Attack Against ROK Ship Cheonan, Seoul: Ministry of National Defense, 2010.

Joint State/Defense message, 'ROKG LEGAL MEMORANDUM ON NORTHWEST COASTAL INCIDENTS (Cable to US Embassy, Seoul)', State Department, 22 December 1973.

Joint Vision 2020, Washington, DC: US Department of Defense, 2000.

Jung, Ha-won, 'Minister: Transfer of Wartime Control May Be Delayed', *JoongAng Ilbo*, 25 June 2010.

Jung, Kyung-min, and Ha-won Jung, 'Two versions of *Cheonan* blast at UN', *JoongAng Ilbo*, 16 June 2010.

Jung, Seung-hyun, 'Inter-Korean Trade Rose Despite New Sanctions', *JoongAng Ilbo*, 30 September 2010.

Jung, Sung-ki, 'S. Korean Army to Deploy 2,000 Wheeled Armored Vehicles From 2013', *Korea Times*, 5 October 2008.

——'USFK Chief Pledges Naval, Air-Centric Reinforcement', *Korea Times*, 1 February 2009.

——'S. Korea, US to Tone Down War Games Next Week', *Korea Times*, 10 August 2009.

——'Minister Vows Preemptive Strike Against NK Nuclear Attack', *Korea Times*, 20 January 2010.

——'S. Korea May Join US Missile Shield', *Defense News*, 17 February 2010.

——'USFK Seeks to Expand Role Outside Peninsula', *Korea Times*, 24 February 2010.

——'S. Korea, Japan Can Build Nuclear Weapons Quickly', *Korea Times*, 18 March 2010.

——'Uncertainty Clouds Prospects of Korean Fighter Plans', *Korea Times*, 24 March 2010.

——'Questions Raised about "Smoking Gun"', *Korea Times*, 20 May 2010.

——'USFK to retake control over drill with ROK', *Korea Times*, 17 June 2010.

Kang, Byeong-tae 'North Korea Does Not Pose a Threat', *Korea Focus*, 28 July 2009.

Kang, Chan-ho, and Gwang-lip Moon, 'China Mulls No-Naming UN Censure', *JoongAng Ilbo*, 21 June 2010.

Kang, Hyun-kyung, 'Nostalgia for Kim Il-sung Rising in N. Korea', *Korea Times*, 21 March 2010.

Kang, Hyun-kyung, and Young-jin Kim, 'Seoul Regrets NGO Sending *Cheonan* Report to UNSC', *Korea Times*, 14 June 2010.

Karnow, Stanley, 'East Asia in 1978: The Great Transformation', *Foreign Affairs* 57: 3, 1978.

Kate, Daniel Ten, and Peter S. Green, 'Defending Korea Line Seen Contrary to Law by Kissinger Remains US Policy', *Bloomberg*, 17 December 2010.

Kay, Bryan, 'Is Collapse of NK Regime Imminent?' *Korea Times*, 15 November 2009.

Kessler, Glenn, 'Analysis: North Korea Tests US Policy of "Strategic Patience"', *Washington Post*, 27 May 2010.

Khalaf, Roula, and James Drummond, 'Gulf States in $123bn US Arms Spree', *Financial Times*, 20 September 2010.

Kim, Bo-keun, 'No. 1 Torpedo Remains Source of Controversy', *Hankyoreh*, 11 September 2010.

Kim, Hyung-jin, 'S. Korea: Nuclear Push Could Bring North's Collapse', *Washington Post*, 17 January 2011.

Kim, Ji-hyun '"Preemptive Strikes Would Be Needed to Stop NK Attack"', *Korea Herald*, 21 January 2010.

——'Nation Divided Over Possible NK Collapse', *Korea Herald*, 23 March 2010.

——'UN Starts Discussions on *Cheonan* Sinking', *Korea Herald*, 15 June 2010.

Kim, Joungwon Alexander, 'Soviet Policy in North Korea', *World Politics* 22: 2, 1970.

Kim, Min-seok, 'Russian Team Wraps Up Probe', *JoonAng Ilbo*, 8 June 2010.

Kim, Min-seok, and Min-yong Lee, 'Drill Under Way to Remove WMDs', *JoongAng Ilbo*, 12 March 2010.

Kim, Min-seok, and Myo-ja Ser, 'Just a Reminder: Seoul's Cruise Missiles', *JoongAng Ilbo*, 8 July 2006.

——'*Cheonan* Probe Detects TNT Type', *JoongAng Ilbo*, 14 May 2010.

——'US Will Command Military Exercise', *JoongAng Ilbo*, 17 June 2010.

Kim, Min-seok, and Jee-ho Yoo, 'North Adopts New War Invasion Strategy: Source', *JoongAng Ilbo*, 27 April 2010.

Kim, Myong Chol, 'Pyongyang Sees US Role in *Cheonan* sinking', *Asia Times Online*, 5 May 2010.

——'South Korea in the Line of Friendly Fire', *Asia Times Online*, 26 May 2010.

Kim, Nari, '*Cheonan* Investigators: N. Korean Torpedo Caused *Cheonan*'s Sinking', *Arirang*, 20 May 2010.

Kim, Samuel S., 'North Korea's Nuclear Strategy and the Interface Between International and Domestic Politics', *Asian Perspective* 34: 1, 2010.

Kim, Se-jeong, 'Kim Jong-il Looking Leaner Than Before', *Korea Times*, 22 March 2009.

——'Is NK the Biggest Threat to Americans?' *Korea Times*, 7 July 2009.

——'Chances of North Korea's Involvement Are Slim', *Korea Times*, 28 March 2010.

Kim, Sue-young, '2 Koreas Open Modern Military Hot Lines', *Korea Times*, 30 March 2009.

——'North Korea Impatient for Dialogue With US', *Korea Times*, 4 September 2009.

Kim, Suk, 'Will UN Economic Sanctions Against a Nuclear North Korea Work?' Institute for Far Eastern Studies, Kungnam University, 20 November 2006.

Kim, Yon-se, 'Roh Sees NK's Economic Boom', *Korea Times*, 15 August 2007.

Kim, Young Jin, '"Russia Unlikely to Back *Cheonan* Findings"', *Korea Times*, 7 June 2010.

Kirk, Donald, 'Rand: 400,000 Troops Needed to Secure N. Korea and Its "Loose Nukes"', *WorldTribune*, 25 January 2010.

Klare, Michael T., 'Twenty-First Century Energy Superpower', Tomdispatch.com, 19 September 2010.

Klein, Ezra, 'California's Scary Sneak Preview', *Washington Post*, 3 January 2010.

Klingner, Bruce, 'US Must Respond Firmly to North Korean Naval Attack', *Heritage Foundation*, 20 May 2010.

Klug, Foster, 'US Intelligence Chief: North Korean Military Crumbling ' Gazette. com, 2 February 2010.

Korean Committee for Solidarity with the World People, 'Joint Military Exercises', by email from Pyongyang, 5 August 2009.

Kotani, Tetsuo, 'Tip of the Spear: The 13 Missions for US Marines in Okinawa', *PacNet* 43, 2010.

Kotch, John Barry, and Michael Abbey, 'Ending Naval Clashes on the Northern Limit Line and the Quest for a West Sea Peace Regime', *Asian Perspectives* 27: 2, 2003.

Kotkin, Joel, 'The China Syndrome', *Forbes*, 24 August 2010.

Krauthammer, Charles, 'Decline Is a Choice: The New Liberalism and the End of American Ascendancy', *Weekly Standard*, 19 October 2009.

Kwak , Junghye, Huisun Kim and Taeho Lee, 'The PSPD's Stance on the Naval Vessel *Cheonan* Sinking', People's Solidarity for Participatory Democracy, Center for Peace and Disarmament, 1 June 2010.

Kwak, Tae-Hwan, 'The *Cheonan* Incident and Its Impact on the Six-Party Process', *IFES Forum* 10–06–04–1, 2010.

Kwon, Hyuk-chul, 'Military Believed N. Korean Submarine Was at Shipyard During *Cheonan* Incident', *Hankyoreh*, 23 October 2010.

——'Joint Drills Will Be Far From NLL, Military Reports', *Hankyoreh*, 27 November 2010.

——'Academics Call for *Cheonan* Reinvestigation', *Hankyoreh*, 12 October 2010.

Kwon, Tae-ho, 'Scope of Carter's Visit Remains in Question', *Hankyoreh*, 26 August 2010.

——'S. Korea and US Chart New Path Following End of Iraq Combat Mission', *Hankyoreh*, 2 September 2010.

——'South Korean Government Impeded Russian Team's *Cheonan* Investigation: Donald Gregg', *Hankyoreh*, 4 September 2010.

Lamb, Christina, 'Elite US Troops Ready to Combat Pakistani Nuclear Hijacks', *Sunday Times*, 17 January 2010.

Landay, Jonathan S., 'China's Thirst for Copper Could Hold Key to Afghanistan's future', *McClatchy Newspapers*, 8 March 2009.

Landler, Mark, 'Clinton Speech Offers Policy Overview', *New York Times*, 8 September 2010.

Lankov, Andrei, 'Kim Jong-un Unlikely Candidate for NK Leader', *Korea Times* 2009.

Lauria, Joe, 'N. Korea: Ship's Sinking Helped US', *Wall Street Journal*, 15 June 2010.

Lee, Brian, 'Behind the Front Line, a Shrouded Military', *JoongAng Ilbo*, 29 April 2010.

Lee, Chang Jae, 'Trade and Investment in North Korea', in *Future Multilateral Economic Cooperation With the Democratic People's Republic of Korea*, Stanley Foundation in cooperation with the German Council on Foreign Relations (DGAP) 2005.

Lee, Chi-dong, '(2nd LD) Main Opposition Heading for Stunning Victory in Local Elections', *Yonhap*, 3 June 2010.

Lee, Eun-joo, 'Six Decades Later, the North–South Gap Grows', *JoongAng Ilbo*, 26 June 2010.

Lee, Hyo-sik, 'Families of Yeonpyeong Civilian Victims Want National Merits', *Korea Times*, 1 December 2010.

Lee, Jae-hoon, 'Clinton Announces New Sanctions Against N. Korea', *Hankyoreh*, 22 July 2010.

Lee, Jean H., 'South Korea Says Mine from the North May Have Sunk Warship', *Washington Post*, 30 March 2010.

Lee, Jong-seok, 'Can the US Afford to "Muddle Through" the N. Korea Nuclear Issue?' *Hankyoreh*, 22 March 2010.

Lee, Myung-bak, 'Full Text of President Lee's National Address', *Korea Times*, 24 May 2010.

Lee, Peter, 'Short Shelf Life for China–US Reset', *Asia Times Online*, 8 June 2010.

——'Good-bye, Mr Insubordination', *Asia Times Online*, 4 February 2011.

Lee, Seunghun, and J. J. Suh, 'Rush to Judgment: Inconsistencies in South Korea's *Cheonan* Report', *Asia-Pacific Journal*, 12 July 2010.

Lee, Sung-yoon, 'Planning For A Life After Kim', *Foreign Policy*, 15 February 2010.

Lee, Sunny, 'China Embraces Soft Power for Image', *Korea Times*, 11 September 2009.

——'*Cheonan* Tragedy: Is There an Exit Strategy?' *Korea Times*, 8 June 2010.

Lee, Tae-hoon, 'Book on China's Soft Power Released', *Korea Times*, 18 January 2010.

——'Jimmy Carter Opposes Sanctions Against North Korea', *Korea Times*, 24 March 2010.

——'Explosives from Torpedo Found on Sunken Ship', *Korea Times*, 7 May 2010.

——'Gov't Seeks to Replace *Cheonan* Investigator', *Korea Times*, 13 May 2010.

——'Would You Pay $1 a Month for Unification Tax?' *Korea Times*, 28 October 2010.

——'Army, Air Force to Stage Largest-Ever Joint Drill', *Korea Times*, 22 December 2010.

Lee, You Ju-hyun, 'Opposition Calls for *Cheonan* Reinvestigation', *Hankyoreh*, 15 September 2010.

Levi, Michael A., *On Nuclear Terrorism*, Washington, DC: Harvard University Press for Council on Foreign Relations, 2007.

——*Deterring State Sponsorship of Nuclear Terrorism*, Washington, DC: Council on Foreign Relations Press, 2008.

Liberman, Peter, 'What to Read on American Primacy', *Foreign Affairs*, 12 March 2009.

Liem, Paul, 'Honor the *Cheonan* Dead with Peace', *Korea Policy Institute*, 3 June 2010.

——'A New Opportunity to Engage North Korea', *Korea Policy Institute*, 14 September 2009.

Lim, Jae-Cheon. *Kim Jong Il's Leadership of North Korea*, Abingdon: Routledge, 2009.

Linzer, Dafna, 'Senate Backs White House Plan for India Nuclear Deal', *Washington Post*, 17 November 2006.

Lister, Tim, 'North Korea's Military Aging but Sizable', CNN, 25 November 2010.

Lopez, George A., and David Cortright, 'Containing Iraq: Sanctions Worked', *Foreign Affairs* 83: 4, 2004.

Lu, Jingxian, and Young-ghil Kwon, 'Multilateral Alliances Critical for Korean Future', *Global Times*, 1 February 2011.

Luo, Yuan, 'All-Out War Unlikely on the Korean Peninsula', *Global Times*, 23 December 2010.

Lynn, Jonathan, 'North Korea Has Plenty of Doctors: WHO', *Washington Post*, 30 April 2010.

Macintyre, Donald, 'The Supremo in His Labyrinth', *Time*, 18 February 2002.

Malcom, Ben S., '"White Tigers" Prowled North Korea', *VFW*, May 2002.

Manyin, Mark E., 'Japan–North Korea Relations: Selected Issues', Washington: Congressional Research Service, 2003.

Markoff, John, 'Chinese Supercomputer Is Ranked World's Second-Fastest, Challenging US Dominance', *New York Times*, 31 May 2010.

Markoff, John, and David Barboza, 'Chinese Telecom Giant in Push for US Market', *New York Times*, 25 October 2010.

Marr, Kendra, 'As Detroit Crumbles, China Emerges as Auto Epicenter', *Washington Post*, 18 May 2009.

Marsh, Peter, 'China to Overtake US as Largest Manufacturer', *Financial Times*, 10 August 2008.

Mayer, Arno, 'The US Empire Will Survive Bush', *Le Monde Diplomatique*, October 2008.

Mazzetti, Mark, and Sang-hun Choe, 'North Korea's Leader Is Seriously Ill, US Intelligence Officials Say', *New York Times*, 9 September 2008.

McCurry, Justin, 'North Korean Hackers May Have Stolen US War Plans', *Guardian*, 18 December 2009.

McGlynn, John, 'Politics in Command: The "International" Investigation into the Sinking of the *Cheonan* and the Risk of a New Korean War', *Asia-Pacific Journal*, 14 June 2010.

——'Banco Delta Asia, North Korea's Frozen Funds and US Undermining of the Six-Party Talks: Obstacles to a Solution', *Asia-Pacific Journal*, 9 June 2007.

McGreal, Chris, 'Obama's State of the Union Address: US Must Seize "Sputnik Moment"', *Guardian*, 26 January 2011.

Melman, Seymour, 'Economic Consequences of the Arms Race: The Second-Rate Economy', *American Economic Review* 78: 2, 1988.

——'In the Grip of a Permanent War Economy', *Counterpunch*, 15 March 2003.

——*Our Depleted Society*, New York: Holt, Rinehart & Winston, 1965.

Meyer, Carlton, 'The Mythical North Korean Threat', (2003), <www.g2mil.com/korea.htm>.

Military expenditure: SIPRI Yearbook 2008: Armaments, Disarmament and International Security, Oxford: OUP, 2008.

Min, Namgung, 'South Korea Splits Along Political Lines', *Daily NK*, 20 May 2010.

Ministry of National Defense, 'Investigation Result on the Sinking of ROKS "*Cheonan*"', Korea.net, 20 May 2010.

Moon, Chung-in, and Sangkeun Lee, 'Military Spending and the Arms Race on the Korean Peninsula', *Asia-Pacific Journal*, 28 March 2010.

——'Military Spending and the Arms Race on the Korean Peninsula', *Asian Perspectives* 33: 4, 2009.

Moon, Gwang-lip, 'Little Enthusiasm for Lee's Unification Tax Proposal', *JoongAng Ilbo*, 17 August 2010.

——'Russia Says Sea Mine Sunk *Cheonan*: Report', *JoongAng Ilbo*, 28 July 2010.

Mosher, Steven W., *Hegemon: China's Plan to Dominate Asia and the World*, New York: Encounter Books, 2001.

Murphy, Melissa, and Wen Jin Yuan, 'Internationalization of the Renminbi and Its Implications for the United States', CSIS Freeman Chair in China Studies, October 2009.

Na, Jeong-ju, 'Lee Regrets Speculations over Ship Sinking', *Korea Times*, 13 October 2010.

——'"We Should Deal Resolutely with N. Korea"', *Korea Times*, 27 December 2010.

Navarro, Peter, *The Coming China Wars: Where They Will Be Fought and How They Can Be Won*, 2nd edn, FT Press, 2008.

Noland, Marcus, *The (Non) Impact of UN Sanctions on North Korea*, Washington, DC: Peterson Institute for International Economics, 2008.

Oh, Young-jin, and Key-young Son, 'NK Sent US Private Cable on Anti-Terrorism', *Korea Times*, 23 September 2001.

Oliver, Christian, 'Theories Why Pyongyang Sank Warship', *Financial Times*, 24 May 2010.

——'Man in the News: Lee Myung-bak', *Financial Times*, 28 May 2010.

Oliver, Christian, and Najmeh Bozorgmehr, 'S Korea Ban Ends Tehran's Kia Imports', *Financial Times*, 13 September 2010.

Park, Myoung-Ky, and Philo Kim, 'Inter-Korean relations in nuclear politics', *Asian Perspective* 34: 1, 2010.

Park, Si-soo, 'Police Hunt for *Cheonan* Rumors', *Korea Times*, 1 June 2010.

Park, Song-wu, 'KAL Bombing Constant Source of Dispute', *Korea Times*, 11 July 2004.

——'48% of Youth Would Support N. Korea in Case of US Attack', *Korea Times*, 21 February 2006.

Pascual, Carlos, Madeleine Albright, Strobe Talbott, Thomas Pickering, Javier Solana and Bruce Jones, 'A Plan for Action: Renewed American Leadership and International Cooperation for the 21st Century', Brookings Institution, Washington, DC, 20 November 2008.

Pastreich, Emanuel, 'Is China the Nemesis in a New Cold War?' Nautilus Policy Forum Online, 6 March 2006.

Perlez, Jane, 'A Visit to a US Ally, but an Increasingly Wary One', *New York Times*, 8 February 2009.

Petrov, Leonid, 'Interview', Radio Free Asia, 28 May 2010.

Pike, John, 'Foal Eagle', Global Security.org, < www.globalsecurity.org/military/ops/foal-eagle.htm>.

——'Garden Plot/CONPLAN 2502 (Civil Disturbance Operations)', GlobalSecurity.org, 31 July 2008.

——'Operation Plans [OPLAN]', GlobalSecurity.org, <www.globalsecurity.org/military/ops/oplan.htm>.

——'OPLAN 5026 – Air Strikes', GlobalSecurity.org, <www.globalsecurity.org/military/ops/oplan-5026.htm>.

——'OPLAN 5027 Major Theater War – West', GlobalSecurity, <www.globalsecurity.org/military/ops/oplan-5027.htm>.

Pollack, Jonathan D., 'The United States, North Korea, and the End of the Agreed Framework', *Naval War College Review* LVI: 3, 2003.

Pomfret, John, 'From China's Mouth to Texans' Ears: Outreach Includes Small Station in Galveston', *Washington Post*, 25 April 2010.

Pomfret, John, and Chico Harlen, 'North Korea Makes Some Gestures Toward Calm', *Washington Post*, 20 December 2010.

Pons, Philippe, 'North Korea, Fortress State', *Le Monde diplomatique*, January 2011.

Powell, Bill, 'China's Amazing New Bullet Train', *Fortune*, 6 August 2009.

Pritchard, Charles 'Jack', 'What I saw in North Korea', *New York Times*, 21 January 2004.

Rachman, Gideon, 'Think Again: American Decline: This Time It's For Real', *Foreign Policy*, 7 January 2011.

Reception, Staging, Onward Movement, And Integration Field Manual, Washington, DC: Headquarters, Department of the Army, 1999.

Richardson, Ben, and Saeromi Shin, 'South Korea Faces Domestic Skeptics over Evidence Against North', *Bloomberg Businessweek*, 29 May 2010.

Richburg, Keith B., 'In Chinese Border Town, Trade with North Korea Can Be Lucrative but Problematic', *Washington Post*, 26 November 2010.

Ritter, Scott, 'The End of Obama's Vision of a Nuke-Free World', TruthDig.org, 16 February 2010.

Roberts, Paul Craig, 'Blinded by Ideology: Cato, Trade and Outsourcing', *Counterpunch*, 9 October 2007.

Rodas, Claudia, 'North Korea Declares Sweden an Enemy', *The Local*, 19 August 2008.

Rogers, Paul, 'The Road to Endless War', *Open Democracy*, 25 November 2010.

Rozoff, Rick, 'Afghanistan: North Atlantic Military Bloc's Ten-Year War In South Asia', *Global Research*, 1 September 2010.

Rubin, Jennifer, 'Stuart Levey Departs', *Washington Post*, 25 January 2011.

Russett, Bruce, 'The Mysterious Case of Vanishing Hegemony; Or, Is Mark Twain Really Dead?' *International Organization* 39: 2, 1985.

Sample, Ian, 'Lunar Eclipse: US Retreat Leaves China Leading Way in Race to Return to Moon', *Guardian*, 2 February 2010.

Sanger, David E., 'North Korea Keeps the World Guessing', *New York Times*, 29 November 2010.

Satoshi, Amako, 'China as a "Great Power" and East Asian Integration', *East Asia Forum*, 4 April 2010.

Segal, Gerald, 'China and the Great Power Triangle', *China Quarterly*: 83, 1980.

Selden, Mark, 'As the Empire Falls: Lessons Learned and Unlearned in "America's Asia"', *Critical Asian Studies* 41: 3, 2009.

Seo, Dong-shin, 'Asians Cooperate to Counter Japan's Rising Militarism', *Korea Times*, 25 March 2005.

Ser, Myo-ja, 'Probe Member Summoned on False Rumor Allegations', *JoongAng Ilbo*, 29 May 2010.

Ser, Myo-ja, and Jung-ae Ko, 'Public Losing Faith in Authority After Sinking', *Chosun Ilbo*, 12 April 2010.

Shanker, Thom, 'Nuclear Deal With India Wins Senate Backing', *New York Times*, 17 November 2006.

Shanker, Thom, Helene Cooper and Richard A. Oppel, Jr, 'Elite US Units Step Up Effort in Afghan City Before Attack', *New York Times*, 25 April 2010.

Shin, Hae-in, 'NK Emerges as Key Election Issue', *Korea Herald*, 20 May 2010.

Shin, S. C., 'Letter to Hillary Clinton, US Secretary of State: There Was No Explosion. There Was No Torpedo', 26 May 2010.

Shorrock, Tim, 'Obama's Only Choice on North Korea', *Daily Beast*, 24 November 2010.

Shultz, George P., William J. Perry, Henry A. Kissinger and Sam Nunn, 'Toward a Nuclear-Free World', *Wall Street Journal*, 15 January 2009.

Sigal, Leon V., 'North Korea's Tactics', *Nautilus Policy Forum Online*, 15 February 2005.

——'North Korea Policy on the Rocks: What Can be Done to Restore Constructive Engagement?' *GlobalAsia* 4: 2, 2009.

——'What Obama Should Offer North Korea', *Bulletin of the Atomic Scientists*, 28 January 2009.

——'Why Punishing North Korea Won't Work ... and What Will', *Asia-Pacific Journal: Japan Focus*, 8 June 2009.

——'Looking for Leverage in All the Wrong Places', *38 North: US–Korea Institute at SAIS*, Johns Hopkins University, 1 May 2010.

——'The Only Way Out: Negotiate With North Korea: An Interview with Leon Sigal on Recent Events and US–DPRK Relations', *Korea Policy Institute*, 16 June 2009.

Slackman, Michael, '5 Years After It Halted Weapons Programs, Libya Sees the US as Ungrateful', *New York Times*, 10 March 2009.

Sly, Liz, 'Amid Arab Protests, US Influence Has Waned', *Washington Post*, 4 February 2011.

Smith, Hazel, 'Overcoming Humanitarian Dilemmas in the DPRK (North Korea)', *United States Institute of Peace*, July 2002.

——'Brownback Bill Will Not Solve North Korea's Problems', *Jane's Intelligence Review*, February 2004.

——*Hungry for Peace: International Security, Humanitarian Assistance, and Social Change in North Korea*, Washington, DC: United States Institute of Peace, 2005.

——'North Korea Shipping: A Potential for WMD Proliferation?' *East-West Center: AsiaPacific Issues* 87, 2009.

Smith, R. Jeffrey, and Joby Warrick, 'Nuclear Aims by Pakistan, India Prompt US Concern', *Washington Post*, 28 May 2009.

Snow, Edgar, and Shao-Chang Hsu, 'Recognition of the People's Republic of China', *Annals of the American Academy of Political and Social Science* 324, no. ArticleType: research-article / Issue Title: Resolving the Russian-American Deadlock / Full publication date: Jul., 1959 / Copyright © 1959 American Academy of Political and Social Science, 1959: 75–88.

Snyder, Scott, House Committee on Foreign Affairs Subcommittee on Asia, the Pacific and the Global Environment 'Smart Power: Remaking US Foreign Policy in North Korea', Testimony by Scott Snyder, Director, Center for US–Korea Policy, The Asia Foundation, 12 February 2009.

——'Symposium on OpCon Transfer and Its Implications for the US–ROK Alliance', *Asia Foundation*, 25 March 2010.

Snyder, Scott, and See-Won Byun, 'The Obama Administration and Preparations for North Korean Instability', *International Journal of Korean Unification Studies* 18: 2, 2009.

Solovyov, Vyacheslav, 'North Korea Flexes Muscles', *Voice of Russia*, 16 June 2010.

Son, Won-je, 'N. Korea Reiterates Innocence, Offers Evidence', *Hankyoreh*, 3 November 2010.

Song, Shengxia, 'Moon Landing Gets Timetable', *Global Times*, 20 September 2010.

Spielmann, Peter James, 'Carter: If no Palestine, Israel Sees "catastrophe"', *Associated Press*, 26 January 2009.

Stahl, Lesley, 'Albright: "Worth It"', UncoverIraq.com, <home.comcast.net/~dhamre/docAlb.htm>.

Stangarone, Troy, 'Korea's Conundrum: Dealing with US Sanctions on Iran', *Korea Insight*, 3 September 2010.

Stares, Paul B., and Joel S. Wit, *Preparing for Sudden Change in North Korea*, Washington, DC: Brookings Institution Press for Council on Foreign Relations, 2009.

Stein, Jeff, 'Analysts Question Korea Torpedo Incident', *Washington Post*, 27 May 2010.

——'Wikileaks Documents: N. Korea Sold Missiles to al-Qaeda, Taliban', *Washington Post*, 26 July 2010.

Steinberg, David I., 'Review: Development Lessons from the Korean Experience – A Review Article', *Journal of Asian Studies* 42: 1, 1982.

Stirrup, Robert, 'Ships Depart Pearl Harbor for RIMPAC 2010 Exercises', *US Navy*, 8 July 2010.

Stone, I. F., *The Secret History of the Korean War*, New York: Monthly Review Press, 1952.

Stossel, Scott, 'North Korea: The War Game', *Atlantic*, July/August 2005.

Subramanian, Arvind, 'Is China Already Number One? New GDP Estimates', *East Asia Forum*, 3 February 2011.

Sudworth, John, 'How South Korean Ship was Sunk', BBC, 20 May 2010.

Suh, Jae-Jung, 'Allied to Race? The US–Korea Alliance and Arms Race', *Asian Perspective* 33: 4, 2009.

——'Confronting War, Colonialism, and Intervention in the Asia Pacific', *Critical Asian Studies* 42: 4, 2011.

Tanaka, Sakai, 'Who Sank the South Korean Warship *Cheonan*? A New Stage in the US–Korean War and US–China Relations', *Asia-Pacific Journal*, 2010.

Tanter, Richard, 'Japanese Militarization and the Bush Doctrine', *Japan Focus*, 17 February 2005.

Terashima, Jitsuro, 'The US–Japan Alliance Must Evolve: The Futenma Flip-Flop, the Hatoyama Failure, and the Future', *Asia-Pacific Journal*, 9 August 2010.

Thompson, Drew, 'China's Perspective of Post-*Cheonan* Regional Security', in *Post*-Cheonan *Regional Security*, Seoul: Asia Foundation's Center for US–Korea Policy and the Asan Institute for Policy Studies, 2010.

Thompson, Mark, 'There's No Business Like the Arms Business', *Time*, 14 September 2010.

Tisdall, Simon, 'Wikileaks Cables Reveal China "Ready to Abandon North Korea"', *Guardian*, 29 November 2010.

——'WikiLeaks Cables: How China Lost Patience with North Korea', *Guardian*, 29 November 2010.

Tjia, Paul, 'The Next India', *The Broker*, 28 May 2009.

Toloraya, Georgy, 'Peace or War? Do We Have to Choose? A Russian Perspective', *38North*, 27 May 2010.

Traub, James, 'The Accidental Domestic President', *Foreign Policy*, 23 March 2010.

Turse, Nick, 'Black Sites in the Empire of Bases', *Asia Times Online*, 11 February 2010.

Underhill, Francis, 'Defusing Western Coastal Island Situation', *State Department*, December 1973.

Van Dyke, Jon, 'The Maritime Boundary between North and South Korea in the Yellow (West) Sea', *38 North*, 29 July 2010.

Van Dyke, Jon M., Mark J. Valencia and Jenny Miller Garmendia, 'The North/South Korea Boundary Dispute in the Yellow (West) Sea', *Marine Policy* 27: 2, 2003.

VanGrasstek, Craig, 'The Benefits of US–China Trade in Services', *United States Council Foundation*, July 2006.

Vick, Karl, 'Children Pay Cost of Iraq's Chaos', *Washington Post*, 21 November 2004.

Vinacke, Harold M., 'United States Policy towards China: An Appraisal', *Far Eastern Survey* 29: 5, 1960.

Von Drehle, David 'Wrestling With History: Sometimes You Have to Fight the War You Have, Not the War You Wish You Had', *Washington Post*, 13 November 2005.

Vorontsov, Alexander, and Oleg Revenko, 'The Conundrum of the South Korean Corvette (I)', *International Affairs*, 25 May 2010.

——'The Conundrum of the South Korean Corvette (II)', *International Affairs*, 4 June 2010.

Wald, Matthew L., 'CIA Denies Being Source of Anthrax', *Los Angeles Times*, 17 December 2001.

Walt, Stephen M., 'Taming American Power', *Foreign Affairs*, September/October 2005.

Warburg, James P., 'United States Postwar Policy in Asia', *Annals of the American Academy of Political and Social Science* 318, July 1958.

Weinberg, Gerhard L., 'Hitler's Image of the United States', *American Historical Review* 69: 4, 1964.

White, Hugh, 'Why War in Asia Remains Thinkable', *Survival* 50: 6, 2008.

——'Power Shift: Australia's Future between Washington and Beijing', *The Quarterly Essay* 39, 2010.

Williams, M. J., 'The Empire Writes Back (to Michael Cox)', *International Affairs* 83: 5, 2007.

Wit, Joel S., 'Don't Sink Diplomacy', *New York Times*, 18 May 2010.

Wolf Jr, Charles, and Kamil Akramov, 'North Korean Paradoxes: Circumstances, Costs, and Consequences of Korean Unification', *RAND National Defense Research Institute*, 2005.

Woods Jr, Thomas E., 'The Neglected Costs of the Warfare State: An Austrian Tribute to Seymour Melman', *Journal of Libertarian Studies* 22: 1, 2010.

The World from Berlin, 'North Korea Seems To Have a Sort of Death Wish', *Der Spiegel*, 21 May 2010.

Wright, Robert, 'China to Loosen West's Grip on Rail Sector', *Financial Times*, 13 September 2010.

Yamaguchi, Mari, 'Japan Capable of Making Nuclear Weapon', *Guardian*, 30 November 2006.

Yang, Sang-hoon, 'Seoul Must Prepare for the Worst-Case Scenario', *Chosun Ilbo*, 17 June 2009.

Yetiv, Steve, 'Reports of America's Decline Are Greatly Exaggerated', *Christian Science Monitor*, 12 March 2009.

Yi, Yong-in, 'Cold War Alliances Reborn with Regional Tension', *Hankyoreh*, 30 November 2010.

Yoo, Cheong-mo, 'Election Defeat Casts Gloom over Lee Administration, Ruling Party', *Yonhap*, 3 June 2010.

Yoo, Jee-ho, 'Korea, US Could Delay Wartime Control Transfer', *JoongAng Ilbo*, 24 March 2010.

——'Scientist Co-Chairs *Cheonan* Probe Team', *JoongAng Ilbo*, 12 April 2010.

Younge, Gary, 'The US is Moving On from Afghanistan, but Its Troops Are Still Dying There', *Guardian*, 30 January 2011.

Youssef, Nancy A., 'As Iraq Winds Down, US Army Confronts a Broken Force', *McClatch Newspapers*, 17 September 2010.

Zacharia, Janine, 'Iraqis Still Reliant on Power Generators as US Prepares to Leave', *Washington Post*, 2 October 2010.

Zakaria, Fareed, 'When North Korea Falls', *Washington Post*, 18 October 2010.

Zakaria, Fareed, and Condoleezza Rice, 'Interview With Fareed Zakaria of CNN', US State Department, 19 June 2008.

Index

In the text, and in the literature generally, there is a mixture of synonyms and abbreviations. The most common of these are

America: United States – US
North Korea: Democratic People's Republic of Korea – DPRK
South Korea: Republic of Korea – ROK
For consistency, only the last versions (US, DPRK, ROK) are used in this index

For a note on spelling variants of common Korea words see http://www.timbeal. net.nz/Crisis_in_Korea/